Anvils, Mallets
& Dynamite

Anvils, Mallets & Dynamite

THE
UNAUTHORIZED BIOGRAPHY
OF LOONEY TUNES

JAIME WEINMAN

sh.
SUTHERLAND
HOUSE
TORONTO, 2021

Sutherland House
416 Moore Ave., Suite 205
Toronto, ON M4G 1C9

First edition, October 2021

If you are interested in inviting one of our authors to a live event or
media appearance, please contact publicity@sutherlandhousebooks.com
and visit our website at sutherlandhousebooks.com for more
information about our authors and their schedules.

Manufactured in Canada
Cover designed by Lena Yang
Book composed by Karl Hunt

Library and Archives Canada Cataloguing in Publication
Title: Anvils, mallets & dynamite : the unauthorized
biography of Looney tunes / Jaime Weinman.
Other titles: Anvils, mallets and dynamite
Names: Weinman, Jaime, author.
Identifiers: Canadiana 20210256850 | ISBN 9781989555460 (hardcover)
Subjects: LCSH: Looney tunes. | LCSH: Warner Bros. Cartoons—History. |
LCSH: Warner Bros. Animation—History. | LCSH: Animated films—
United States—History and criticism. | LCSH: Animated television
programs—United States—History. | LCSH: Cartoon characters—United States.
Classification: LCC NC1766.U53 L669 2021 | DDC 791.43/340973—dc23

ISBN 978-1-989555-46-0

Contents

To my mother, who remembers that when I was a child,

I would point at a cartoon gag and ask,

"Why is that funny?"

CHAPTER 1

Who Are These Talking Animals, and Why Do We Care?

Mickey Mouse is not a funny character. He neither tells jokes nor does anything funny, he has no point of view, no real character, and his girlfriend is an uptight bore. Bugs Bunny, on the other hand, is a brilliantly inventive comic genius, sharp-witted, physically agile, a fearless wise-guy who thinks nothing of donning a dress, producing an anvil out of thin air, kissing his enemy on the lips, and, in the face of death and torture, calling out a cheery, "What's up, Doc?" Bugs is much funnier than Mickey, no contest. Why, then, is Mickey the billionaire movie star? People don't seem to be able to get their fill of that little rat, him with his squeaky voice and gee-whiz attitude. Mickey is completely inoffensive, involved in a long-term, caring relationship, optimistic. Bugs is the opposite: he's a wild man with a raging carrot-dependency, big with the exploding props and the verbal abuse, and one of these days he's going to go over the edge. Mickey never will. He and his girlfriend will spend their days in inoffensive, unfunny bliss. But it is Bugs who makes us laugh, and isn't that, after all, enough?

Rob Long, *Conversations with My Agent*[1]

1

THE FIRST THING WE NOTICE about *Looney Tunes* on a movie theater screen is that the characters are looking down at us. When Daffy Duck looks out into the audience and apologizes for the fact that a giant eraser almost removed him from the picture, he's not looking directly in front of him. His eyes are focused on a position below the camera, an acknowledgment that he is up there, on a large screen, and we're down here.

I knew that about the old Warner Bros. cartoons with Bugs Bunny, Daffy Duck, Porky Pig, the Road Runner, Tweety, Sylvester, Speedy Gonzales, Foghorn Leghorn, and that singing frog in the top hat. Even though I had watched them on television on Saturday mornings, I knew that they hadn't been made for television, but for movie theaters. The Warner Bros. studio had cranked out hundreds of them between 1930, when the franchise began, and 1963, when it officially shut down. I knew all that, but I didn't really *feel* it until I saw them on a big theater screen.

It was my second time seeing this touring festival. I had gone to see it in Ottawa, where I grew up, and when it came to Montreal, where I was studying. Having seen it twice, I considered going out on the road to see it in other cities, but I wasn't as big a fan as that, although I still kind of regret not traveling considering how hard it's become to see these cartoons as they were intended to be seen.

Warner Bros. had sent this festival package out to repertory theaters with good 35 mm prints drawn from the cartoons it owned. It mixed a bunch of classics, like "What's Opera, Doc?" (Bugs Bunny and Elmer Fudd do Wagner) and "One Froggy Evening" (the singing frog) with seemingly random shorts featuring other popular characters, plus two bonus shorts with the Tasmanian Devil, an ugly, slobbering beast who had only appeared in five cartoons but somehow became one of the studio's most popular characters in the 1980s and 1990s, even getting his own TV show for a while.

It was a good but not great selection of cartoons, thanks in part to one big limitation, the necessary fact that it was restricted to the cartoons Warner Bros. owned. It sounds strange in our era of entertainment company consolidation, but the rights to *Looney Tunes* cartoons were divided, and Warner Bros. didn't own half the films it had made. In the 1950s, when television was new and movie studios were desperate for extra money, Warner Bros. sold its pre-1948 film library to a distribution company that needed cheap filler to sell to TV stations. This decision cost the studio many times over the $21 million it received,[2] and while the library changed hands many times afterward, it was still in the hands of a Warner Bros. competitor, Ted Turner, who used them as cheap filler on his cable channel Cartoon Network.

All of this meant that the festival could only choose from cartoons released after 1948. A lot of the best shorts couldn't be included, and the ones on the program tended to be a bit too similar in style: the 1950s were not a period that had much use for anarchy, so Bugs Bunny and Daffy Duck had lost most of the wildness they displayed in the 1940s. It was a bit too easy to predict what they were going to do in every cartoon. Watching them one after the other, they seemed the work of skilled artists who were maybe a bit too familiar with what got laughs and a little too willing to repeat themselves.

But then these cartoons were never meant to be watched one after the other, even though that was how most of us grew up watching them. The original Warner Bros. cartoon studio was in the business of making short animated films to play before the studio's live-action movies, back when most movie theaters would show a cartoon, a newsreel, and other short films before the main feature. The cartoons were meant to be consumed one at a time. Because the creators only had six or seven minutes to tell their stories, there was none of the slow build that you see in comedy features, or even in the twenty-minute shorts by live-action comedians like the Three Stooges or Laurel and Hardy. Almost every long comedy film has some quiet moments, or moments that aren't intended to get big laughs. Otherwise, the audience would get exhausted. A *Looney Tunes* cartoon wasn't worried about exhaustion. Each cartoon bombards us with jokes, gags, explosion effects, and weird sounds to force us to laugh as hard and as often as we can before it gets the hook. This is why, in every screening I saw, the laughs were less enthusiastic in the second half of the program. This was mostly because you can't laugh equally hard at twelve cartoons in a row. When you add them all together, you don't get a feature film, you feel as if you're watching twelve two-hour features in a row without a break.

Still, on this particular night, the audience was enthusiastic. There's nothing like seeing an old film with a good audience, and that's especially true of comedy, which is timed for audience reaction. What surprised me was that with a receptive crowd, the cartoons were even funnier than I remembered. Stuff you watched as a kid usually becomes worse the older you get and the more you know. But *Looney Tunes* had clearly been diminished by TV, and the big screen revealed qualities that I had never really appreciated before. TV had always made it apparent that Maurice Noble, the layout artist who designed the scenery for many of Chuck Jones's cartoons, had outdone himself on "What's Opera, Doc?," with his uniquely stylized approach parodying the look of operatic stage sets while also looking as imposing as real mountains. But I hadn't been aware of why, when Elmer Fudd gets angry, Noble and Jones bathed the entire screen, including Elmer, in magenta red. In a dark theater, the sudden colour change has a physical impact. No one could have imagined that from television.

Bits of these cartoons that never got much of a response on television became huge laugh-getters when the lights were down, the screen was big, and the sound reverberated through a large space. "Rabbit Seasoning" is the second of three cartoons that director Chuck Jones and writer Michael Maltese made based around a simple gimmick: Daffy Duck tries to get Elmer Fudd to shoot Bugs Bunny; Bugs tricks Daffy into making the demand in a way that causes Elmer to shoot him instead. In this film, Daffy keeps getting the terms "you" and "me" mixed up, and winds up asking Elmer to "shoot me now." When he realizes what's happened, Daffy turns to the audience—again, with his eyes moving downward—and says, "Pronoun trouble!"

On television this was a mildly funny line, a creatively literal description of what was going on in the scene. In the theater, it was an explosive laugh, resounding everywhere. A little moment turned out to be a big one when seen under the conditions that the creators had in mind.

Another huge moment that had seemed like nothing on TV came in "Bully for Bugs," a Jones/Maltese collaboration released in 1953. (This director/writer team was responsible for most of the studio's best cartoons after 1948, so this show was more heavily slanted toward their work than an ideal selection ought to be.) The cartoon drops Bugs Bunny into a bullring where a huge, vicious bull has just caused the matador to run away in fear.

Bullfighting was one of those premises that, for reasons no one has figured out, was overused in classic cartoons. Every studio did a bullfight cartoon: Metro-Goldwyn-Mayer had "Señor Droopy"; Warner Bros. had put Daffy Duck into the ring in "Mexican Joyride"; Disney had done "Ferdinand the Bull" and then put Goofy in a matador outfit in "For Whom the Bulls Toil." The premise was so tired that Eddie Selzer, the producer of the Warner cartoons at the time, reportedly told his staff:

"I don't want any cartoons about bullfights. Bullfights aren't funny!" Selzer, a company man who had been installed by the studio, was disliked by most of the animation people. The way Jones told it, he and Maltese assumed that there must be something funny about bullfights if Selzer didn't think there was.[3]

It's not immediately clear that they were right. The limitations of a short cartoon's budget are on display as the film opens: the filmmakers aren't actually able to show us the crowd; there's only so much the background noise can do to compensate for its absence. Jones, a master of small, precise facial expressions, shows us the matador's fear. His first reaction to the bull is to force his face into a thin, brief smile. But it's still basically a stock scene. We know its only purpose is to establish the bull as a fearsome creature that terrifies even professional bullfighters so that when Bugs shows up, it will seem impressive that he's not afraid of the bull.

Even if we hadn't already seen the cartoon, we would probably guess, by the laws of cartoon formula, that Bugs would not be afraid of the bull. Still, the audience is not prepared for what happens when Bugs steps into the ring via a famous gag that Maltese invented in the mid-1940s and used many times thereafter: trying to burrow to some place or event (in this case, "the Coachella Valley and the big carrot festival therein"); Bugs fails to make "that left turn at Albuquerque" and winds up wherever the cartoon takes place. He tries to ask the matador for directions, but the matador is busy getting the hell out of the ring. As Bugs tries to figure out what's going on, the bull stops behind him, looking furious, breathing ferociously on him. Bugs turns around . . . and slaps the bull in the face. "Stop steamin' up my tail!"

That slap was the biggest moment of the entire night. The laugh was huge, it was loud, but it was also a laugh mixed with and in some ways indistinguishable from cheers. People didn't only think it was *funny* that

Bugs was unafraid of the bull. They thought it was cool. Bugs was, in that moment, both comic and fearless action hero, and the reaction was a mix of laughter and hero worship.

Jones had also timed the lines perfectly for a theater audience. Bugs pauses after he delivers that line to the bull, and starts his next line ("What are you tryin' to do, wrinkle it?") as the laugh is still reverberating through the theater, but has receded enough for the line to be heard.

It's like music.

I was always a fan of *Looney Tunes*, but I walked out of the theater that night more convinced than ever that I'd picked the right thing to be a fan of. There are some things I love that I don't think are that great, and others that I know are an acquired taste. *Looney Tunes* is different. To me, it is the greatest achievement of American film comedy in the sound era. I knew it better than ever after that screening, hearing the applause for the creations of long-dead animators and storywriters. These were not just entertainments that diverted me on Saturday morning. They were the greatest kind of "classic," one that never loses its power over audiences no matter how much time passes since the day it was made.

* * *

Of course, I didn't know that night that the cartoons, and the characters in them, had just passed their peak of popularity, and that their owners would spend the next two decades looking in vain for a way to make them big stars again. I didn't know, but I should have known. It's not the natural order of things for great classics to also be popular.

In my defense, I'd grown up in a period when it seemed normal that a child born in 1976 would prefer to spend his Saturday morning watching cartoons from the 1940s and '50s. A lot of the people I met, in that theater and elsewhere, had enjoyed the same experience. And the reason we'd had that experience is that *Looney Tunes* cartoons were phenomenally popular among children, even though almost none of them were new. Between 1964 and 1988, Bugs Bunny only starred in four all-new productions, each one a television special lasting twenty-five minutes, which amounts to about four minutes a year. The company didn't need to make more than that, because they were making so much money off the old material.

"For more than three decades, Warner has claimed a No. 1 rating for its Saturday morning reruns of the classic cartoons originally made for the Silver Screen," the *Los Angeles Times* said in 1992.[4] Sure, they could have been doing better. These old cartoons were making millions every year from broadcast and cable sales, and it was "nearly all profit," since the films had already been paid for. If Warner Bros. hadn't sold off half its cartoons all those years ago, there would have been still more profits to boast about.

There was even a very popular live-action movie dedicated to the idea that Warner Bros. once made the best cartoons in the world. In the late 1980s, Warner Bros.' rival, the Walt Disney Company, produced *Who Framed Roger Rabbit*, a movie about a detective investigating the world of animated cartoon characters, or "toons," in the 1940s. The film was conceived as a tribute to the cartoons of the era, and the filmmakers had Disney's entire stable of cartoon characters to draw on, but it wasn't enough. *Roger Rabbit* was about the world of zany, violent cartoons, with a title character who will do almost anything for a laugh. That wasn't the way of most Disney characters. For *Roger Rabbit* to actually deal with cartoons as the creators knew them, it needed to borrow another studio's characters, and often treat them as substantially more interesting than the Disney stars. For the first joint appearance of Bugs Bunny and Mickey

Mouse, Bugs got to inflict all the violence on the film's human star, played by Bob Hoskins, while Mickey mostly watched Bugs work.

The movie's elevation of Warner Bros. cartoons over Disney was originally supposed to extend to the very end, which had Porky Pig delivering the catchphrase that ended almost every Warner Bros. cartoon from 1930 onward: "That's all Folks! To avoid ending a Disney production with a Warner Bros. star, the creators had Tinker Bell from Disney's *Peter Pan* fly in as the screen did an iris out on Porky. No one was fooled. This was not a Disney movie with some Warner Bros. cameos. It was a movie that held up the Warner Bros. cartoon style as the ideal of what a cartoon should be.

A character being world-famous almost entirely on the basis of repeats is not normal. Old work has usually been a minority taste. So why did several generations watch old *Looney Tunes* alongside new work, and actually prefer the stuff made before they were born? It was partly a historical accident, caused by television's unique demand for an endless supply of material. Material is difficult and expensive to create. On radio, you can fill twenty-four hours cheaply; on TV, even the cheapest filler needs cameras, lights, and makeup. So what every television station needed was a supply of preexisting material, something that might cost money to run but not to produce. The pre-1948 Warner Bros. cartoons were available cheap and, compared to other cartoons available to stations for the same money, they were a steal: some of the world's best-loved animation for the price of the worst-loved.

Once Warner Bros. realized it had made a mistake by selling so many cartoons, it decided to exploit the TV possibilities of the cartoons it still owned. In 1960, the company sold *The Bugs Bunny Show* to the ABC network, which ran it in prime time for two years. The studio's three longest-serving directors, Chuck Jones, Friz Freleng, and Bob McKimson, created a few minutes of new animation every week, but the bulk of every episode was three six-minute cartoons from the post-1948 period.

ABC removed the show from prime time after two years, and the package of post-1948 cartoons spent many decades as Saturday-morning children's programs. It changed titles a few times (the final incarnation was *The Bugs Bunny and Tweety Show*), but one thing that never seemed to change was that these cartoons were massively loved even by children who hadn't been alive when they were produced. *Looney Tunes* became a TV success impervious to time and changing standards. In 1990, celebrating the fiftieth anniversary of Bugs Bunny's sort-of-birth ("A Wild Hare" [1940] was his first official cartoon, although there had been prototypes with different voices and designs), the Warner Bros. corporation proudly announced that *Looney Tunes* reruns were beating all other programming on Saturday morning. It was as if kids preferred art house revivals to blockbusters: not wrong, just unexpected.

Part of *Looney Tunes*' enduring success reflects the simple power of money. Cartoons made for the big screen had higher per-unit budgets than television cartoons, for the same reason feature films have bigger budgets than television episodes: the crew didn't need to make as many of them. So, on television, the *Looney*s were up against shows that had to turn out twenty-two minutes per week and looked like it: *Kissyfur* and *The Smurfs* and *Rubik, the Amazing Cube*. The beauty of TV reruns is that you can watch lavishly made movies instead of cheaply produced TV shows if you don't care how old something is. Kids didn't care how old *Looney Tunes* cartoons were, and televisions weren't sophisticated enough to expose the age of the films or the poor condition of some of the prints.

Also, *Looney Tunes* seemed edgier and freer than the new material. Unlike feature films from the 1940s and '50s, which had strict censorship rules forced upon them, short cartoons were so obviously silly and unreal that they could get away with things that wouldn't be allowed in a live-action movie. Suicide, for example, was hard to slip into a dramatic motion picture, but *Looney Tunes* used suicide as a recurring punch line, often having characters react to a strange sight by saying, "Well, now I've seen everything!" and blowing their brains out. The sight of a talking animal pulling a gun out of nowhere was so obviously absurd that it couldn't be taken as actual advocacy of suicide as a means of escaping your troubles. Cartoons did sometimes run into censorship problems, but mild ones compared to what anything live-action usually had to deal with. Bob Clampett originally ended a Bugs Bunny cartoon he directed by having Bugs shoot his opponent, but the version finally released just had the villain shoot himself in the head, which apparently sent no bad messages at all.

Another advantage old cartoons had over new ones was that network executives mostly wanted cartoons to be as bland and nonthreatening as possible. It's much easier to impose blandness on something before it's made than after. No matter how much the censors cut out of a *Looney Tunes* cartoon, they could never quite censor their spirit. The cartoons where Bugs Bunny tricks Elmer Fudd into shooting Daffy Duck would get chopped a little more with every year of parental complaint. But even with the violence excised, they were still cartoons about a man with a shotgun, and two popular characters scheming to get each other shot. That concept would never have made it out of a pitch meeting for a new cartoon.

So kids watched *Looney Tunes*, and loved them, and because they were actually good, most of us never grew out of loving them. But however much we loved them, they never got the credit they deserved. There hasn't been much mainstream film criticism about them. When they were being made, they were almost totally ignored by all but two critics: James Agee wrote an appreciation of a music-themed Bugs Bunny cartoon, "Rhapsody Rabbit," and the great contrarian Manny Farber wrote a longer article where he hailed *Looney Tunes* producer Leon Schlesinger's output as the best in the business.[5] Later, after the cartoons started appearing on TV, younger critics got interested in them, and *Film Comment* magazine in 1975 devoted a whole issue to classic Hollywood cartoons and Warner Bros. cartoons in particular. There have been interesting things since then from historian/critics like Michael Barrier, author of *Hollywood Cartoons*, which devotes a lot of space to the Warner Bros. directors. But there is still much that hasn't been said, particularly outside of animation fandom, about *why* they're great.

* * *

So why are *Looney Tunes* so great?

First, let's admit their limitations. Some great comedy is also serious, or moving, or profound even while it does all the things a comedy is supposed to do. There are a few *Looney Tunes* cartoons that can be sort of taken seriously, like "One Froggy Evening," which very much wants us to know that it's a parable about human greed. But most of the cartoons are comedy for its own sake, with no underlying message or theme.

And unlike the great silent comedians, Warner Bros. characters have no depth. Charlie Chaplin, Buster Keaton, and Harold Lloyd all created characters who were not only funny, but also embodied the human desire for love and respect. They seem real, and we can like them even when they're not doing anything funny. They also were classic underdogs, struggling against society or natural disasters or all the other things that put us in our place. Comedy is usually taken most seriously when it's on the side of the underdog. Some classic cartoon characters fit that mold, like

Popeye, who (both in comics and animation) lives to punch back against bullies. The case has sometimes been made for the great *Looney Tunes* characters as classic underdogs, but it's never a convincing case because the characters aren't actually struggling against anything. They seldom have to try hard: as long as it's funny, they can produce a weapon out of nowhere, and the most horrific acts of violence cause them no stronger reaction than irritation. In a more serious comedy, the characters feel an exaggerated version of what we might feel in their shoes, whether anger, fear, or determination. We can't usually identify much with a *Looney Tunes* character, because we know that nothing has consequences for them, and they seem to know it too.

It's not a criticism of *Looney Tunes*, just a description, to say that the cartoons will do anything for a laugh. As a result, a lot of the cartoons suffer when judged by standards of fictional storytelling. One rule that most fiction creators follow is that the hero must have a villain who is his equal. It's not good storytelling if the villain is an idiot. *Looney Tunes* villains are the biggest idiots in fiction. They always believe that Bugs Bunny is a woman when he dresses up as one. They get tripped up by the most obvious devices, and allow themselves to be tricked into doing anything the hero wants them to do.

Even when the villains initially seem like an actual threat, that's just to make it funnier when they turn out to be no threat at all. In "The Hasty Hare" (1952), Bugs Bunny faces off for the second time with a tiny Martian who has no face, just a pair of eyes in a void. The character was never named in the cartoons, but is usually called "Marvin the Martian" for marketing purposes. Like any good 1950s Martian, Marvin possesses a destructive ray gun, and seems to terrify Bugs when he shows it off. But immediately afterward, Marvin and his Martian dog sidekick fall for every one of Bugs's tricks, including turning the two of them against each other by merely suggesting that the dog is a mutineer ("Mutiny makes me so angry!" Marvin replies, blasting K-9 in the face). Bugs was never really in trouble.

Another recurring Bugs Bunny villain, Yosemite Sam, was created because director Friz Freleng thought Elmer Fudd wasn't enough of a threat. But Sam is never presented by Freleng as an actual danger to Bugs either. Instead, Sam usually starts out by intimidating bit characters. In one of his early appearances, *Bugs Bunny Rides Again* (1948), he makes his entrance by walking into a Wild West bar, where everyone is terrified at the sight of him. When Sam says, "All of you skunks clear out of here," they run, including an actual skunk. Unlike Elmer, who was just a middle-class idiot out of his depth in the woods, Sam is a genuine villain, a criminal, someone who deserves everything he's going to get in the course of the cartoon. But we're never left in any doubt that Sam's going to get destroyed by Bugs. Again, Bugs only shows fear for the purpose of setting Sam up, and Sam is so stupid he will do anything Bugs wants as long as it is framed as a challenge. Two different cartoons have Sam walk off a precipice when Bugs dares him to "step over this line."

Running on the principle that a story is better with a weak villain is only one violation of the normal rules of structure that a good *Looney Tunes* cartoon habitually commits. Even the idea that characters should be consistent is usually not followed. A *Looney Tunes* character may have one or two traits that define him, and everything else can change depending on what's funnier in the moment. Daffy Duck almost seems like a different character from picture to picture. During World War II, he was a brave commando who flew to Berlin and hit Hitler over the head with a mallet. Another cartoon had him as a cowardly draft dodger who tried to murder the little man who was giving him his draft notice.

This all falls under the general heading of "anything for a laugh." It isn't what we expect of first-rate art. Even popular art isn't supposed to pander to the audience by giving them anything for a laugh; it's supposed to leave out things that violate the world the artist is trying to create. That's how things were done at United Productions of America (UPA), the cartoon studio usually considered the most artistic and ambitious. UPA was willing to make a big show of how much it left out. Its most successful recurring character, the nearsighted old man Mr. Magoo, was the deliberate antithesis of the Warner Bros. style: not only was Magoo a human, he was a human whose life was governed by something resembling real-world physics. When he blundered into dangerous situations, the comedy depended on the fear that he could actually die unless lucky (as he always was). Everything was more restrained and realistic than at Warner Bros. When Jim Backus performed the voice of Mr. Magoo, he sounded like a slightly exaggerated version of a cranky old man from our world, and the animation was similarly restrained. When Backus did a voice for a WB cartoon, as a genie in the Bugs Bunny short "A-Lad-In-His Lamp," he gave a loud, outrageously hammy performance, matched by the performance of the animators, who had him swinging his huge hands to emphasize every cadence of his speech.

UPA people generally thought that this willingness to avoid the easy gag and the sudden disregard for reality made their product superior to Warner cartoons. Bill Scott, who co-wrote cartoons at Warner Bros. for several years and then moved to UPA, said that "the kiss of death at UPA was to be considered a Warner Brothers writer." *Looney Tunes* writers, he added, were dismissed as "clothesline gag" writers, for whom a story was just a cheap, insubstantial way to support the gags."[6]

That description, which Scott didn't agree with, wasn't exactly wrong. It is absolutely true that in a lot of Warner cartoons, the story is an excuse for gags. If the creators have a choice between telling a joke and giving the film a consistent style, they'll almost always choose the joke. A lot of cartoon gags are like the cliché phrases that composers use to link their best material together. They're there because they're easy, and every *Looney Tunes* cartoon has a few bits that clearly came easy.

There are some Warner Bros. cartoons that strive for something different, something more coherent, but are constantly pulled back by the ideology of anything for a laugh, and the willingness to fall back on stock gags. Friz Freleng's "Three Little Bops," a retelling of the familiar story with the pigs as progressive jazz musicians and the wolf as a bad trumpeter who wants to sit in with them, is one of his best-loved cartoons, and it shows some signs of wanting to be more than just another Warner Bros. cartoon: the music is by jazz musician Shorty Rogers instead of the regular music team, and the film ends with a simple "THE END," eliminating the usual "That's all Folks!" Even the use of sound is a little different; only one effect from the Warner sound effects library is used, and all the other sounds are indicated through music alone.

But Freleng can't bring himself to commit to something truly different from the average *Looney Tunes* cartoon. So as the short goes on, more and more stock Warner Bros. gags start sneaking in. After the pigs start playing at the House of Bricks (a fancy club that is too well-built for the wolf to blow down), the short turns into a series of blackout gags about the wolf trying to sneak into the club and being foiled in his attempts, which could just as easily be used for Sylvester the Cat or Yosemite Sam. In fact, some of them *were* used for those characters. The last big gag, where the wolf tries to blow up the club but the pigs blow out the fuse before he can get close enough, is recycled from Freleng's "Southern Fried Rabbit," where it was used for Sam and Bugs Bunny. When the UPA gang did an unconventional cartoon, they committed to it; every joke had to be a joke that sprang from the unique nature of the film. Every Warner Bros. cartoon, even the most experimental, includes jokes that could have been used in any other picture, and often were.

This all sounds like I'm hedging my bets when it comes to proclaiming the greatness of *Looney Tunes*. I'm not. To celebrate the greatness of works of art, you have to acknowledge their limitations, the sides of the world that they don't or can't see. *Looney Tunes* cartoons leave out a lot of human experience, and speak to only one kind of mood. But what we ask of art is not that it tell us everything, but that it tell us *something*, that it have a style and a viewpoint that makes sense to us. Every good *Looney Tunes* cartoon has that.

Take "A Tale of Two Kitties," a 1942 short directed by Bob Clampett and written by Warren Foster. The title characters are cats named Babbit and Catstello, based on the comedy team of Abbott and Costello. After this film, they would be changed from cats to mice in a few cartoons under other directors. The third character in the picture was quite a bit more successful than that. He's a tiny, baby-talking bird who would later be named Tweety. He's colored pink in this cartoon, suggesting that he's featherless; to avoid the suggestion of bird-nudity, he would later be colored yellow.

This is a good cartoon, but more than anything else, it's a completely *typical* Warner Bros. cartoon, which has all the elements we expect from the studio. Here are the elements.

The formula. You can see why Warner Bros. cartoon writers were considered unsophisticated by the UPA crowd. This story follows a formula that had been slowly establishing itself as *the* Warner cartoon formula, and would pretty much dominate the company until the studio shut down. The premise is that someone goes hunting for someone else, repeatedly tries to catch them, and repeatedly fails. That's the whole story of this cartoon.

It opens with Babbit (voiced by Tedd Pierce, a storywriter at Warner Bros. who did some voice work on the side) talking to Catstello (Mel Blanc). Even if you haven't seen an Abbott and Costello movie, their relationship is understandable just by looking at them and listening. Catstello is small, fat, whiny, and easily talked into anything by the tall, scheming Babbit, who gets his partner to take all the risks on any plan he comes up with. In the first few seconds of dialogue, we establish that they're hungry, and that they're standing under a tree with a bird's nest in it. Babbit gives Catstello his objective: "Get the bird out of that nest, and we'll eat."

The next six minutes consist of a series of gags where Catstello tries to get to the nest to catch Tweety, and fails in humiliating ways. Although each gag has its own identity and structure—some are longer, others are shorter, and Tweety doesn't participate in thwarting all the attempts—there is not much attempt to weave them together into a plot. There isn't even an ending, exactly. The closest thing to a plot resolution comes when Tweety, after the last gag, gets down from the tree onto the ground and scares the cats by shouting, "TURN OUT THOSE LIGHTS!" (a stock phrase during wartime air-raid drills). This slight break in the formula, Tweety joining his would-be predators on the ground, is enough of a change to pass for an ending.

Heavy borrowing from radio and live-action comedy. The origin of many cartoon characters is someone saying, "Hey, you know what I heard on the radio last night?" (Or, later, "Hey, you know what I saw on TV last night?") Sometimes their sources are still familiar today, like Abbott and Costello. But just as often, we get what the website TV Tropes calls the "Weird Al Effect," where the parody or borrowing remains famous while the source is forgotten.

In Tweety's case, the source is Red Skelton. Skelton is not completely forgotten, thanks to some Hollywood movie roles and his paintings of sad clowns, part of the pantheon of twentieth-century kitsch along with dogs playing poker. But his radio show featured a number of characters who influenced other media, and Junior, the "Mean Widdle Kid," was the most influential of them all. Junior was an excuse for Skelton to talk in exaggerated baby talk while doing mean things and spouting catchphrases. His most famous catchphrase, which turns up in this picture and many other Warner cartoons, was "I dood it!" Foster claimed that this cartoon was inspired by a real-life child who pointed at a squirrel and yelled: "I tawt I taw a twirl!," which he turned into Tweety's "I tawt I taw a putty tat!"

Amorality. There's a memorable fake out near the beginning of the cartoon, where we're led to think that Catstello might have some kind of conscience. "I don't wanna hurt no birds," he tells Babbit. "I like birds! I'll go hungry first." Then Babbit reassures him that the bird is tiny and helpless, and Catstello instantly changes his mood (everyone's emotions can turn on a dime in this world), revealing that the only reason he was reluctant to kill the bird is that he thought it might hit back:

> *Catstello*: You mean a poor little teensy-weensy, itsy-bitsy, defenseless bird?
> *Babbit*: Yes!
> *Catstello*: Let me at him! Let me at him! I'll get him, Babbit! Gangway! I'll murderlize him!

Of course, the "defenseless" bird isn't so defenseless. There's probably not a viewer in the world who doesn't expect that. But a new viewer might not be prepared for the vigor of Tweety's defenses. He's more vicious than his would-be tormentors. Like Skelton's Mean Widdle Kid, the joke with this version of Tweety is that he pretends to be innocent and cute, but he's a total bastard.

In the most famous gag in the film, which animator Mark Kausler later adapted for Tweety's appearance in *Who Framed Roger Rabbit*, the little bird walks up to someone who is hanging from a wire by his fingers, and starts unfastening the fingers, one by one, while playing a game of this little piggy (or "this widdle piddy" in Tweety-speak). Other cartoon directors believed, at least to some extent, in the idea of innocence, that there are some people who mean no harm and look at the world in a charmingly ingenuous way. Even Jerry in the *Tom and Jerry* cartoons is sometimes portrayed as an innocent, or at least someone who is just too happy and cheerful to realize that he's doing vicious things. Clampett never leaves us in doubt that Tweety is mean, and enjoys it. Clampett might be described as a cynic, but not necessarily an unhappy or unhealthy one. Tweety is his way of thumbing his nose at the idea, familiar from Disney cartoons, that cuteness equals goodness.

Voices. American animated films are often richer in visual humor than dialogue. Mickey Mouse started out as a silent character and usually had very few lines. Donald Duck's dialogue was (intentionally) almost impossible to understand. Popeye muttered as much as he talked, and Tom and Jerry, the most popular characters from Warner Bros.' rivals at Metro-Goldwyn-Mayer, almost never talked. In a typical Warner Bros. cartoon, on the other hand, talk is almost nonstop. "A Tale of Two Kitties" begins with the two cats talking behind a fence, invisible but audible to the audience, and they never stop talking throughout the film, each visual gag preceded by a verbal joke. Mel Blanc, who voices two of the three characters and performed the voice of virtually every major Warner Bros. cartoon star, was a dominant force in *Looney Tunes* in a way that no other voice actor was until television came along. His delivery of Tweety's lines never sounds like a Red Skelton impression, and his voice has enough of an adult, sarcastic edge to it that it is always easy to listen to, where other baby-talk voices wear out their welcome really fast. Tweety's final scream in the movie only works as an ending because of Blanc and his ability to go from a cute little-bird voice to an adult scream that tests the limits of the microphone.

Warner Bros. cartoon writers knew what they had with Blanc, and tried to supply him with dialogue that would be worthy of his skill. Foster's dialogue mostly holds up because it rarely strains to be clever and is mostly a succession of lines that get a laugh based on sheer sound and delivery, like Tweety's catchphrase, or Babbit and Catstello imitating pilots while trying to launch Costello into the air ("Contact . . . contact . . . contact . . ."). There are some more typical punch lines, including a memorable censor-baiting joke: Babbit says, "Give me the bird!" and his worn-out partner tells us, "If the Hays Office would only let me, I'd give 'im the bird, all right!" but the cartoon never spends so much time setting up a verbal joke that it would leave the animators with nothing to do.

Looney Tunes dialogue has the wise-guy tone and fast pace of radio comedy, the medium Blanc came from and the writers all borrowed from while condensing and simplifying so that it never interfered with the visual humor. Incorporating dialogue without losing visual interest is something movies struggled with from the moment sound was introduced. For decades, *Looney Tunes* managed to do it better than any other sound comedy.

Violence. You can't talk about *Looney Tunes* without talking about violence. The Warner cartoons didn't start out as particularly violent—less violent, certainly, than *Popeye*, where every cartoon ended in a huge fistfight, and even less violent than the early Mickey Mouse cartoons, where he could be a bit of a psychopath. But by 1942, violence was a standard device in most *Looney Tunes* cartoons. This film has most of the ones you remember from childhood. Dropping an anvil on a character is perhaps the iconic *Looney Tunes* gag, combining an attack that would be fatal in real life with a device that hardly anyone has seen outside of a cartoon. This is one of the few cartoons where the anvil does actually drop. After causing Catstello to fall from the wire, Tweety throws him a rope, but the rope is attached to an anvil, and it smashes Catstello into the ground, leaving him as a squashed, thin layer under the anvil.

Tweety also greets Catstello by repeatedly hitting him with a club. When he gets tired of the club, he switches to blowing him up with a stick of dynamite, which is second only to anvils as the most iconic cartoon weapon. All of these items, of course, are produced from nowhere. And a tiny little bird can brandish a club that's several times larger than he is. Which brings us to . . .

Cartoon logic. Possibly the best-known aspect of the classic *Looney Tunes* cartoons is that they seem to break the laws of physics in ways that suggest they exist in an alternative physical universe with its own rules. Anything can be pulled from anywhere if a character needs it. Gravity doesn't work until you look down, and even then, it's sometimes possible to resist gravity and crawl back to safety. Distances and weights are never consistent. Catstello falls more quickly than the anvil, racing it to the ground before it smashes him and pulls a few acres of ground into a hole behind it.

Cartoon logic also allows things to happen that are completely contradictory to the actual story. In this film, these leaps of logic involve food. In one scene, Catstello is shown eating an apple while Babbit prepares to launch him up to Tweety's nest. Later, after the anvil falls on Catstello, we see Babbit planting a "victory garden." Almost since the beginning of YouTube, commenters have pointed out that these moments go against the premise of the cartoon, which is that the cats are so hungry they'll do almost anything to catch one little bird.

They're right, but it doesn't matter. Catstello is eating an apple to set up a gag: Tweety takes the apple from him, pulls out a worm, eats the worm, and throws away the apple. Babbit is working on a victory garden as a topical reference to the home front in World War II. The question of why Catstello wants to eat a bird if he can get an apple is no more important than the classic issue of why Coyote doesn't buy food with all the money he spends on ACME products. These cartoons break the most familiar storytelling rule of all, that of internal consistency. Logic bends to the demands of the joke.

Director individuality. Warner Bros. was the studio where the "auteur theory," the premise that films are reflections of their directors' personalities, was most applicable. Disney set up American animation as a producer-dominated system, much like the American live-action film industry at the time. At Warner Bros., the directors worked almost autonomously, being asked only to deliver cartoons that were on budget and made theater audiences laugh. Each director had his own style and his own personal take on the overall formula, so much so that fans can learn to spot a director's work instantly just by his approach to storytelling and gags.

In "A Tale of Two Kitties," Clampett is using a story that Foster could have sold to another director, and a bunch of gags that anyone at the studio could have handled, but he has his own take on every one of the gags. Some directors like an anvil drop to be quick and sudden. Clampett stretches it out as long as possible, and prolongs the impact of the drop. He also subverts an expected gag when Catstello takes another fall: Clampett keeps cutting to a pitchfork on the ground, setting us up to expect the cat to fall on it . . . but instead, Catstello defies gravity to his own benefit (for once) and slides sideways out of the way. Clampett happened to like nonstandard resolutions to standard gags, and this is one of the reasons why he's the favorite director of many cartoon fans who like their cartoon comedy more subversive than that of Chuck Jones or Friz Freleng, the directors who remained at the studio after Clampett left.

The point is not that one approach is better than another, but that at Warner Bros., you can see everyone's approach clearly. It was an auteur studio in a way that the producer-focused animation studios could never be, as Chuck Jones found out to his despair when he spent a few months at Walt Disney's studio in the 1950s: "He had a sheet of typewritten suggestions he tried to hold forth, and Walt was not interested," a Disney co-producer wrote in his diary. "Chuck is going to have to learn to work with Walt. I presume that he feels he was called in for his creative thinking and ability. He will soon have to learn that Walt sets the direction, the pace, and even the topic of conversation."[7]

The attitude. This is the most indelible part of the Warner Bros. cartoon style, hard as it is to define. Every director had his own idea of how far a character could go without forfeiting audience sympathy. Clampett, as noted, would go farther than any other director, which is why his version of Tweety is a vicious sadist. But *all* Warner Bros. cartoons, at least after the studio found its style in the 1930s, have at least an element of sadism, and contempt for normal morality. People who overreacted to cartoon violence aren't really overreacting: cartoon violence carries the slightly antisocial message that the most horrifying things imaginable are funny if they happen to someone else.

Of course, Clampett isn't just saying that violence is funny. The war is funny. Air-raid readiness is funny. Childish innocence is a lie, and so are friendship and compassion. The Warner Bros. attitude is that Disney has been lying to you.

* * *

Are there other animation studios, then or now, that could offer something like the Warner Bros. mix of elements? Yes, and at least one other classic studio that did it with consistency: MGM is in the same class as Warner Bros. when it comes to making funny cartoons. MGM had a somewhat similar structure. Fred Quimby, the producer, put his name in huge letters on every cartoon, but its two most famous animation units were headed by strong directors who supervised every aspect of their work. Tex Avery, the director who shaped the Warner Bros. style and defined the personalities of Daffy Duck and Bugs Bunny, quit Warner Bros. and joined MGM, where he did his very best work, and it was unquestionably his work, not Quimby's. The studio's other top unit, which made the *Tom and Jerry* series, was directed by William Hanna and Joseph Barbera, who created much of their own story material.

Hanna and Barbera would eventually become the kings of television animation. They were in some ways the most successful in combining the brash, violent Avery style with some of the respectability of Disney; no Avery cartoon ever won an Oscar, but *Tom and Jerry* won several. And even Bugs Bunny is not as strong a brand as Tom and Jerry, especially worldwide. The cat and mouse are better known internationally than any single Warner character, probably because they almost never talk, making them easy to translate into other languages and removing the problem of Bugs Bunny's accent, which seems (because it is) foreign to English speakers outside of North America. When the CIA declassified the files that were on Osama bin Laden's computer before he was killed, 138 of those files were Tom and Jerry cartoons.[8] There is no similar celebrity endorsement for *Looney Tunes*.

Still, while the best MGM cartoons rank with the best Warner Bros. cartoons, the studio's output doesn't compare to WB's when it comes to character creation. Hanna and Barbera, once they struck gold with Tom and Jerry, pretty much gave up trying to invent new recurring characters, and made nothing but Tom and Jerry cartoons for over a decade. Avery seemed uninterested in recurring characters at all. His real heart was in cartoons with new characters who mostly weren't intended to appear again, and the majority of of his MGM cartoons were like that.

Most studios had one or two good stars: Universal had Woody Woodpecker; Max Fleischer had Betty Boop and Popeye; Terrytoons are still vaguely remembered for Heckle and Jeckle and Mighty Mouse. But when it comes to a stable of characters, Warner Bros. was the clear winner, which is probably one of the reasons the cartoons were so successful on TV. You can fill an hour of programming with Warner cartoons and never run out of good characters to spotlight.

There's something else that sets the Warner Bros. cartoons apart from even the best work from other studios. More than other cartoons, maybe even any other comedy films, *Looney Tunes* have a power over the audience that goes beyond the quality of the individual gags. *Looney Tunes* cartoons are full of inexplicable laughs—like "pronoun trouble!"—where all the elements add up to a laugh that is much bigger than the same bit would get in anyone else's film. This mystery—why is an anvil drop funnier in a Warner Bros. cartoon than in almost any other cartoon that has ever tried to imitate the style?—reminds me of a comment by a symphony conductor who said that, given all the clichés and derivative tricks in Mozart's music, a computer analysis of his work would probably decide that Mozart was a second-rate composer. Obviously, only a computer would ever come to that conclusion. The point is that the whole is greater than the sum of its parts. Mozart's greatness is hard to analyze but easy to feel. You also *feel* the greatness of a great Warner Bros. cartoon.

The comparison of Warner Bros. cartoons to music is deliberate. There is a strong connection between animation and music. The *Looney Tunes* series was approved by Warner Bros. in part as a way to plug the songs owned by the company's music publishing division. Even after cartoons no longer had to be built around individual songs, many sequences were timed to music, and the movements of the characters had a steady, specific rhythm to them. This made the director of a cartoon a bit like the composer of a musical score, providing instructions to all the performers about what to do, but also like a conductor, making sure that everyone stays on the beat.

A good *Looney Tunes* cartoon also has the inexplicable, almost abstract appeal of music. Music can't say anything specific unless you put words to it. Its power is in making us feel things without being able to say, in any ordinary language, what we feel or why we feel it. *Looney Tunes* also have a power beyond words. Analyze a lot of the big gags, and none of the phrases we have developed to describe comedy greatness seem to explain why they're special. In Freleng's "Buccaneer Bunny," Bugs deals with a parrot who keeps pointing out his location to the villain. Bugs says, "Polly want a cracker?" and when the parrot says yes hands him a firecracker that blows up. An explosion gag. We've seen this bit in every cartoon, from every era, at every level of animation quality. Why is it so much funnier when Bugs does it than when anyone else does it? And why do we laugh even though we know what's going to happen, even when we've seen this bit already?

It's like music. The laughs come from timing and rhythm. Freleng was not known for fancy cinematic work or unusual camera angles—a lot of his best scenes take place in static shots with no camera movement—but he was legendary for knowing exactly how long to hold a beat for the maximum number of laughs. The gag is divided into three basic beats: Bugs hands the firecracker to the parrot; the firecracker explodes; the smoke clears, showing the ashen but otherwise unharmed bird. This all happens in just a few seconds, but each of these beats is held just long enough for it to play properly. We react not so much to the explosion or to the parrot's one line ("Me and my big mouth"), as to the subconscious feeling that each of these things is happening at the right time.

Freleng also knows enough to have Bugs duck down, out of the shot, before the firecracker explodes. You can't really say that it's for any particular reason; he doesn't look any more or less sympathetic because he ducks, and cartoon logic would certainly allow him to be unharmed even if he was in the shot. But the ducking provides the nonessential action we need to cover the very brief moment between seeing the firecracker and seeing the explosion. If the explosion happened immediately, with no time for us to react, it wouldn't be as funny. If it happened even a half second later, it wouldn't be as funny. And in other studios' cartoons, a lot of explosion gags do seem to happen a moment too soon or a moment too late. Not in *Looney Tunes*. They had it down to a science, and music, rhythm, and timing are all sciences of a sort.

Some of this has to do with the cartoon characters' direct relationship with the audience. In "Gee Whiz-z-z-z-z-z" (1956), Coyote puts on an ACME Bat-Man outfit that allows him (unlike the other Batman) to fly. After flying around beautifully and flawlessly he turns to us with a smug look on his face, as if asking us to acknowledge that this plan is actually working. And, of course, because he's busy looking at us, he slams into the side of a cliff. What makes the moment work, apart from the precise timing and the excellent use of sound (while Coyote is flying, there is no music; then there's a loud, dissonant chord to punctuate his latest screwup), is that he does not look over to someone else to approve his achievement. He looks at us, again, his eyes going downward rather than directly at the camera. The look on his face suggests that he is aware, on some level, that we expect him to fail and that we're surprised he hasn't failed yet. It's the interplay between him and us, between our expectations and the delayed payoffs, that make the violence funnier than it would be in a less self-conscious kind of film.

(A better example of the complicated games that these films could play with the invisible space that separates the action from the audience, the so-called fourth wall, is "A Hound for Trouble," where Mike Maltese does the voice of a customer at a restaurant in Italy. The obnoxious Charlie Dog is posing as his waiter. The customer gives him a ridiculously long, complicated order in pidgin Italian. Charlie then repeats the exact words of the order back to the customer, exactly as he said it. After finishing, Charlie sticks out his tongue at the audience. The joke wasn't the order itself; it was that we thought Charlie would get it wrong, and he gets to gloat over our mistake.)

Silent comedy can be analyzed, and has been at great length since it appeared. We know why the house falling down and just missing Buster Keaton is funny, and we know that the joy is in seeing a real person take that kind of risk and come out completely unharmed. That can't happen in a cartoon, but *Looney Tunes* creates a different kind of joy: the joy of seeing something so incredibly difficult—the creation of movement and action through thousands of individual drawings—add up to something so simple, so seemingly effortless, so very right, even if we don't know exactly why it's so right.

This special quality, this power that defies analysis, helps explain why there have been so few successful projects with the *Looney Tunes* characters since the original studio shut down (and there have been a lot of projects, as we will see later on). It's possible to analyze what makes non-*Looney* characters work and replicate it for a modern audience. Disney's most popular character worldwide is probably Donald Duck, and his adventures, especially in comic books, have a sort of template that a modern creator can follow. Superman has a formula for a successful story, as does James Bond. Bugs Bunny is much trickier, and a lot of what this book is about is people trying to figure out what exactly made Bugs Bunny work, and how they could revive him with something that wasn't just a cut-rate copy of the old stuff.

It might be that there is no way to do that. Or it might be that as you're reading this, someone has come to Warner Bros. with the perfect solution for modernizing Bugs and Daffy and Porky and turning them back into money machines. But that's the heart of the story this book will tell. These characters have experienced decades of strange management decisions, ill-advised revivals, and changes in technology and taste. Any other pop culture figures would have been completely forgotten after that kind of treatment, but *Looney Tunes* will never die. The cartoons are just too good to disappear.

CHAPTER 2

Bosko Beginnings

THE STORY OF SHOW BUSINESS is the story of people who accidentally create art that lasts.

Looney Tunes producer Leon Schlesinger was not someone who ever intended to create art for posterity. He came to Hollywood and started a business, Pacific Title & Art Studio, tailored to the needs of the Hollywood studios, which needed title cards for their silent movies. Then talking pictures came along and drastically reduced the market for title cards, so Schlesinger adapted his company to the things the studios still needed and moved his company into things like main title design and postproduction services.[1] Schlesinger also started a new company, one that would provide a Hollywood studio with six-minute animated sound cartoons or, as he might have described it, the next big thing in the graphic design business.

Schlesinger looked and dressed the part of a self-made businessman and producer, with expensive white suits, and an all-too-obvious comb-over. People who remembered him usually mentioned the scent of cologne.[2] He was budget-conscious, like many independent producers, always trying to make films for as little as possible so that they could earn back their money when he sold them to a distributor. His production facilities were so run-down that one place became known as "Termite Terrace," a nickname that eventually stuck to his entire cartoon studio. Shortly after getting into animation, he produced a series of live-action Western movies with a young John Wayne, where the shooting schedules were around three days and the expensive action was recycled from silent movies.[3] He never attempted anything as ambitious as an animated feature film.

But Schlesinger was also an appreciative audience for a good joke and a funny cartoon. He seems to have been one of those producers who had few pretensions to being a creative artist himself, but believed that his own tastes matched up with the mass audience's tastes in a way that highbrows and self-conscious artists couldn't hope to match. His own tastes ran to fast, funny films that didn't try to be too artistically ambitious or groundbreaking, and he was probably right to think that this was what the public wanted, even if he wasn't under any illusion that he knew how to create those cartoons on his own.

The reason for getting into the animation game was simple. It was a seller's market: every studio was looking for its own Walt Disney, a producer with a cartoon-production factory. The animated cartoon had probably benefited more from the introduction of sound than any other type of motion picture. Walt Disney's "Steamboat Willie," the 1928 film that introduced Mickey Mouse, had demonstrated what the synchronization of animation with music and sound effects could do, and how audiences would go wild to see characters moving to the beat of recorded music.

Warner Bros. was particularly interested in the "music" part of it. The studio was best known for having patented the Vitaphone process for synchronizing recorded sound with motion pictures. After its production of *The Jazz Singer* created a market for musical movies, Warner Bros.

invested heavily in music publishing, partly with a view to promoting original songs from its films. When Schlesinger arrived to pitch *Looney Tunes* (a title now much more famous than the Disney series it was ripping off, *Silly Symphonies*), he sold it as yet another way of plugging Warner-owned songs. Instead of being featured in only one movie, a song could appear in a live-action film and then be used as the basis for a cartoon, theoretically increasing the amount of exposure it got and thereby increasing the sheet music sales. Synergy, we'd call it now.

When the studio started up, Schlesinger had a creative team in place and a character to build his studio around. Both were influenced by Disney. But then, everything was influenced by Disney in Hollywood animation around this time, even the things that rebelled against what Disney would have done. "We didn't do anything," *Looney Tunes* director Frank Tashlin once said. "It all came from Disney's."[4]

Tashlin was exaggerating, but it's true that everyone in the American cartoon business looked to Disney to teach them not only technique— Disney's studio would come up with a technical innovation, and everyone else would run with it—but also character types and subject matter. Disney's "The Three Little Pigs," for instance, taught a lot of US animators how to use movement to differentiate characters who looked the same, and it also kicked off decades' worth of "Three Little Pigs" cartoons from every other animation producer, all of which took some cues from Disney in how the pigs and the wolf were portrayed.

A rival studio, of course, couldn't get their own Walter E. Disney. But Schlesinger acquired two of the next best things: Hugh Harman and Rudolf-Ising, or "Harman-Ising" as they were usually referred to due to the unintended play on the word "harmonizing." Like many animators, they were from Disney's hometown of Kansas City, where Harman's brother Fred had worked with Disney at Kansas City Film Ad

Service, an advertising company whose animated ads became a training ground for many local animators. When Disney moved to California and opened his studio there, Harman and Ising were among the Kansas City animators who joined him, working on his cartoon character, Oswald the Lucky Rabbit. When Disney asked for more money from Charles Mintz, who distributed the Oswald films, Mintz cut ties with Disney's studio instead and took over the rights to Oswald. Several Disney staffers, including Harman and Ising, chose to continue working on Oswald for Mintz, but Disney bounced back by co-creating Mickey Mouse, a character similar to Oswald, but owned outright by the Disney studio. Once Mickey became the most popular character in the world, Harman and Ising were inspired to go off on their own and try to create their own cartoon star, trading on the prestige of their past association with Disney.[5]

When Harman and Ising met with Schlesinger, they already had a film to show him: "Bosko, the Talk-Ink Kid." Created and copyrighted by the pair in early 1928, Bosko was a cheerful child of indeterminate age, described in the copyright filing as a "negro boy." The pilot film was a live-action/animation hybrid where an animator's drawing of Bosko comes to life and interacts with him. While drawing animation on top of live-action footage was not new, the specific combination here was influenced by "Out of the Inkwell," a series created by Max Fleischer's studio in New York, which had emerged as the most important rival to Disney.

The Harman-Ising team had already pitched the Bosko film to other producers who passed on it, but Schlesinger liked it. He took Bosko to Warner Bros., which agreed to distribute Schlesinger's cartoons. Beginning in 1930 with the first *Looney Tunes* short, "Sinkin' in the Bathtub," Bosko became the first star of Schlesinger's studio.

The main thing to note about the cartoon itself, apart from the start of the long *Looney Tunes* tradition of punny titles (the cartoon is built around a song called "Singin' in the Bathtub"), is that it drops the elaborate live-action/animation combination of the pilot film, and makes Bosko a character in an all-animated world. A recurring theme of the Warner Bros. cartoon studio: if an approach costs extra money, don't expect it to last.

In staffing their new studio, one of the animators Harman and Ising brought in was a cartoonist named Isadore Freleng. (He hated that first name and preferred to be called "Friz.") Freleng was also an alumnus of Kansas City Film Ad who had moved out to Hollywood to animate for Disney. A Kansas City colleague described him as "this little red-haired Jewish guy, everybody picked on him." Sensitive about his height, Freleng found California people even more inclined to joke about it, and Disney would sometimes join in. "When he'd make a remark," Freleng recalled to Joe Adamson, "I'd take exception, and I'd make a nasty remark back to him."[6] His red hair, small stature, and headstrong nature would eventually make him the basis for one of his most popular characters, Yosemite Sam.

Freleng lasted only a few months at Disney. One reason was that his boss was impatient with his lack of skill as an animator. Before he was hired, Freleng was assured that he would have time to practice and learn his craft, but Disney was a perfectionist who wanted great results from his young animators right away. A demanding style worked for Disney, but his competitors had to accept that they would be staffed with people still learning their craft. Animation was a younger medium than live-action film, and conventions on how to animate in sound cartoons were still being codified when Freleng went to Schlesinger's. Rules of timing, of making the characters look like they have weight, of synchronizing dialogue to mouth movements were all being worked out on the job. There was potential in this, because audiences were still so thrilled with this new form that they would accept crude technique or deficient plots. But it also meant that few of Disney's rivals could seriously hope to match him when it came to technical innovation. They had to settle for people who could draw and would learn on the job, if not as quickly as Disney would have demanded.

Still, Schlesinger, along with Harman and Ising and his brother-in-law Ray Katz, managed to staff the studio with good young talent. And Bosko was successful enough that Schlesinger launched a second series of cartoons, titled *Merrie Melodies*, which was intended to focus on "one-shots," meaning cartoons without recurring characters, although characters from one-shots could sometimes become popular enough to get a series.[7]

The Schlesinger studio's early years did not produce a lot of outstanding cartoons, and it's doubtful that many people would be talking about them today if Bosko had remained the studio's biggest star. Harman and Ising's approach was nothing like the punchy, gag-filled comedy that Schlesinger came to prefer. There was too much singing. Harman and Ising may also have made a miscalculation in trying to decide what would set them apart from Disney. They imitated the blandest things about Disney cartoons, while changing the things that rescued those cartoons from blandness.

It was normal for pop culture creators to look at the best works in their field in hopes of inventing a lead character similar enough to be popular, but also different enough to stand out. Disney was the leader with his funny animals, but Max Fleischer and his director brother Dave had established themselves as solid competitors by emphasizing human stars like Betty Boop, and unusual technical gimmicks, like the combinations of animation and live-action in their "Out of the Inkwell" series. The obvious route for the *Looney Tunes* creators was to take bits and pieces from both studios and see if the combination would lead to something new.

And so Bosko was as close to Mickey Mouse as you could get without being sued. Carleton University film studies professor Mark Langer notes that Bosko resembled Mickey "in terms of his physical proportions, simple black on white 'inkblot' design, squeaky voice and musical routines." What made him different from Mickey was "the use of long trousers and the lack of tail and mouse ears."[8] In other words, it's Mickey, but more human than funny animal.

Copying characters is nothing to be ashamed of in the world of cartoons. It would often work for Warner Bros., and it had already worked for Mickey himself, since he was hastily created after Disney lost the rights to Oswald (who had some resemblance to Felix the Cat, the original American cartoon hero). But Bosko, popular enough at first, was no Mickey Mouse, or even Oswald. No one could really tell you what his gimmick was, or what his personality was supposed to be.

Bosko also demonstrated why animation studios usually preferred to use animal characters: while Mickey doesn't resemble a mouse in any way, and Oswald was only slightly more like a rabbit, you could at least identify them by their species. Even Popeye, while human, had a job and a uniform. Bosko wasn't anything. After his early appearances, Harman and Ising mostly dropped the minstrel-show dialect and became unclear about whether they thought he was supposed to be Black or not, but if he became less offensive, he never stopped being generic. Mickey Mouse started out as a mischievous little anarchist and only gradually lost his personality to become the unfunny character that Rob Long complains about; Bosko skipped the intermediate stage and had no personality from the beginning.

Nor was there anything technically impressive about Bosko. What makes the early Disney cartoons work, at their best, is the tremendous quality of the animation. Disney's studio was partly a movie studio and partly a research and development firm, where technical innovations were formulated and then applied to animated storytelling. The Fleischers offered their own innovations, like creating backgrounds that gave the illusion of being in three dimensions. Warner Bros. didn't have the budget or the staff to create such dazzling visuals. Their animation and production were of good quality, but they were never going to be the first studio to do anything that cost extra.

Perhaps Harman and Ising could have done better with Bosko if Schlesinger wasn't always taking budgetary shortcuts, like reusing animation. For the most part he didn't care if his cartoons looked beautiful, while Disney was constantly showing the world how beautiful animation could look with extra money and training. Harman and Ising must have found it frustrating, because their talents were really more in the Disney vein than what we think of as Warner Bros. style. The best-known work from either man is a cartoon Harman directed for Metro-Goldwyn-Mayer near the end of the 1930s called "Peace on Earth," the story of talking animals who repopulate the world after humans wipe themselves out. It gave Harman a generous budget that proved he could match Disney or anyone else when it came to lighting effects, realistic-looking backgrounds, and detailed character animation. At Schlesinger's, these were frills.

So in 1933, Harman and Ising left Schlesinger, and took Bosko with them. They could do that because they had created Bosko before bringing him to Schlesinger; the character wasn't owned by the studio. (Any character produced on the job was assumed to be owned by the studio, but a pre-existing character was a different matter.) Bosko's post–Warner Bros. career was not impressive. His creators took him to Metro-Goldwyn-Mayer, where they tried to reestablish him as an out-and-out minstrel show caricature. When they were let go from MGM, Bosko was finished.

All this left Warner Bros. in need of a new headliner who was like Mickey Mouse or Bosko, although not enough like either of them to result in a lawsuit. The studio tried Buddy, who was basically the same character without any obvious minstrel show influence. Unfortunately, he looked as though the animators couldn't decide if he was a short adult or a heavily built child. And on the theory that characters are cuter if their eyes are bigger, Buddy was given eyes that looked big enough to be on some other character's face. ("Buddy was a character with round eyes," recalls an old animator in the TV cartoon *Animaniacs*. "Big, huge, gigantic, *enormous* round eyes!") No personality and an unappealing look was not going to compete with Disney, or for that matter with the Fleischer studio, where Popeye was demonstrating the advantages of a human form with an unambiguous, easily described personality.

The studio started to look around tentatively for ideas for recurring characters less like Bosko. The first cartoon that seemed to show some promise was "I Haven't Got a Hat," a 1935 Friz Freleng effort in the *Merrie Melodies* series. It is about a school talent showcase, where kids get up and recite poetry, play the piano, or sing. All the characters are new, and most of them are anthropomorphized animals, suggesting that Warner Bros. is looking for the next Mickey or Donald instead of trying to come up with humans like Buddy. There's a cute owl, identical-twin dogs named Ham and Ex, a cat named Kitty, and Beans, who has a tail but who may or may not be a cat himself. The film seems like an audition for the position of Warner Bros.' next cartoon star. Each character does a turn that suggests what might set them apart as the star of their own series: Kitty is cute and nervous and forgets the words to "Mary Had a Little Lamb," mild stuff like that.

The one character from "I Haven't Got a Hat" who might actually be recognized now is a pig named Porky, who gets up to recite Henry Wadsworth Longfellow's poem "Paul Revere's Ride" and ends up segueing into Alfred, Lord Tennyson's "The Charge of the Light Brigade." Bob McKimson, the future director who animated the scene,[9] delivers some promising animation of Porky trying to act out Revere's galloping steed, but the main thing that stands out about the character is that he has a stutter. It's not a very funny stutter at this point. His voice originally sounded too much like a real person struggling to get the words out, which makes the scene cruel rather than amusing.

Still, stuttering Porky was the only character to make an impression in "I Haven't Got a Hat," and Warner Bros. was starting to realize, as other animation studios already had, that voices were as important as design for cartoon characters in the sound era. Successful characters often had some vocal quirk. It didn't always have to be a speech impediment: it could be an accent, like Popeye's, or just a very distinctive way of talking, like Goofy. But the speech impediment would become the Warner Bros. stock-in-trade for identifying a character.

The studio now had a plan: find a funny-animal character instead of a human, and in "I Haven't Got a Hat" they had a group of characters, or at least character designs, that could be the inspiration for a series. But Freleng was not the director to take one of those characters and make him a star. In a roundabout way, the man who finally made that happen, the man who is generally considered the true founder of the *Looney Tunes* style, was Tex Avery.

* * *

Again, popular art is imitative. Every superhero is a version of Superman, an attempt to be the opposite of Superman, or both. Every American animated cartoon of the sound era is at least partly a response to Disney. And the thing that would ultimately define Tex Avery as a creative artist was his hostility to Disney, or at least to the conventions that Disney's studio had created for the animated cartoon. He would later be responsible for a film in which a cute, Disneyesque squirrel is beaten by an ugly, sadistic creature known as Screwy Squirrel. But the Tex Avery who arrived at Warner Bros. around 1935 was just a down-on-his-luck animator who had been fired from drawing Oswald the Lucky Rabbit.

Avery might have stayed an animator if it hadn't been for an accident in 1933. In the spirit of pranks and horseplay common in early animation studies, a colleague used a rubber band to shoot a paper clip at Avery. It hit him in the eye. Within a few months, he had lost all vision in the eye, and eventually he had it removed. Animation historian Tom Klein speculates that this tragedy "may also have been something of an impetus for change, spurring him on to new milestones and achievements," and others have suggested that maybe his lack of depth perception accounted for his lack of interest in conventional visual beauty in animation.[10] The latter may be a stretch, but it's hard to resist imposing origin stories onto real-life humans. Avery's accident has become his origin story, if only because it may have placed a limit on how far he could go as an animator. Two years after the accident, bored and no longer doing his best work, he was let go. He found himself in Leon Schlesinger's office, applying to be a director or, as Schlesinger always insisted on billing it, a "supervisor."

Avery had been the de facto director on some Oswald cartoons,[11] but he had no directorial credits. He claimed that he lied to Schlesinger about his experience during his job interview. "I said, 'Hey, I'm a director.' Hell! I was no more a director than nothing, but with my loud mouth, I talked him into it," he told Michael Barrier.[12] The truth of these tales of old Hollywood can be elusive, but Schlesinger did give Avery his own unit to direct. Schlesinger, too, might have been short of options. There weren't many experienced animation directors in such a young business, and they wouldn't come to a studio that had yet to produce a truly successful character. So Avery got the job and began looking for characters he could work with.

In his interview with Barrier, Avery recalled that Schlesinger screened some of the studio's cartoons for him, including "I Haven't Got a Hat." Avery picked three of the funny-animal characters out of that film and made them the stars of his first cartoon as a credited director. "Gold Diggers of '49" was a play on Warner's popular series of musicals about metaphorical gold diggers, applied to the literal gold diggers of the nineteenth-century gold rush.

"Gold Diggers of '49" is a milestone cartoon, one that reference books always identify as a key moment in the development of *Looney Tunes*, not just because it was Avery's debut, but because of two other names on the title card: the animation is credited to Bob Clampett and Chuck Jones (billed as Robert Clampett and Charles Jones, because Schlesinger or someone else at Warner Bros. seemed to find nicknames undignified—Avery was billed as "Fred"). Both Clampett and Jones had lived in Los Angeles since they were children, both went to art school there, and both had worked their way up to becoming full animators: Clampett was a favorite of Schlesinger, who hired him in the early days of the studio based on a viewing of a 16 mm film he created. Jones, who was never very friendly with Schlesinger, had a slower climb up the ladder, doing odd jobs for Ub Iwerks (Disney's ex-partner, who had his own studio for a while), and earning his promotion to full animator just before Avery arrived.

Those weren't the only members of Avery's unit. Schlesinger had a rule that only two animators, and later only one, could be credited on a film, no matter how many animators worked on it. But Clampett and Jones would both soon be promoted to directors, and between them would be responsible for much of the studio's greatest work. Both of them were heavily influenced by Avery, and if there is such a thing as an Avery school, "Gold Diggers of '49" is where it begins.

Another, more dubious reason for considering this cartoon a milestone is that it is sometimes considered the first true Porky Pig vehicle. It's dubious because, although Porky is in it, he has almost no resemblance to the character he would become. In fact, he bears no resemblance to the version Freleng had introduced, except for the stutter. This version is an adult, with a marriageable daughter. This cartoon also attempts to give Porky his own catchphrase, which involves letting out a piercing scream of "WHOOPEE!" at random moments. For every "What's up, Doc?" there are several catchphrases that never catch on.

"Gold Diggers" showed poor judgment in trying to pick the "I Haven't Got a Hat" character most likely to become famous. The star is Beans, who is basically identical to Bosko in every way except that he has a tail. Kitty also returns from the "I Haven't Got a Hat" roster as Beans's girlfriend.

"Gold Diggers of '49" is more interesting for what it led to than what it is. Jones and Clampett were better directors than animators, and the whole picture suggests a team that is still learning how to get the results it wants, like early CGI animated films where the creators hadn't figured out how to make characters move like people. In "Gold Diggers," there are some nice visual bits, like a pan across an entire Western town, but the character animation is stiff, and the backgrounds move at different speeds than the characters, creating a jittery look common in early animation.

All of the timing is off in "Gold Diggers." Avery has the germ of a good gag in a scene where a bunch of grizzled prospectors rush away from the bar, revealing that they've been drinking sodas, not liquor. But Avery holds the shot too long, and the composer, Norman Spencer, can't come up with music to sustain the extra seconds. Cartoons and other film comedies do have to pause after gags to let the audience laugh, but if the pause lasts half a second too long, the audience has time to decide that the joke wasn't funny after all, one of the worst offenses in comedy.

Not that "Gold Diggers" had a lot of gags that could be sold even with the best timing. Warner Bros.' writers were weak at this point, and it shows. Beans saves what he thinks is a bag of gold, but it turns out to be Porky's lunch. Beans's car drives past two stereotypical Chinese guys, spraying them with dirt and turning them into two stereotypical Black guys. (A lot of stock racial jokes assumed that it was inherently funny just to see someone who wasn't white.) One of the few gags that might get a laugh today has Beans and Porky open a book called *How to Find Gold*, where the text consists of the words "DIG FOR IT." Even that was tired by 1935.

Still, if you watch "Gold Diggers" for signs of an emerging Warner Bros. style, you can see it here and there. There's a touch of the combination of realism and fantasy that Avery's cartoons would become noted for. While he's spraying bullets at the bad guy's behind, Beans's automobile (an anachronism no one bothers to comment on) begins to sputter and slow down. He pulls out a jug of moonshine, labeled, as black-market liquor always is in cartoons, with three *X*s, and pours it into the car. The car hiccups, briefly acts drunk, and then gets a huge burst of speed, even shifting shape from a jalopy into a sleek Art Deco car. The sequence parodies, or at least exaggerates, one of the standard cartoon conventions of miracle foods and drinks, like the spinach that makes Popeye unbeatable.

As Avery got used to being a director and his team got used to working with him, he increasingly used this kind of gag, playing on our familiarity with cartoon conventions, and stretching those conventions to maximum absurdity. If Disney or Fleischer characters will punch the villain, Avery will riddle the villain with bullets. If spinach can make Popeye strong, then alcohol or other substances will do the same for Avery's inanimate objects. In a later Avery cartoon, a character feeds pills to a gun that has lost its ability to shoot; the gun immediately stands up erect and starts firing. The Avery style is not about subtlety, it's about pushing at the limits of everything. Most cartoon directors would pull back when they were being too crazy, too cruel, or too self-aware. Avery would double down instead. The story of Warner Bros. animation in the late 1930s is Avery and some of his younger colleagues pushing hard when everyone else is pulling back.

The other important thing about the better bits of "Gold Diggers" is that, even with their outrageousness, they're somehow plausible. "Outrageous but plausible" is as good a short description as any for the classic *Looney Tunes* style that Avery would help build. He wasn't the only one doing big, violent gags, which Schlesinger seemed to like. The next Porky and Beans cartoon, "Boom Boom," from director Jack King, is much more violent than "Gold Diggers." It's set in a war zone with Porky and Beans as soldiers, and characters get blown up, shot down, and attacked by guided missiles.

But while that description makes it sound like the *Looney Tunes* that audiences would come to know and love, the actual cartoon comes up short. The violent gags are violent in an unpleasant way, like the "Itchy & Scratchy" cartoons on *The Simpsons* (only there it's intentional). Some of the gags fail because they are too realistic: a plane crash looks like an actual plane crash. And others stretch reality too much even for a world of talking animals. There's a guided missile that not only follows people wherever they go, but sometimes grows a face. What would come to set Warner Bros. cartoons apart from the competition was not that they were more violent, because anyone can do violence. It was that they could create gags like Avery's car bit: a drunk, shape-shifting car somehow has a weird internal logic (after all, cars *do* need liquid, and cars *do* sometimes get renovated). It's believable in the context of the cartoon, and funny.

* * *

If "Gold Diggers" is the cartoon we can point to if asked to name the exact moment when the Warner Bros. style took hold, the studio's first classic came in 1936, also from Avery and his team. This is "I Love to Singa." Or as people are likely to refer to it, "that cartoon with the cute little owl whose dad doesn't want him to sing jazz music." Or they might not even describe it: they might just hum the song, and we'll know which cartoon they mean.

Animation historians never considered "I Love to Singa" a major work of Avery's, and there's no indication that he thought it was important. It became famous through TV. No one could watch it without remembering it. On the old Usenet newsgroup alt.animation.warner-bros, it was common for new users to ask the name of that cartoon they had seen— they couldn't remember much about it, but there was this owl, and he sang a song . . . "I love to sing," maybe? When the creators of *South Park* made their first full-length half-hour episode, they included a scene where a character briefly starts singing "I Love to Singa," with his voice borrowed from that cartoon's soundtrack. The cartoon then turned up on Warner Bros.' second *Looney Tunes* DVD collection on a disc with more established classic musical cartoons like "What's Opera, Doc?" and "One Froggy Evening."

The plot is simple, a funny-animal version of *The Jazz Singer*. That movie starred Al Jolson as a man who wants to be a popular singer, even though his father wants him to become a synagogue cantor and can't accept his boy's sinful musical preferences. "I Love to Singa" features "Owl" Jolson, a big-eyed little owl who wants to sing popular music, while his dad would prefer him to sing old-fashioned salon music. Plugging Warner Bros. songs was still part of the cartoon studio's mission, and part of the reason for this film's popularity is simply that it picked the right song. It was written by composer Harold Arlen and lyricist E. Y. "Yip" Harburg, a team best known for creating the songs for *The Wizard of Oz*, and it spoofs the clichés of American popular songwriting, where "moon" always rhymes with "June" and lovers retire to a cottage by a waterfall. Arlen and Harburg were two of the elite names in a golden age of American popular songwriting, and a small cartoon had access to one of their catchiest numbers. It was the musical equivalent of a B-movie recycling a set built for films with many times the budget.

Although a Disney cartoon wouldn't have been able to use music from a Warner Bros. film, "I Love to Singa" certainly could have been a Disney cartoon. It's cute enough, and its attitude to art is typical of the middlebrow world that Disney and Avery and many other Hollywood creators occupied: respectful of high culture (the opening scene drops the names of the classical musicians Caruso, Kreisler, and Mendelssohn, and assumes that the audience will know who they are), but suspicious of the highbrow stuffiness that goes along with it. They take the side of the common person who wants good unpretentious entertainment. Owl Jolson is the unsophisticated but commonsensical normal person who will attract audience sympathy.

What makes it different from a Disney cartoon is that there is a note of cynicism. The father doesn't learn to respect his son's musical preferences. He changes his mind only after seeing that Owl Jolson has won a trophy and a radio contract for his jazz singing, and may be headed for stardom.

The message of the cartoon is that your parents will only accept you if you have a chance of making them rich.

The cynical tone extends to the radio show Owl Jolson auditions for, and which winds up making him a star. It's a talent showcase loosely based on the *Major Bowes* radio program, except if the host doesn't think the auditioners are talented enough, he hits a gong and a trapdoor opens beneath them. One character, inevitably, is too fat to fit through the trapdoor and the host has to hit her on the head to get rid of her. There's even a reference to what would later be called sexual harassment, as a messenger keeps trying to grab a secretary, who finally pushes him away so hard that we hear an offstage clattering noise, which tells us that someone has gotten hurt even if we can't see it. Cruel or dark gags were a normal part of early animation, but Warner Bros. had a way of giving this type of gag a hint of satire. In a short cartoon, otherwise intended to provide an escape from the real world, a hint of satire seemed grown-up.

Finding his voice as a director, Avery experimented with what would become one of his trademarks: gags that play on the conventions of film storytelling in general and animated cartoon storytelling in particular. Like most short cartoons, this one ends with an iris out that leaves the screen black, only Owl Jolson's trophy is accidentally left in the foreground, and the little owl has to open up a hole in the screen and pull the trophy in with him.

Avery loved jokes that addressed particular points of film grammar or film technology or things that happen in a movie theater. In a famous gag from his later years at MGM, it looks like a hair has gotten into the film and is flickering across the screen until a character plucks the hair and throws it away. A famous stock gag, which all the Warner Bros. directors began to use from 1937 on, involved a silhouette on the screen that was supposed to look like the real shadows theater patrons cast on the screen when they get up.

Avery also assumed his audience was familiar with the clichés of the short animated cartoon, so that he could subvert them, parody them, or pull them apart. The convention of having a bland hero with no particular personality—the convention that Warner Bros. had been following for much of its existence—would be spoofed in Avery's "Little Red Walking Hood," where a short, bulbous-nosed character known as "Egghead" keeps wandering in and out of the cartoon. When the villain finally asks him what he's doing there, Egghead replies, "I'm the hero of this picture," pulls out a mallet, and knocks the bad guy out.

Avery also loved to do parodies of the live-action, nonfiction films that Warner Bros. and other studios produced regularly for movie theater packages. Several Avery cartoons were satirical versions of news shorts: we see documentary footage as a narrator describes the scene. That type of film is still familiar enough that the jokes will play, but they probably played even better in the 1930s and '40s, when the cartoon might be appearing on the same bill as a film that played those clichés straight. "Daffy Duck in Hollywood" is a cartoon made of live-action newsreel footage redubbed with incongruous voice-overs, and title cards that don't match the action they're supposed to be introducing. The purpose of it might not have been anything more ambitious than saving money, but it's a funny example of Avery reaching out from the cartoon and taking hits at the whole moviegoing experience.

A cartoon from a couple of years later, "Cross Country Detours," is a parody of nature films, done in what was known as the "spot-gag" style. Avery made a lot of spot-gag films, where instead of a plot or characters, the short would just have a series of jokes around a theme, with titles like "Car of Tomorrow" or "T.V. of Tomorrow." These shorts were almost always uneven, showing how much cartoon gags can suffer without at least some character interest to support them. But this one managed to include one of the definitive Avery gags. The camera pans to a realistically drawn frog, not doing much. The narrator says: "Here is a close-up of a frog croaking," and the frog pulls a gun out of nowhere and shoots itself in the head. This is immediately followed by a title card reading "The management is not responsible for the puns in this cartoon." This one little gag has a lot of laughs packed into it: shock laughter at the sudden outburst of bad taste, groaning laughter at the pun, laughter at the disconnect between the sweet world of nature shorts and the intrusion of the violence that they ignore.

With such gags, Avery started to establish a style for the Schlesinger studio, one defined by its attitude to what most of the other studios were doing. Anything others played straight, Warner Bros. would subvert or question. Any convention that was unquestioningly accepted was fair game. With that contrarian attitude established, it may have become easier for Warner Bros. to start developing some characters with staying power, because instead of looking for someone who was just like Mickey Mouse, only different, they started looking around for characters who were the *opposite* of Mickey Mouse, or at least the opposite of the mild-mannered icon he had become.

Developing that type of character takes time, and some lucky breaks, which Avery and his team would soon have. In the meantime, they found a character who could ease the transition away from Buddy and Bosko. Porky Pig became the new star of the black-and-white *Looney Tunes* series, a position he would hold for several years until the series was retooled to include other recurring and one-shot characters. Though his design was always a little old-fashioned, a round head on a round body, similar to other early cartoon characters, the animators found ways to improve his look, mostly by simplifying it and eliminating almost all resemblance to an actual pig. And his voice was sped up again, to make it clear that he was supposed to be young, though the actor doing his voice, a man named Joe Dougherty, who by some accounts had an actual stutter, was not quite right, and would soon be replaced.[13]

Whoever was voicing him, Porky was clearly there to stay, the flagship character of the studio. He had his picture displayed not only at the beginning of his cartoons, but also at the end. Schlesinger's cartoons had always concluded with the catchphrase "That's all Folks!" Starting in 1937, Porky got to say the line at the end of every *Looney Tunes* production (the *Merrie Melodies* series just spelled it out on the screen). In a famous closing sequence that lasted until the mid-1940s, Porky would burst out of a bass drum and stutter, "Th-th-that's all, folks!," even if he hadn't actually appeared in the cartoon itself.

Porky would appear in more Warner Bros. cartoons than practically anyone else, thanks to a huge number of black-and-white *Looney Tunes*. He was a useful utility character who stuck around even after his solo series was canceled in the early 1950s. In some ways, he resembles the later Mickey Mouse, since he's not exactly funny in and of himself. He's a straight man, and a good one, normal enough to react to strange things the way we might react to them, but eccentric enough that he didn't seem out of place among characters still more eccentric than he was.

Bob Clampett, the first member of Avery's team to be promoted to director, was the most prolific creator of Porky cartoons, and his usual formula was to have Porky wander into some kind of strange situation or exotic setting and observe what happened around him. The most famous Clampett Porky cartoon, "Porky in Wackyland," casts Porky as a modern Alice in a modern Wonderland of weirdly designed creatures. The real star of the cartoon is a dodo bird ("The last of the do-dos") who spends most of his screen time warping reality to mess with Porky, including riding in on the Warner Bros. shield, and manifesting a brick wall for

Porky to crash into. Other Clampett cartoons had Porky pop in at the beginning and end while the bulk of the action focused on new characters, none of whom became popular enough to appear again.

It may seem strange that a studio, having finally found its breakthrough character, would immediately start auditioning his replacement. But that was part of what would make the Schlesinger gang special: Avery, Clampett, and other key people were too restless to settle for something that worked; there was a sense that even though Porky was better than Bosko or Buddy, there had to be something out there better than Porky. They found it in a cartoon that introduced the next major Warner Bros. star, a cartoon that also provided the first big job for the actor who would voice nearly all the *Looney Tunes* stars to come. After years of trying to establish a personality, Warner Bros. suddenly had personality popping up everywhere.

CHAPTER 3

Daffy

DAFFY DUCK IS THE definitive *Looney Tunes* cartoon star. Bugs Bunny may be more famous, and Tweety may be more merchandisable, but Daffy is the Warner Bros. cartoon barometer, always at the heart of whatever the studio is doing with its characters. If you want to understand the style of Warner Bros. cartoons at any particular moment from 1937 to the present day, look first at what they're doing with Daffy.

The company was always a bit protective of the image of its biggest star, Bugs Bunny, not wanting to involve him in anything that would tarnish it, but they never had that problem with the duck. Everything about him, including his basic personality, can be adjusted to fit whatever the creators and executives want a cartoon to be. If a TV or comic strip hero was popular, Daffy would pretend to be him. When it became too expensive to make anything more complicated than chase cartoons, Daffy started chasing Speedy Gonzales. The success of *Ghostbusters* led to *Daffy Duck's Quackbusters*. When Mel Tormé got popular again in the 1980s, he was invited to sing a song coming out of Daffy Duck's beak. While Bugs and Tweety are fairly stable characters in the public mind, like Tom and Jerry and Donald Duck and most other cartoon stars, Daffy is anything and everything.

Even casual *Looney Tunes* viewers are aware that Daffy has at least two different characterizations, so different that if you describe both of them, they sound unrelated. There's the wild, wacky screwball character who lives only to torment his enemies and laugh insanely at them. That's the version who appeared in most of the cartoons in the old pre-1948 TV package. Then there's the Daffy who appeared in the 1950s and in *The Bugs Bunny* show of the 1960s. He is not really daffy, but bitter and angry, obsessed with being a hero or getting the better of his more successful colleague, Bugs. He almost always fails, and deserves to fail. The 1940s Daffy is known for leaping around and yelling "Woo-hoo! Woo-hoo!" The 1950s Daffy's most popular catchphrase is "You're despicable." The only thing they really have in common is that both are sociopaths, but Daffy #1 is actually daffy, and Daffy #2 rarely is. This may be part of what made him such a useful character: he never completely settled into a single characterization, and the studio could adjust him to whatever the current fashion or marketing plan demanded.

Because these cartoons have no continuity and every film is a fresh start, there are variations within Daffy's two broad characterizations. The later version of him, driven by envy of the less maladjusted cartoon characters he is forced to co-star with, is actually anticipated in a few early cartoons, most famously "You Ought to Be in Pictures," Friz Freleng's animation/live-action hybrid, where Daffy becomes jealous of Porky Pig's popularity and tricks him into leaving the studio. Daffy then tries to get an unimpressed Leon Schlesinger (playing himself) to make him the flagship star of the studio instead of Porky. The slight metatextual joke here is that Daffy had already stolen that status from Porky. His first cartoon was called "Porky's Duck Hunt," created by Tex Avery and his unit and released in 1937. The story of "Porky's Duck Hunt" is just what the title implies. Sometimes the writers would run out of pun titles and go with simple ones, which often worked better.[1] Porky goes out duck hunting with his dog, but all his attempts to shoot a duck go wrong; he gives up and goes home. At home he finds the ducks are outside his house, taunting him with his failure to shoot them. He tries again and fails one last time, to provide the obligatory closing gag.

It doesn't seem, at first, like a cartoon that is going to launch a new star. For the first half of the cartoon, the duck who gives Porky the most trouble just acts like a cartoon version of a regular duck, swimming, quacking, and flying away when Porky shoots at him. And then the duck breaks the rules that appear to have been set for him. Porky finally shoots the duck, who falls from the air and into the lake. Porky's dog swims out to fetch the bird, but by the time the pair of them swim back to the shore, it's the duck who is carrying the unconscious dog and dumps him at Porky's feet.

Avery loved to have cartoon characters step in and out of their roles, so he has Porky respond to the duck's antics by pulling out a script and complaining that that last gag was not written. The duck, suddenly revealing that he can talk, replies, "Oh, don't let it worry you, skipper! I'm just a crazy, darn-fool duck!" and lets out a strange combination of screaming and laughing, happy and threatening at once, while bouncing across the water and out into the distance. And that is Daffy Duck. The rest of the cartoon repeats his wild laughter and bounding several more times, including at the very end, where Daffy jumps in front of the "That's all Folks!" title and becomes the last character we see. Avery seemed to want him to steal the picture from Porky, and he did.

Although the pig would remain a useful character, Daffy stole the entire spotlight from Porky at Warner Bros. Within a year, he was co-starring in some of Porky's black-and-white cartoons and getting his own series of color cartoons, and Schlesinger's directors and story men were trying to develop new characters who resembled "the little black duck."

"Porky's Duck Hunt" shows how much funnier Avery had become in the short time since his arrival at the studio. He already has some of his favorite jokes playing out here, including self-deprecating metajokes. A short scene where Daffy swallows an electric eel and becomes electrified himself is probably the best-animated scene in the picture, but what makes it special is what precedes it: when we see the eel, a hand emerges from the side of the screen, holding up a sign that says, "THIS IS AN ELECTRIC EEL, FOLKS." Providing exposition while also making fun of blatantly obvious exposition would become an Avery trademark.

Avery's unit, including credited animators Virgil Ross and Bob Cannon and uncredited animators Bob Clampett and Chuck Jones, isn't free from growing pains. When Porky's neighbor knocks at his door, the impact is mostly shown with motion lines and a sort of lump that appears and reappears on the door; only a few years later, Warner animators would find better visual equivalents for the impact of hands and legs and entire bodies. Still, their staging of gags is better, the timing sharper, than even a year before.

Some of the gags from "Porky's Duck Hunt" would become stock gags in *Looney Tunes* and in Avery's MGM work, like the bit where Porky fires his gun into the air and the thrust of each shot causes him to sink deeper into the ground. Or where Porky and his dog are getting shot at by hunters who have mistaken them for ducks: Porky holds up a white flag, which is immediately shot to pieces. These gags are predictable but work if they are well-timed and don't give us a chance to predict them, and if the characters' reactions are amusing in themselves.

The cartoon also benefits from the fact that the studio's soundtracks were becoming increasingly sophisticated. Treg Brown, who was in charge of sound effects and what would later be called sound design, had a knack for finding the funniest possible sound for a gun backfiring. Brown had also helped introduce the studio to Mel Blanc, who was signed up for small voice parts in 1936, and quickly became such a hit with the creators that he took over the voice of Porky Pig starting with "Porky's Duck Hunt."[2] Other actors had made Porky's stutter sound painful, but Blanc made it sound just as stylized and remote from real life as Brown's sound effects; finally, audiences could laugh at Porky's pronunciation jokes (finding himself out of bullets, he cries, "No more b-b-b-shells!") without feeling like they were mocking actual speech impediments. Blanc also does the voice of Daffy here, including the laugh. The voice is not quite perfected yet: he doesn't have much of what would soon become his own personal speech impediment, the lisp, which is often claimed to have been borrowed from Schlesinger. Even though it is the same man doing both voices, they sound like two very distinct characters with different outlooks.

Porky is stolid, straightforward. When he tells Daffy that his last bit "wasn't in the script," he doesn't sound like he's defying convention by breaking the fourth wall. Instead, he sounds like a *defender* of convention, a guy who wants to put an end to all this unauthorized foolishness. Daffy is written as a true wild man, a screwball, and Blanc makes him sound like that every second. His high-pitched laughing and whooping sounds like an actor testing the limits of his throat, and it became so identified with Daffy that he occasionally kept on laughing like that even when he was no longer crazy. At minimum, he sounds like he's just about to break out into that laugh, and has to get the words out before the laughing fit takes over.

* * *

"Porky's Duck Hunt" helped establish Warner Bros. as a home for what Jerry Beck and Will Friedwald, in their illustrated guide to Warner Bros. cartoons, call the "screwball hunting picture."[3] The formula features a more or less normal character, like Porky, hunting a character who doesn't follow the rules. One advantage of this type of plot is that it finds a middle ground between realism and surrealism. A lot of earlier cartoons were famous for presenting a world where anything could happen at any time, where inanimate objects constantly came to life, and there was almost no resemblance to real life. This is the type of cartoon parodied in the movie *Who Framed Roger Rabbit* when Bob Hoskins's detective character drives into "Toontown," and is greeted by literally everything in town moving and singing. Then there was another type of cartoon that had something resembling real-world physical rules. Popeye isn't exactly realistic, but it is at least implied that if he fell from a tall building *without* spinach-driven superpowers, he would die.

In a screwball hunting cartoon like "Porky's Duck Hunt," real-world logic is mostly suspended, but not totally. Porky represents real-world logic. He thinks that when you shoot at a duck and hit it, the duck is supposed to fall down. Porky is also a funny-animal character like Mickey, drawn as an animal but behaving like a human in every other way. The fact that he can talk, or that he's a pig who owns a dog, is not strange, because we know he's not really supposed to be a pig; it's just more fun to draw a pig than to draw a man.

But Daffy is a talking animal who is clearly not human. While he's not unprecedented, most of the biggest cartoon stars to this time had been either human-acting animals or humans. Donald isn't really a duck, and no one even bothered to give Mickey the physical proportions of a mouse, and Porky wears a jacket and bow tie in most of his films. When we first meet Daffy, he's not wearing clothes, and he's living in a pond. He's definitely a duck, yet he can talk, and his wings sprout human hands whenever they need to. It is strange and surreal that he can talk, yet for a clothes-wearing quasi-human like Porky, it seems normal.

Most of the Warner Bros. cartoon stars who followed Daffy would be this kind of talking animal: not quite human, but not quite animal. Bugs Bunny, Tweety, and Sylvester almost never wear clothes, and they usually begin a picture in a situation that sort of resembles a situation an animal might find themselves in: most Bugs cartoons start with him living in a forest and being chased by hunters, and while Foghorn Leghorn is too big to be a real chicken, he almost invariably lives on a farm. You will very rarely see Bugs living in a house, or Sylvester owning one; there are cartoons that break this rule, but so few that the creators must have sensed, on some level, that it was wrong. The *Looney Tunes* world is a world dominated by animals who shouldn't talk and walk on two feet and have access to weaponry, but somehow do.

The screwball hunting cartoon provided the Schlesinger crew with a durable template for many of their cartoons. Hollywood studio animated shorts depended heavily on formula, and to create a successful formula, you need effective stock plots. Warner Bros.' was the predator-vs.-prey story. Someone tries to catch someone else. He fails repeatedly. The end. Most of the series Warner Bros. developed from this point on would fit this formula. Some, like Bugs Bunny or Tweety cartoons, focus on a character in danger (theoretically, anyway) of being eaten almost every time we see them. Others rely overtly on the hunting format, which before long was so familiar that writers were coming up with weirdly specialized variations on the formula, like a giant chicken being stalked by a young chicken hawk no bigger than his foot (Foghorn Leghorn), or a predatory French skunk chasing a cat he has mistaken for a female skunk (Pepe Le Pew), or a cat hunting a baby kangaroo he has mistaken for a giant mouse (Hippety Hopper). Not every Warner Bros. cartoon is about hunting, but "who is chasing what, and why, and where" was the starting question for more Warner cartoons than any other premise.

The hunting format worked because it was just enough plot to hang the gags on. The *Looney Tunes* creators were becoming increasingly adept at creating gags that theater audiences would respond to, and they knew that people enjoyed their gags, not their plots. But there usually needed to be *some* plot. Avery sometimes experimented with the spot-gag format, a completely plotless cartoon where the gags are organized around a theme, with a running gag or recurring character to give some semblance of unity: "Cross Country Detours" has a running bit about a husky dog running away from Alaska and toward California, and it pays off at the end when the dog arrives in California and exclaims "Thousands and thousands of trees, and they're mine, all mine!"[4] But almost none of the spot-gag cartoons were as good as the cartoons with plots.

The gags needed a story to link them, and all of the gags became more effective when related to that story and the character motivation behind it. And yet, even though a story is essential, the baseline rule at Warner Bros. was that the barest minimum of storytelling was best. That's what the hunt, or the chase, provides: a story for a film that doesn't have time for a story.

Schlesinger's other cartoon directors were quick to notice how they could use hunting as a peg for gags. After being assigned to the Porky series, Bob Clampett built a distinctive style combining Avery's gags and wise-guy attitude with the wild surrealism of the best early sound animation. In "Porky in Wackyland," Clampett is free to pour on as many absurd gags as he wants, knowing that the underlying structure of Porky's attempt to catch the last dodo will keep the short from seeming formless, like a lot of equally weird early sound cartoons do.

It also helped that hunting cartoons were very budget-friendly. They really only needed two characters: the pursuer and the pursued. Anyone else was incidental. This was a perfect fit for a short cartoon at a studio that didn't have the top budgets in the business. Dividing a cartoon into scenes, and assigning each scene to individual animators, was easier when most of those scenes had only two important figures. And it also helped that the antagonist in a hunting cartoon isn't an out-and-out villain, someone who might be more scary than funny. Warner hunting cartoons start with a sight that's inherently funny: a fool who thinks he's intimidating just because he bought a gun. Porky in "Porky's Duck Hunt," and his successor as Warner Bros.' hunter-in-chief, Elmer Fudd, are middle-class, present-day characters who could go to the supermarket to get a duck or rabbit for dinner. Exactly why they want to hunt is, like everything else, inconsistent. In one cartoon, Elmer Fudd says he's a vegetarian and hunts only for the sport of it; two years later the same writer and director has him say he's hunting for "fwesh wabbit stew." But the implication is usually that they're hunting because that's what men do.

A theme that runs underneath a lot of hunting comedy is that hunting is a faintly pathetic way for modern men to prove their manliness. A lot of American popular culture in the twentieth century deals, in one way or another, with the fact that the old pioneer and frontier ways have died out and modern men will never do anything risky unless there's a war. Stories like James Thurber's "The Secret Life of Walter Mitty," and even a modernist classic like James Joyce's *Ulysses*, deal with the contrast between heroic myths of what a man should be, and the repressed contemporary male.

"Porky's Duck Hunt" mocks this type of male right from the first shot of Porky's house, with the camera panning across the various items he's assembled for his mission, including a book on how to hunt ducks and "One Wear-Well hunting suit." Then we pan over to Porky, wearing the suit and looking at himself in the mirror. It's the suit that gets the first laugh in the cartoon. Porky looks ridiculous in it. It's too baggy, the shotgun shells in his belt look silly, and his tall hunting hat with a bow on top looks silliest of all. But the laugh is connected to our view of all those boxes of equipment and the how-to book. We know what we're looking at is someone who is *not* a hunter, either for food or for sport, but someone who thought it would be cool to dress as a hunter and shoot ducks. Elmer Fudd would wear almost the same outfit when he hunted Bugs Bunny, and no matter what Fudd's job (if any) is in a hunting cartoon, he always looks like a pampered suburbanite doing all the things that he thinks a real sportsman ought to do.

Still, if Porky is funnier than usual here, it's the duck who gets most of the laughs. And more important than how many laughs he gets is *why* he gets them. He's the first *Looney Tunes* character who is funny because of who he is. What Avery stumbled into in "Porky's Duck Hunt" was the thing that had eluded the studio for so long, and would lead to its greatest successes: personality comedy. Unlike Bosko, unlike Buddy, Daffy has a personality. He is a screwball, a character who would be a frightening psychopath if he weren't funny. But he's also, crucially, a bit self-aware about being a psychopath. Remember, his very first line has him admitting that he is "a crazy, darn-fool duck."

Another of Daffy's early signature lines comes from the 1938 Clampett cartoon "Porky and Daffy" (Daffy is a boxer, Porky is his trainer, and, as in all cartoon boxing matches, no rules are enforced), in a scene that has him floating in the air and riding around a boxing ring on an invisible bicycle. He turns to the audience and says, "I'm so crazy, I don't know this is impossible!" It's not the sight of a cartoon character defying gravity that gets the laugh–even then, that was a common sight. What gets the laugh is Daffy's explanation of *why* he can defy gravity, and his strange objectivity about his own wildness.

* * *

The great comedians in vaudeville, silent movies, and radio, the comedians every American animation studio borrowed from, knew the importance of character. It's a proprietary interest, if nothing else. Comics steal jokes and routines from each other all the time, but it's much harder to steal a persona.

Not that they don't try. You could tell that Schlesinger's studio had finally arrived with this character because other studios tried to copy the Daffy Duck persona. Walter Lantz, an independent producer who mostly distributed his cartoons through Universal Pictures, came up with a similar character in Woody Woodpecker and even hired Blanc to do the voice (until he became exclusive to Warner and abandoned the part). Woody had a signature laugh that became more even famous than Daffy's, but he was never the equal of Daffy. Even Disney would occasionally try to feature a Daffy-type character (most notably a manic South American bird in the 1944 film *The Three Caballeros*), although it went against most of what that studio had become.

Creating Daffy, with Porky to handle the straight-man job, brought Warner Bros. cartoons into the major leagues, but it wasn't enough to put it at the very top of the field. Daffy was a great character, but another thing "You Ought to Be in Pictures" seems to acknowledge is that he doesn't have what it takes to be the number-one star of a cartoon company. Porky was better than Bosko, and Daffy was better than Porky, but neither could represent Warner Bros. the way Mickey Mouse represented Disney.

Schlesinger's directors must have thought they could improve on Daffy, because they spent several years trying to develop the character who ultimately became Bugs Bunny. In a follow-up to "Porky's Duck Hunt" called "Porky's Hare Hunt," and extending through two years of cartoons, the studio tried to take what it had learned from Daffy and apply it to other characters with more potential. The inherent limitation of Daffy was that he was dangerous, and dangerous characters can seem threatening. He would harm allies as well as enemies; he would do anything to anyone as long as it was funny.

A 1938 Clampett cartoon called "The Daffy Doc" makes Daffy the assistant to a surgeon at a big hospital; a human atmosphere makes him wilder than usual. After the doctor delivers his clichéd request for surgery tools—a lot of Warner Bros. cartoons start out by using the clichés of a serious movie, and immediately mock or subvert them—Daffy starts handing the instruments faster than the doctor can take them, then screams, whoops, and starts throwing the tools around.[5] Soon after the doctor tosses him out, Daffy decides to be a doctor himself. To get his first patient, he stalks an unsuspecting Porky, walking down the street to the beat of the tune he's whistling, clubs him on the head, and dumps him into a hospital bed. The last minute of the cartoon has Daffy trying to operate on Porky by producing a saw out of nowhere and attempting to cut Porky's stomach open.

Even for Clampett, the director who was most willing to disobey convention, including the convention that your lead character should not be trying to disembowel an innocent person, this was a risk. It works because Daffy doesn't actually manage to do it, but also because he's not the kind of character we need to like. He's a jerk, but a funny jerk.

This is one of the few things that has remained consistent about Daffy from 1937 until today, despite the many variations and reimaginings he's gone through. He is uncontrollably selfish. He doesn't care about anything except what is most fun for him at any moment. Even when he's not acting crazy, he's consistently out to amuse or profit himself, and nothing but amusement and profit control his behavior. Donald Duck is also a funny jerk, but as a quasi-human funny animal, he still belongs to our society. He gets mad, but unlike with Daffy, we can expect that his first resort will not be to try to kill the person he's mad at.

CHAPTER 4

Timing

ONE OF THE PLEASURES of watching *Looney Tunes* from the late 1930s is seeing a studio's mature style evolve quickly. Not long after "Porky's Duck Hunt," everyone seems to grasp that the studio's future is in gag production, and the different units are in an arms race to create the funniest gags. Craft is polished, techniques are refined, even in the smallest things. To simulate a camera movement in animation, the drawings had to be photographed against the backgrounds at just the right rate. In some of the cartoons of 1937, this isn't done right, and it looks like the characters and surroundings are moving at different speeds. You rarely see this in cartoons made closer to the end of the decade.

As the units learn from one another and borrow from one another in this era, we see stock gags refined in a way that makes them distinctively Warner Bros. gags. A 1937 cartoon by director Frank Tashlin, "The Case of the Stuttering Pig," features a running gag where the villain looks out into the audience and taunts a spectator in the third row, calling him too much of a "big softie" to stop him. At the end of the picture, the bad guy is about to "do away" with Porky and Petunia Pig (even back then, there was a squeamishness about letting cartoon villains say "kill") when he's defeated by a heavy object thrown from the audience. Mel Blanc's voice booms out from a distance: "I'm the guy in the third row, ya big sourpuss!"

That's funny enough, but there's something missing that would make it even funnier. We only hear the guy in the audience; we don't see him. In most subsequent cartoons, a gag like this would include a silhouette at the bottom of the screen, suggesting that an actual person is standing up in the theater we're in, and we laugh because it looks real. But it is not unexpected.

A year after the release of Tashlin's cartoon, Avery brought out "Daffy Duck and Egghead," a color re-creation of "Porky's Duck Hunt" with Egghead, a short, bulbous-nosed, humanoid hunter, replacing Porky. Egghead repeatedly tries to get a silhouetted audience member to sit down and stop interrupting the picture. The third time the guy stands up, Egghead shoots him, and the silhouette (provided by writer/actor Tedd Pierce) does a very elaborate, over-the-top death scene, spinning around and finally falling flat on his back, in an odd but pleasing mix of realistic and cartoony animation. The idea of characters interacting with the audience, combined with Avery's love of surprise and the increasing knowledge that censors would allow cartoons to get away with a level of violence that they would never approve in any other kind of film, brings the studio one step closer to maturity, and it only took a year.

Above all, the timing is constantly improving, to the point that a fast and precisely timed cartoon from 1939 can seem slack by 1940 standards. Everyone seems to understand that to make a perfect gag cartoon, everything has to happen at just the right speed: a split second of space between an action and reaction can decide how much of a laugh it gets.

In Avery's 1939 "Thugs with Dirty Mugs," a spoof of gangster movies, he and writer Jack Miller came up with an impressive number of good gags that no other medium could do at the time, like a bit where a bank robber pockets his money and casually leaves his guns floating in the air. This film demonstrates how far Avery had come in a short time as a director. It uses the silhouette gag yet again, with a man in the audience tipping off a cop as to where the thieves are (in revenge for an earlier scene where the head gangster forced him at gunpoint to sit down). The cop thanks him, leaves the room, and immediately comes back in again to call the silhouette a "little tattle-tale." It's probably the best interactive gag so far, in part because Avery uses the right length of pause between the cop's departure and return, just long enough that we can start to predict that he'll be back, but not so long that we can finish making that prediction.

The laughter is so dependent on the inexplicable power of something happening at exactly the right moment that it brings us back to the notion that a good *Looney Tunes* gag is like music. We can't understand the mature *Looney Tunes* style without understanding the unique nature of cartoon timing: every time the characters move, they are moving to something resembling a musical beat.

* * *

That beat usually came from Carl Stalling, who became the musical director and chief composer of Warner Bros. shorts in 1936. He started out accompanying silent movies in (that place again) Kansas City. Though Stalling didn't score Disney's first sound cartoon, he later became Disney's musical director and helped codify a lot of the standard techniques for animation scoring, which he continued to use and refine after he left Disney.

Those techniques were heavily influenced by the way silent films were scored. One holdover from the silent days was quoting preexisting pieces of music to emphasize the meaning of the scene or simply to create an in-joke for anyone who was familiar with the song's title. Stalling's favorite thing about working at Warner was having access to its song-publishing catalog, and he mixed that with classical music and early twentieth-century tunes to develop his own little library of stock quotations, like playing "The Lady in Red" for a cartoon about Little Red Riding Hood, or "A Cup of Coffee, a Sandwich, and You" for any scene where someone sat down to eat.[1] When Warner Bros. got the publication rights to the compositions of jazz bandleader Raymond Scott, Stalling fell in love with them, using the central section of a piece called "Powerhouse" as his all-purpose theme for assembly lines, factories, and any other heartlessly mechanized environment.

But his main job was to make sure that the music was constantly responsive to action and to the characters' movements. His work at Disney had used this technique so conspicuously that it is still almost universally known as "Mickey-Mousing." It's also known as "hitting" action. When a character touched his feet on the ground, Stalling would hit that footstep with a chord, with the orchestration and dynamics suggesting how heavy or light the footstep was supposed to be. The music would descend on the page if a character fell down, and ascend if he was flying. Stalling would even play chords when a character merely blinked his eye, and his usual orchestrator, Milt Franklyn, would most often score it for xylophone. There are people to this day who think of a xylophone when they picture someone blinking in an overly emphatic way.

Part of the reason for scoring like this was to allow the composer of a sound cartoon to create what we might call a sound dimension in films that had no real-life sounds to guide them. Stalling worked closely on the soundtracks with Treg Brown, and while Brown's main job was sound effects, he was also a professional musician who had played guitar and banjo.[2] Together, they made sure music and effects were never redundant. If a bomb exploded, Stalling would stop or tone down the music and let the sound of the explosion carry the moment. But Brown rarely put the sound of a character's feet on the ground as they walked, the way most live-action movies do. It would have been too realistic, too literal, for cartoons that never pretended to be literal representations of reality. The job of accompanying the character's movements went to Stalling.

Stalling also helped plan those movements in advance. Films in the sound era used a standard projection speed of twenty-four frames per second, and Stalling found out, early in his Hollywood career, that this made it possible for the tempo of the music to be matched precisely to the frames of film: one beat every eight frames, or every ten frames, or every twelve frames, and so on. When a cartoon was in preproduction, Stalling would meet with the director to work out the tempo of every scene before any animation was created, and the director would use that as a basis for creating the action, with the characters' movements timed to the rhythm of the scene.[3]

This process allowed Stalling to write or even record a score without seeing a frame of film. "I just recorded from our beat," he explained. "By the time they had the picture ready, I had the recorded music ready."[4] Both Stalling and the animators had all the action and movement laid out for them on an exposure sheet, a device that was so important to animation that Schlesinger's in-house newsletter was called *The Exposure Sheet*.[5]

An understanding of the importance of exposure sheets requires a familiarity with the basic process of making cartoons in Hollywood, which had already been codified by the time *Looney Tunes* started. The story would be plotted on a storyboard, like a comic book in rough form. Most cartoon writers drew well enough to create a rough storyboard, which they would then present to the director, often with funny voices and anything else they could think of to explain why it would be funny. Once the storyboard was finalized, the voice actors would record the dialogue, and the director would plan the action of the film. Scenes or shots were assigned to individual animators, whose job was to create all the key drawings, with "in-betweeners" providing fill-in drawings to make the action move fluidly. When the animation was finished, it was inked, colored, and painted onto transparent sheets, known as "cels." The layout and background department worked separately to create the environment in which the animation took place, in the form of painted backgrounds. The camera operator was then left with the tedious but essential work of photographing every cel against the appropriate spot on the background, to create the illusion of motion. The director supervised all the departments, but perhaps the most important aspect of his job was establishing the timing, which was where the exposure sheet came in.[6]

Studios initially found it hard to make it seem like their pictures matched up with the soundtrack, and the more dialogue and singing they introduced, the more difficult it became to ensure the animation matched the characters' voices. It was the Disney director Wilfred Jackson who first synced up sound and animation on paper before any of the animation had been completed. The early Disney sound cartoons used a system known as "bar sheets," where the film would be summarized on music paper, parallel to the musical score. Eventually this developed into the exposure sheet, the animated film equivalent to the score of a symphony. The sheet had to indicate everything that happened in the film, down to the smallest twitch, and exactly when it would happen. The pretimed cartoon became standard for the industry.[7]

The strict timing of most sound cartoons made it difficult for animators to control the scenes they were animating. The exposure sheets they worked from told them every gesture a character made, the rhythm of their footsteps, even those emphatic eye-blinks. Animators could use their individual talents to convey those movements in a unique way, and part of a director's job was to use the animators the way a live-action director uses actors, but great live-action actors can get away with changing the timing or extending a scene, and animators could not.[8]

For a budget-conscious studio like Warner Bros., it was even more important to get the timing right; unlike live action, animation doesn't provide much leeway for editing. The footage is so expensive and time-consuming to create that even the most extravagantly budgeted productions try to avoid producing any animation that doesn't get used. So the timing stage in a *Looney Tunes* cartoon was also the editing stage.[9]

This was a system that cried out for a director to come along and make use of it. Even the most powerful and controlling live-action directors could never make actors do exactly what was asked of them at all times, or guarantee that every person on the production would follow instructions. Sound animation should have been a showcase for brilliant, megalomaniac directors. But a lot of Hollywood animation directors didn't have enough institutional power for that. Walt Disney didn't direct his studio's films, but every director knew that if they disagreed with Disney about something, Disney would prevail.

Schlesinger, by contrast, was a hands-off producer who cared mostly that his crews stayed on budget and delivered cartoons that would be popular enough in theaters to pay back their investment. So his directors wound up as de facto producers, or at least co-producers, on his films. They not only supervised the exposure sheet and the physical production, knowing the strengths and weaknesses of the animators when assigning their scenes, but also brought their own very specific ideas of what made a good story, a funny gag, and a good character. This meant that as

71

Looney Tunes developed its formula—the hunting plot, the screwball hero, the increased emphasis on violent gags—the directors were developing distinct individual styles, fueled by their own notions of how a cartoon gag should be paced and timed.

In the late 1930s, Bob Clampett and then Chuck Jones were given their own units to direct while still in their twenties, and these directors established their own individual approaches within a few months of starting the new job. Their different approaches are evident in the character designs: Clampett liked characters with a gleam of insanity in their eyes and some kind of design quirk (buck teeth, hair over their eyes) that made them look a little grotesque, while Jones inclined more toward cute characters with sympathetic eyes. It's also evident in the camera angles, the decisions about when to cut between characters and when to show them in the same frame, and in the gags that are chosen and the way the animators are asked to draw them.

Clampett liked distorted bodies, wild reactions, and rude humor even in places where no one else would think to be rude: in the cartoon "Porky's Naughty Nephew," Daffy (or another duck with a similar character design) announces the beginning of a swimming race by flashing a "NOW!" sign tattooed on his backside, which he shoves into the camera and waggles back and forth. He was also, even by the standards of animated comedy, a surrealist. In "Porky in Wackyland," the camera pans across an entire row of bizarrely designed characters, each doing something that is a warped parody of something we might see in real life or in a movie: a guy pouring water on himself while holding up an umbrella that doesn't work; a peacock with playing cards for feathers; a man with a tie rack for a body using a special holder to smoke a cigar, a cigarette, and a pipe at the same time; a man holding up a grate of iron bars in front of his head just so he can demand to be let out.

If Clampett was a rebellious young man using the resources of a Hollywood cartoon studio for his own ends, Jones was more sentimental and more inclined to observational portrayals of how people and animals behave and react. His early cartoons aren't as funny as Clampett's, and he got a reputation as the Warner Bros. director who couldn't quite let go of the idea of imitating Disney. His most famous creation from this period, Sniffles the mouse, is an adorable critter with a cute voice, the kind of character who would instantly get beaten up in an Avery cartoon. But Jones was working out some ideas about timing and pacing that were different from those of his colleagues, and it would eventually help him find his own way to funny.

Both Clampett and Jones would produce some great comedy, but they were two very different comic personalities operating under the *Looney Tunes* umbrella. They got so used to this kind of power that they found it hard to operate without it, which is why Jones felt so lost during his brief stint at Disney. Between Schlesinger's hands-off producing and the rigid, timing-based format of animation, Clampett and Jones could be mini-Disneys in their own units, and because they were timing and supervising everything themselves, they could stamp their own preferences on everything they did to a degree even Disney never could.

* * *

Meanwhile, another director was working his way forward to greatness by using timing as the focal point not only of preproduction but almost everything, including gag writing. Friz Freleng returned to Warner Bros. in 1939 after a stint at MGM, and stayed with the studio until it closed down.

Of the major Warner Bros. cartoon directors, Freleng was the most risk-averse, the director who thought most like a producer. But Freleng was a world-class timing director, especially in the form he became best known for: the classical-music cartoon, where the humor comes from seeing cartoon characters move to the rhythms of a familiar piece of instrumental music. In 1941, he released his first Warner Bros. cartoon in this format, "Rhapsody in Rivets." It was an orchestral arrangement of Liszt's Second Hungarian Rhapsody for piano (which might be the most-used piece of classical music in all animation). The characters were construction workers, acting as if their tools were musical instruments. The short earned Warner Bros. an Academy Award nomination and inspired Freleng to make an immediate follow-up, "Pigs in a Polka," where the story is "The Three Little Pigs," and Liszt is replaced by Brahms.

Classical music was in its last period of prominence in American popular culture, with NBC broadcasting regular concerts by its in-house symphony orchestra under Arturo Toscanini, and movie studios putting out films like *The Great Waltz* and *100 Men and a Girl* (where the girl was Deanna Durbin and the hundred men were a symphony orchestra). In 1940, Charlie Chaplin's *The Great Dictator* featured two memorable scenes built around orchestral classics, and that same year, Disney released *Fantasia*, an ambitious suite of very expensive, mostly serious interpretations of classical pieces.

Freleng's film has been referred to as "a working-class *Fantasia*."[10] While Disney dealt almost exclusively in scenes from the past or fantasy, including prehistoric dinosaurs, mythological gods, and sorcerer's apprentices, much of the fun of "Rhapsody in Rivets" comes from seeing Disney's music-appreciation project applied to a modern city. If Disney was striving to make animation highbrow, Freleng was stripping away some of its pretensions and connecting it to everyday life. He and Maltese, who wrote many classical-music stories for Freleng and Jones, both approached the classics in the spirit of an American who listens to

Toscanini broadcasts and records of Liszt and Rossini and Wagner but refuses to be highbrow about it.

"Rhapsody in Rivets," like many such films, puts the emphasis on the music by including no dialogue and no sound effects while the music is playing (except sounds that can be created by musical instruments, such as a triangle imitating a hammer on a nail). It also has a plot that, even for a Warner Bros. cartoon, is simple. With their foreman acting as the "conductor," a construction crew erects an entire skyscraper in sync with Liszt's famous piece. After they finish the building, it falls down. It's the ultimate "clothesline gag" plot, providing a minimal structure for several minutes of gags.

A few of those gags are about classical music in general. The foreman's long hair and solemn manner are a reference to the famous conductor Leopold Stokowski, who had just conducted the music for *Fantasia*. But the majority are synchronization gags, derived from how the action relates to the music, sometimes moving with it, sometimes contradicting it.

Freleng's film is a showcase for how rhythm and motion alone can create laughter when the timing is perfect. A bricklayer puts down an entire row of bricks in time with the music, and then pants in exhaustion, also in time with the music. A little man tries to climb up a ladder to a few bars of music, only to be forced back by someone else climbing down to the next few bars. The foreman holds up a "STOP" sign to signal that the first section is over; everyone and everything freezes until the recapitulation begins. In a sequence where light chords are answered by heavy chords, the visual equivalent is a tiny worker leaning in to hammer on a big wooden peg, and then leaning back again as his co-worker smacks the peg with his own, gigantic hammer. We all know the little guy is going to get hit with the hammer, but the biggest laugh comes from the matching of movement and character design to music.

Liszt's piece ends with a trio of notes, right after the loud chords that we think are final. Here, those notes work with a running gag about the foreman hitting a goldbricking worker on the head with a brick: after that same worker is responsible for the building collapse, the foreman is about to throw one more brick when three other bricks fall on his own head to the accompaniment of those three notes. Freleng and his crew carefully developed funny visual equivalents for each event in the music.

Such a strongly rhythmic, timing-based approach to storytelling calls for a similar type of animation, more concerned with precision than the fluid, beautiful movement of *Fantasia*. Freleng's animators often worked in a style that lacked fluidity, with characters popping from pose to pose; they'll turn their heads sideways and down and then, on the beat, bounce back to an upright position. It isn't always beautiful, but it emphasizes the rhythm on Freleng's exposure sheets. Freleng is also perfectly happy to repeat animation when the music repeats: it may save a bit of money, but it's also funnier to watch the exact same thing happen more than once, and the literal repetition also makes it funnier when something different happens on the third or fourth try.

Animation that accentuated sharp, split-second timing instead of striving for fluidity became part of the studio's collective style. When Chuck Jones got past the cuteness of his early cartoons and learned to be just as funny as the other directors, he made "The Dover Boys," a parody of a turn-of-the-century series of children's books about three nice young lads triumphing over vile villains. The cartoon is most famous today for its pioneering use of limited or stylized movement. Characters go between poses with movement indicated by only a frame of "smear" animation, a drawing that creates a subliminal feeling of movement between the poses, even though the character is distorted beyond recognition when you freeze-frame it. They also have offbeat ways of walking: the heroine glides as if she were on wheels, because a proper young lady would never think of showing her feet. This was an artier version of the revolt against fluid, Disney-style animation.

By the time he made this film, Jones had found ways to insert fast, strongly accented timing into scenes that might otherwise have been slow. A famous moment in "The Dover Boys" comes when the vile villain Dan Backslide (referred to twice as a "coward, bully, cad and thief") screams that the Goody Two-shoes title characters "drive me to drink!" In the space of a few seconds, he runs to the bar, gulps down several drinks in succession, watches helplessly as the bartender drinks one of the glasses meant for him, and rushes back to where he had been standing to continue his monologue. Treg Brown matches the drinks with perfectly timed sound effects, one drinking sound for Dan and a slightly different sound for the bartender, plus a very quick sound that plays every time Dan puts his glass down.

What we're witnessing in a scene like this is the development of a new comedic language, and every Warner director has his own variant of it. The precision of the movement, the sudden slowing down and speeding up, the surreal warping of time where many things happen in an absurdly short moment. And above all this, the constant promise that the next gag will happen when we don't expect it, combined with the assurance that whenever it does happen, it will feel as right as the soloist's entry in a piece of music.

"Rhapsody in Rivets" and "The Dover Boys" were special projects with no recurring characters, and a cartoon studio couldn't live on those. What Schlesinger's studio really needed was a star like Chaplin's Little Tramp who could get laughs without doing anything particularly funny, just by the way he posed or walked or held a trademark prop. So the Warner Bros. gang got together and decided that their studio's future would have something to do with a rabbit.

When animation historian Joe Adamson sat down with Tex Avery for a long interview in the early 1970s, he asked how Bugs Bunny came to be created.

"Oh," Avery replied, "we wanted a rabbit."[11]

Virgil Ross, one of Avery's animators (and later one of Friz Freleng's top animators), told an interviewer in 1990 that the studio was looking for a rabbit: "We received orders from the story department that they needed a drawing of a bunny. We all did drawings, and tacked them on the wall, and the story men voted on them."[12]

They didn't know what this rabbit would do, or even his name. But they knew they wanted a rabbit. That was a start.

CHAPTER 5

Birth of a Bunny

P. G. WODEHOUSE WROTE a short story in the 1930s about a cartoonist looking for inspiration to create the next cartoon animal star, in the tradition of Mickey Mouse. Having rejected Hilda the Hen and Bertie the Bandicoot, and discovering that Sidney the Sturgeon has already been done, he finally comes up with his meal ticket, Ferdinand the Frog. Wodehouse evidently did not get to the movies enough to know about the actual cartoon character Flip the Frog, who appeared in Metro-Goldwyn-Mayer cartoons around the same time that Warner Bros. was making do with Bosko. But the point was fair enough: to most moviegoers, a cartoon star was a species and a first name, preferably alliterative.

In addition to all the other reasons why Daffy Duck could never be a true flagship character was the fact that Disney already had the most famous cartoon duck in the world. It may have been, then, that one reason the studio wanted a rabbit was that there was an opening to create the number-one rabbit character in the world. Oswald the Lucky Rabbit's fame had been obliterated by his replacement, Mickey Mouse, and Oswald had gone into decline after Disney lost his rights to Universal, which stopped using him in 1938. While at Disney, he had been successful enough to keep other studios from trying a rabbit character, but as a semi-retired, semi-forgotten character, Oswald was replaceable.[1]

Once it was decided that a rabbit, hare, or bunny (the terms were used more or less interchangeably in cartoon titles) would be its next big thing, the creative people behind Warner Bros. cartons made their most elaborate and successful effort to manufacture a cartoon star. While some characters, like Porky, become famous by accident, Bugs Bunny was no accident. He exists because the studio, as a collective entity, had an idea of what it wanted, and they spent several years making mistakes until they got it right.

So what were they looking for? Obviously, a follow-up to the success of Daffy Duck and the hunting format. Rabbits, who can get shot for sport or food, fit that format well. It also seemed to be vaguely understood that this new rabbit would be what is loosely referred to as a trickster.

There were a number of rabbit characters who fit this description, taking qualities of a real rabbit's movement—the speed, the unpredictability, the difficulty of following their movements with the human eye—and transmuting it into a way of living. In his book *Bugs Bunny: Fifty Years and Only One Grey Hare*, Joe Adamson argues that Bugs was influenced by Zomo, "the trickster rabbit from Central and Eastern Africa who gained audience sympathy by being smaller than his oppressors and turning the tables on them through cleverness." Zomo was "a con artist, a masquerader, ruthless and suave, in control of the situation. Specialized in impersonating women."[2]

One of Zomo's American descendants, Br'er Rabbit from the Uncle Remus stories, has similar trickster qualities, and in his book *The Colored*

Cartoon, Christopher P. Lehman points out that Bugs and Br'er Rabbit share "confidence and cleverness, and both are willing to feign humility in the process of outsmarting their adversaries."[3] Also, illustrations usually show Br'er Rabbit as physically the size of a human, anticipating Bugs's final form as a very tall rabbit. This forfeits some of the sympathy he would get if he were small, but it makes it easier to play the stories for laughs, because he never looks like he's in actual danger of being treated as hunters treat a real rabbit.

As usual, there was a bit of borrowing from the industry leader. Not Oswald, who was just Mickey before Mickey. Disney's short "The Tortoise and the Hare" had provided a better example of what a cartoon rabbit would look like. It featured a character named Max, who played the role of the cocky, speedy rabbit whose overconfidence causes him to lose a race to a laconic turtle. The design of a bipedal rabbit with buck teeth and oversize ears was appealing, and so was his tall and thin body in a mostly short and pudgy world.

"Bugs Bunny is nothing but Maxie Hare," Frank Tashlin said late in his life. "We took it—Schlesinger took it, or whoever, and used it a thousand times."[4] Avery himself told Adamson that Bugs was similar to Max, at least as far as his design went. "Mr. Disney was polite enough never to mention it, because he didn't have to. People had been copying him for years, his bears and everything else, but he never did complain. He evidently looked at us as parasites. But if you look back, why, my goodness, there's a rabbit that looked a heck of a lot like Bugs Bunny, as far as the drawing goes."[5]

* * *

Even with the studio deciding it wanted a rabbit, and that he should be a bit like Daffy, and a bit like Max, and a bit like the rabbit tricksters of folklore, there was a lot of leeway for the people who took part in creating him, and there were a lot of people. Most of the Warner Bros. characters who debuted after Bugs were created by one unit alone, with directors gaining unofficial proprietary rights to their creations; after Friz Freleng came up with Yosemite Sam, other directors didn't use him. But several different directors took a crack at this rabbit character and he evolved rapidly as those directors tried to figure him out, while identifying his enemies and his stock gags. The result was a character much more popular and versatile than he might have been under only one director.

That's not entirely something to celebrate, since it's an outgrowth of the fact that *Looney Tunes* characters were created under an unfair system. Every new character created after Bosko was owned by the studio. The creator had no ownership stake in him or his future. The wrongness of this work-for-hire system became more apparent over the years as the characters endured and made more money than anyone could have anticipated. Most of the Warner Bros. directors could have gotten rich if they had owned a piece of Bugs Bunny or received a few cents from each of his broadcasts. Instead, all his development was done for a paycheck and nothing else, with no residuals.[6] The system made Bugs a more rounded character than if he were just one person's creation, but at the expense of truly rewarding anyone for their work.

The first stage of Bugs Bunny's development, the first cartoon with anything that resembles him, came from people whose directorial careers at Warner Bros. didn't last. Studio animator Cal Dalton was teamed with Ben Hardaway, a story man, to take over Friz Freleng's unit when he left to join MGM. When Freleng returned, Schlesinger gave him back the unit and demoted Dalton and Hardaway. The best cartoon they would produce in their short tenure was a one-shot called "Katnip Kollege," about a swing-music university where the professor acts like bandleader Kay Kyser and the students all have to prove they're "really in the groove." Hardaway, directing on his own, also made a black-and-white Porky cartoon that isn't exactly the first Bugs Bunny cartoon, but isn't exactly *not* the first.

As the title indicates, "Porky's Hare Hunt" is a straightforward follow-up to "Porky's Duck Hunt" with Porky pointing his gun at a different type of animal: instead of a crazy black duck, a crazy white rabbit. There are a few differences. This rabbit is influenced by wisecracking comedians like Groucho Marx. One of his lines to Porky—"Of course you know this means war!"—is a line Groucho had used in *A Night at the Opera*, and it's delivered as a Groucho impression.

This rabbit is too much like Daffy to be what the studio was looking for. He even has a version of Daffy's wild laugh: a strongly rhythmic laugh by Mel Blanc, something you could almost notate on music paper. This laugh was rejected for the rabbit (it would eventually catch on when Hardaway left Warner Bros. for Walter Lantz's studio, where Blanc applied it to the Daffy Duck imitator, Woody Woodpecker). What did stick was the rabbit's name. Hardaway's nickname at the studio was "Bugs," and the rabbit became known around Warner Bros. as "Bugs's Bunny," which eventually turned into "Bugs Bunny."[7] The name splits the difference between two different cartoon naming conventions. Disney's biggest stars had conventional human names like Mickey and Donald. Daffy's first name described what he was like. "Bugs" works as a description ("buggy" would have been the term someone might actually have used in conversation to describe a crazy rabbit) and can also pass as a nickname, as it did with Hardaway.

Hardaway got a little closer to the rabbit the studio was looking for in his unit's next cartoon, which he and Dalton directed together. In "Hare-Um Scare-Um," a human hunter and his dog go out rabbit hunting to save on the price of meat. It was a color cartoon (at a time when half the studio's output was still in black-and-white), and while the "Porky's Hare Hunt" rabbit was all white, this rabbit has a mostly gray body with a white stomach. This became the prototype for all subsequent designs of Bugs. He still has the Woody Woodpecker laugh, and a personality too close to Daffy's obnoxiousness, but some of the gags are working. Several bits in "Hare-Um Scare-Um" would become permanent stock gags for Bugs Bunny.

One is the disguise gag: all Bugs has to do is put on a cop's hat and some glasses, and the hunting dog pulls over to let Bugs see his driver's license. The disguise itself isn't as funny as the fact that the dog momentarily thinks he is a highway driver in a car. For decades afterward, Bugs Bunny cartoons would show his enemy caught up in some kind of ritual, whether arguing, opening doors, or obeying authority, in situations where it makes no sense.

"Hare-Um Scare-Um" also features the first appearance of Bugs's cross-dressing act. One of his disguises is as a female dog, establishing the rule that he's always irresistibly attractive to his enemies when he pretends to be a female of their species. And one more stock Bugs bit makes its first appearance near the end of the cartoon, when Bugs pretends to have been shot and performs an elaborate death scene, tricking the hunter into feeling guilty. This combination of hammy showmanship and psychological warfare was so perfect that it would be recycled by different directors in two subsequent early Bugs cartoons.

The next big step in the rabbit chronology was a cartoon called "Elmer's Candid Camera," from the Chuck Jones unit. You can tell that it's an early Chuck Jones directorial effort because it's less violent and more kid-friendly than what the other directors were creating. Instead of using the formula of someone hunting rabbits, this one has Bugs's antagonist using a camera for nature photography. You can also tell that it's an early Jones cartoon because it's slow. Painfully slow. Pauses last a beat longer than they should, every gag takes so long to unfold that we guess the punch line before it arrives. Even Bugs's voice is slow: he speaks with a measured drawl, sort of a cross between Goofy and Jimmy Stewart, and nothing like the energetic character Schlesinger probably wanted.

Still, there are things that Jones figured out here that had eluded Hardaway and Dalton. One of them is that Bugs is not crazy. Like Daffy, he's a jerk. More so, in fact, because he's harassing someone who isn't trying to hurt him. But he's a subdued jerk, capable of holding a conversation with Elmer. He lets out that Woody Woodpecker laugh at the end of the film, and he has a few other weird nervous tics like muttering to himself under his breath ("The SPCA will hear of this!"), but he's no longer a Daffy clone.

Also introduced in this film is the rabbit's foil, Elmer Fudd. Like Bugs, Elmer was developed by a number of different units, but he's essentially a combination of two Tex Avery characters. In "Dangerous Dan McFoo," a 1939 parody of Robert Service's "The Shooting of Dan McGrew" (a poem which used to surpass even Poe's "The Raven" for the number of cartoons based on it), Avery assigned the voice of the title character to radio actor Arthur Q. Bryan. Bryan used an ineffectual-sounding, meek voice with a speech impediment that makes *r* and *l* sound like *w*: "Hewwo," and so forth. Avery had another character, a roundheaded man named Egghead who had gone up against Daffy Duck. Elmer takes elements of Egghead's design and combines it with the Bryan voice, making him one of the few important *Looney Tunes* characters not performed by Mel Blanc. It's probably his voice that makes Elmer such a perfect comedy antagonist. It sounds different from the voices around him and stamps Elmer as someone who doesn't quite get what's going on.

Jones's next cartoon with the Bugs-Elmer team was called "Elmer's Pet Rabbit," where Elmer buys Bugs at a shop and takes him home. The only distinctive things about this effort are that it takes Bugs out of the woodland setting, and gives him yet another voice that doesn't fit. He sounds like an outright simpleton. It didn't matter: the release of "Elmer's Pet Rabbit" was delayed and by the time it came out, it was obsolete. Tex Avery's "A Wild Hare" (1940) had been released and even before the film was rewarded with an Academy Award nomination, everyone at the studio knew this was what the rabbit should be.

* * *

Avery is often referred to as the creator of Bugs Bunny, though he was convinced that this was something Warner Bros. started talking up just so they could prevent Schlesinger from getting the credit for creating him.[8] While it's not as simple as that, Avery's "A Wild Hare" is the film that established Bugs's accent, his catchphrase, and his attitude. Avery created the blueprint that all directors would follow.

"A Wild Hare," written by Avery's frequent collaborator Rich Hogan,[9] doesn't break new ground with plot. It is a hodgepodge of elements from the prototypical Bugs Bunny shorts other units had made. Elmer Fudd goes out hunting. He notices rabbit tracks and follows them to Bugs (like the hunter in "Hare-um Scare-um"). When Bugs appears and asks Elmer what he's looking for, Elmer replies that he's looking for a rabbit, not realizing at first that he's talking to a rabbit (this joke was done in "Elmer's Candid Camera"). Bugs plays tricks on Elmer, including putting his hands over Elmer's eyes and making him play guess who (this happened in "Hare-um Scare-um"). Bugs then gives Elmer a shot at him and melodramatically pretends to be dying (a much better version of the bit from both "Hare-um Scare-um" and "Elmer's Candid Camera."). Then Elmer walks off into the distance, yelling and screaming and barely hanging on to his sanity, like the "Hare-um Scare-um" hunter, and Bugs ends the cartoon with a gag lifted from "Porky's Hare Hunt," where the rabbit walked away playing the song "The Girl I Left Behind Me" on a fife, although in this version, he's playing an imaginary fife, which is funnier.

The cartoon nevertheless advances the Bugs Bunny project in several ways, starting with the introduction of Bugs's stock bits:

- The opening long shot of Elmer, in his hunting costume and carrying his rifle, tiptoeing through a peaceful forest, followed by a closer shot where Elmer notices us and addresses us directly: "Shh! Be vewwy, vewwy quiet. I'm hunting wabbits!"
- Elmer uses a carrot to tempt the rabbit out of his hole. The first we see of Bugs is his white-gloved hand sticking out of the hole to feel the food. Avery, always trying to get things past the censors, has Bugs suggestively stroke the carrot.
- When Bugs first meets Elmer, he's chewing on that carrot, giving him his most iconic pose. It's usually said to have been inspired by a scene in the 1934 Academy Award winner *It Happened One Night*, where Clark Gable ate a carrot with the stalk sticking out of it, but it instantly became associated with Bugs.
- The first thing he says is, "What's up, Doc?," a phrase Avery had picked up back home in Texas ("We called everyone doc," he recalled) and introduced to the world. Few catchphrases have ever sounded so right so quickly, and almost every cartoon that followed would include it.
- Bugs ties the two barrels of Elmer's rifle into a knot.

Avery also strengthened the gags that had come before, shaping the way they would be used by other directors. He recycles the gag where Elmer talks to Bugs without realizing that he's a rabbit, but adds what became a long-running bit where Elmer describes the rabbit he's looking for and Bugs gives him every chance to figure it out:

> BUGS: What do you mean, "wabbit"?
> ELMER: Wabbits! Wabbits! You know, with big wong ears.
> BUGS: Oh, like these? (Indicating his ears)
> ELMER: Yeah, and a wittle white fwuffy tail.
> BUGS: Like this? (Points to his tail)
> ELMER: Yep. And he hops awound and awound.
> BUGS: Oh, like this? (Hops around)

This particular gag would take many forms in many pictures. It became so familiar that in 1944's "The Old Gray Hare," Bob Clampett gets a big laugh by subverting it and letting Elmer realize immediately that Bugs is the rabbit he's looking for.

The most important new element in "A Wild Hare," the thing that nailed the character so far as the studio was concerned, was Mel Blanc's approach to the character's voice. He now has a New York accent, which Blanc explained as a mix of Bronx and Brooklyn. Bugs is now instantly distinguished from Daffy, and the urban accent is somehow inherently funny in this woodland atmosphere. Matched up against Bryan's Elmer Fudd voice, it tells the story of a tough big-city rabbit having fun with a meek man out of his element.

Avery's is also the most attractive rabbit we've seen to this point. Robert Givens, an artist who would work on character designs and production layouts for much of the studio's history, designed a model sheet for Avery's version, making the rabbit cuter and happier; he's smiling in almost every drawing. He still isn't quite what he would be (later designs would make his cheeks puffier and straighten out the crooked posture he has here) but this is a rabbit who could be your friend, as long as you don't cross him.[10]

The new voice and shape are joined in "A Wild Hare" with a clearer personality for Bugs. Avery, Hogan, and Blanc present a character who is smart. "Elmer's Candid Camera" had already experimented with the idea of having Bugs act more or less sane for most of the picture but, even then he went around muttering non sequiturs under his breath. Avery's rabbit is intelligent and shrewd: until the very last gag, everything he says or does is calculated to get him the upper hand over Elmer. The only time he yells in the picture is to taunt Elmer over his failure to notice that he's a rabbit ("Don't spread this around, but confidentially . . . I AM A WABBIT!"). His mock death scene is expertly staged to bring Elmer to tears. Bugs evades Elmer's "wabbit twap" with no apparent effort. He sportingly agrees to let Elmer take a free shot at him, but on realizing that he's standing under a bird's nest, asks Elmer to let him step a few inches to the side to make sure the bird won't drop something on his head. Most cartoon characters are too simple or too crazy to notice things. This guy notices everything going on around him.

Bugs also likes to play mind games with his opponents. His signature gesture in this film is to kiss Elmer on the lips, which will become part of the rabbit's repertoire for the rest of his career. He's always trying to confuse, disorient, and humiliate Elmer. Daffy seemed to have no particular plan against his opponents except to annoy them as much as possible; he's the ancestor of characters like the gremlins in the movie of the same name, who only want to run around and be obnoxious. Bugs doesn't have that wild energy or love of heckling for its own sake. He wants to drive Elmer mad in a systematic way. This is something new: the screwball as strategist.

It follows that Bugs is smug. Look at the way he tries to make Elmer notice that he's a rabbit. He could easily have run for safety, but he doesn't. Avery has realized that one of the things audiences like about Bugs is his near-total lack of fear. "What's up, Doc?" got a huge audience response right from the beginning, not because it's inherently funny, but because Bugs would say something so banal to a man with a gun who is trying to kill him.

That calmness in the face of danger, what someone's mother would have called "phlegm," made Bugs a special kind of cartoon hero. Mickey Mouse or Porky Pig would react to danger like a person. Donald Duck would react like an angry person. Popeye would need to increase his strength. And Daffy Duck would be too screwy to know what was going on. Bugs in "A Wild Hare" gives us a special kind of wish fulfillment: not only the wish to be able to get out of trouble (all cartoon heroes can do that) but the wish to *know* we'll be able to get out of trouble.

Bugs knowing that things will turn out all right is another example of how these cartoons break the normal rules of storytelling and get away with it. In a regular story, with stakes, it's considered bad form to have protagonists who react to danger as if they've already read to the end. In a seven-minute cartoon that only wants to make us laugh, it works, and this was what "A Wild Hare" crystallized. Elmer thinks he has all the advantages over the timid woodland creature. He thinks the rules of storytelling are in force. But Bugs knows that he is actually the one with the advantages. He is a strange combination of underdog and bully, and this cartoon would define him forever because it finds that combination and presents it to the world.

Of course, having established these rules about Bugs, Avery immediately broke them all in his second Bugs cartoon, "Tortoise Beats

Hare." This made Bugs a flustered loser in a comedy remake of the story "The Tortoise and the Hare," with Bugs playing Max Hare to a new character, a slow-talking, lethargic but clever turtle named Cecil. Avery returned to the hunting format and the more familiar characterization of Bugs with "All This and Rabbit Stew," but replaced Elmer with a gross minstrel caricature of a Black man, creating one of the cartoons that would be pulled from television in the 1960s due to what is euphemistically called "changing sensibilities."

By this time, most of the Warner Bros. directors were under orders to make Bugs cartoons, and they were starting to push the character in directions that Avery might not have gone. And these competing visions, more than anything else, are what turned Bugs into a cartoon superstar, the flagship character Schlesinger had been seeking all those years. They are what saved Bugs from the fate of Pepe Le Pew.

* * *

Pepe was considered one of the weakest Warner Bros. stars even before it became common to notice the creepy subtext of his cartoons. His problem was that he was exactly the same, entirely predictable, each time out. With just his third cartoon, "For Scent-imental Reasons," Pepe won the Academy Award. He deserved it, and if he'd never made another film, he would be remembered for one of the studio's most perfect films. But he did make many more films, and his creator, Chuck Jones, paralyzed by the success of "For Scent-imental Reasons," repeated its plot and gag formulas every year until no one could remember why Pepe had been popular. Joint ownership of Bugs ensured that no Warner Bros. director would settle into a formula quite so soon. Each was free to find his own way with the character and put his own stamp on the studio's new star.

A lot of their experimentation revolved around Bugs's motivations. The directors couldn't agree on *why* Bugs was committing mayhem. It was a fundamental question about the character that no one has ever answered definitively: Is he reactive or proactive? Does he commit violence because he's provoked, or because he likes to commit violence?

With Daffy, there's no doubt. He's a proud sociopath who doesn't care how much others suffer as long as he gets what he wants, and the main difference between early and later versions of the character is whether he's trying to hurt people for fun or for money. "A Wild Hare," on the other hand, is ambiguous about why the rabbit does what he does. You can read it as Bugs fighting back against someone who threatens him: Elmer has a gun and Bugs doesn't, so Elmer deserves what he gets for trying to kill Bugs. But you can also see Bugs as a sociopath with an alibi. He knows he's not in any real danger, and he could ignore Elmer or scare him off quickly. But once he gets provoked, he is free to indulge his love of tricks and mind games, and amuse himself at the suffering of his enemies. If you look at him that way, he's not any less cruel than Daffy, he just uses provocation and retaliation as respectable veneers for his cruelty.

No Bugs Bunny cartoon comes down completely on the side of one of these interpretations, but they do lean more toward one side or the other. Bob Clampett preferred Bugs to be an anarchic force. In one of his early Bugs cartoons, "The Wacky Wabbit," Elmer isn't hunting Bugs or even interested in hurting him. In the plot of this film, Elmer is a prospector looking for gold, and singing more verses of "Oh, Susanna" than anyone ever knew existed. After he meets Bugs, he shrugs, says, "Oh, well," and goes back to digging for gold. But Bugs won't let him alone. He spends the cartoon throwing Elmer's dynamite back at him, or cutting off Elmer's pants to reveal he wears a girdle ("Don't laugh!" he tells the audience, "I'll bet plenty of you men wear one of these!"), and finally trying to bury him alive. After this last trick, Bugs gets a line that soon became another one of his catchphrases: "Ain't I a stinker?" And he definitely is. Clampett's version of Bugs is a trickster god who likes to abuse his power over mortals, for no better reason than that he can.

In a later cartoon, Clampett repeats the gag of Bugs burying Elmer alive, and then has Bugs pop into the grave to hand Elmer a bomb, which explodes after the final iris out, causing the "That's all Folks!" card to shake. And that's not even the most horrific ending he tried to create for a Bugs cartoon. In a 1944 release called "Hare Ribbin'," the villain, having fallen for Bugs's fake-death act, says, "I wish I were dead!" and Clampett got all the way to the completed animation stage with an ending where Bugs obliges by pulling out a gun and shooting the guy. After clashes with management, Clampett changed it so that Bugs just offers him a gun, which he uses as his suicide weapon.

Chuck Jones preferred the rabbit to be a force for good, or at least as good as you can be while still being funny. The same year as "The Wacky Wabbit," Jones made a cartoon called "Case of the Missing Hare." Today it's known for its innovative design, getting away from the realistic, detailed look of the forest in "A Wild Hare" and the desert in "The Wacky Wabbit." Jones and his design team fill this picture with simplified, deliberately flat-looking designs and nonliteral color: the sky is yellow, the trees are purple, and the backgrounds sometimes change color behind the characters to punctuate an act of violence. It's also notable as the first example of the justified-revenge cartoon, something Jones would return to again and again.

It begins with Bugs minding his own business, until an obnoxious magician defaces his home by nailing flyers to it. Following the rule of three, our protagonist gives the antagonist two chances to back down: the first time, Bugs politely asks him to stop; the second time, he angrily accuses the magician of violating "the inalienable right of the sanctity of the home." The magician responds by producing a pie out of nowhere (following another cartoon rule: if someone is defined by his profession, we'd better see him do something associated with it) and shoving it into Bugs's face. Over Stalling's ominous drumroll, Bugs says, "Of course, you realize this means war!," a paraphrase of a line from "Porky's Hare Hunt," now transformed into one of his most iconic catchphrases.

The rest of the cartoon takes place at a magic show, where every gag involves Bugs humiliating the magician onstage, while also stealing the show, and the laughs, from the theater audience. To emphasize that this is a revenge story, Bugs's last act is to produce a pie out of nowhere and hit the magician in the face: he's only doing to the antagonist what was already done to him.

Jones's rabbit leans toward being a force for good, but only so far. He genuinely needs to be provoked, but once he is justified in retaliating, he loses all sense of proportion. If anything, he's meaner than Clampett's version and more prone to violence, whacking the bad guy on the head with a mallet, blowing him up with an exploding cigar (in cartoons, they always actually explode), and flaunting his ability to be anywhere and do anything. Like the Marx Brothers in some of their later movies, you get the feeling that he enjoys doing harm, and if he couldn't find someone around who deserved it, he would start hassling people who didn't.

Another rule that begins to develop in these cartoons is that Bugs can't be allowed to win nonstop for the whole picture. There is usually a moment when he gets scared or when something backfires on him. In "The Wacky Wabbit," he buries Elmer and struts away singing, clearly thinking that this adventure is over. He next bumps into Elmer, who has dug himself out. Bugs actually looks scared of Elmer here. He gets over it quickly, but we get the feeling that he's not totally in control of what happens in this film. He can be surprised; he can be momentarily frightened of his adversaries, and sometimes they can even hurt him, although never as hard and often as he hurts them. This bit of vulnerability keeps Bugs from being obnoxious.

For two years after the Bugs formula was set up in "A Wild Hare," the directors poked holes in it, monkeyed with it, and subverted it, eventually reaching a point where it needed to be deconstructed. Friz Freleng's best Bugs cartoon of 1942 is "The Hare-Brained Hypnotist," written by Michael Maltese. Cartoon writers always treated hypnosis as functionally identical to magic, so Elmer decides he is going to hunt his prey by using hypnotism to mentally enslave them. It works on a bear, but, as we expect, Bugs turns the tables and causes Elmer to be hypnotized. And now something new happens. Bugs makes a mistake that will leave him on the defensive for the rest of the cartoon. He brainwashes Elmer into thinking he's a rabbit. Without missing a beat, Elmer becomes more aggressive and obnoxious than Bugs, while also taking on Bugs's ability to come out on top in every situation. Bugs, furious that Elmer is stealing his act, yells, "Who's the comedian in this picture anyway?" Soon he grabs a gun and starts hunting the trickster Elmer. It's a reversal of roles that are barely two years old, and it's good for the character, keeping him from becoming predictable.

As these directors were building on Avery's discoveries, Avery was stepping away from the studio whose style he had done so much to establish. Although he worked in a form that depended on constant repetition, he wasn't a fan of repeating himself, and tired of the formula he had helped create. His last Bugs cartoon before leaving the studio, "The Heckling Hare," had some good laughs, but the only audacious bit tested the limits of the audience's endurance: at the end of the film, Bugs and his antagonist step off a precipice and fall, screaming all the way, for forty seconds, which, in a seven-minute cartoon, feels like an hour. Avery was testing out the comedy principle that if you stretch out a gag forever it stops being funny, until it becomes funny again.

Schlesinger didn't appreciate his cartoons being used as an avant-garde comedy lab, and he especially didn't like Avery's original ending, where the two characters fall off another precipice and start the whole thing over again. That part of the film was deleted (it is lost, like most cut footage from classic Hollywood movies), and Schlesinger suspended Avery[11], who soon left the studio.[12] After briefly working at Paramount, Avery signed a contract to direct an animation unit at Metro-Goldwyn-Mayer, where he remained until 1953 despite being nostalgic for the freewheeling atmosphere at Warner Bros., fondly recalling moments like the time he lost $10 to Schlesinger in a poker game and paid him off in pennies.[13]

Avery's departure didn't hurt Warner Bros. creatively, but it did change the balance of power at the studio. Avery had been the top man, the one all the other directors looked up to and learned from. With Avery's old animator Bob Clampett taking over his unit, there wasn't a single director with the most creative influence, since to some extent they were all imitating the guy who had just left. The atmosphere at the studio became incredibly competitive, with each unit trying to outdo the others, get the biggest laughs from audiences, and make sure that if Jack Warner ever cut back on cartoons, their unit wouldn't be the one to get shut down. There would be few collaborative, multi-unit attempts to develop a character the way Bugs had been developed. The thing now was for directors to create their own characters to prove their value.

Despite his success at MGM, this was something Avery was rarely able to do there. MGM was not a studio where there was a lot of pressure to create a big family of characters. Avery mostly lost interest in the kind of character work he'd been a part of with Bugs Bunny. One of his few recurring characters at MGM was Screwy Squirrel, an ugly, obnoxious jerk who seems to represent how we would view Bugs Bunny if we were the targets of his abuse. But if Avery was ambivalent about what he'd helped make, he was always aware that he and his colleagues had created something important, even if they'd started out just looking for a rabbit. After talking to Adamson about the resemblance between Bugs Bunny and Max Hare, he added: "But he wasn't Bugs Bunny without the gags that we gave him."

And speaking of gags . . .

CHAPTER 6

Gags

THE RELEASE PERIOD from 1942 through the end of 1946, shortly after Bugs Bunny finally gave them a top-tier star, represents the absolute peak for Warner Bros. cartoons. Everyone was working with confidence, decent budgets, and a freshness that is only possible when characters are relatively new. Erskine Johnson, who wrote "Hollywood Today" for the Newspaper Enterprise Association, informed his readers early in 1943 of a trade magazine poll that showed Schlesinger surpassing Disney to become the second-most popular producer of short subjects, just behind Pete Smith, who made live-action mock-documentaries with sarcastic narration.[1]

This was the period that saw the introduction of characters like Tweety, Sylvester, Yosemite Sam, Pepe Le Pew, Beaky Buzzard, and Foghorn Leghorn. It was when Bugs Bunny ended one cartoon by tricking the entire theater audience into thinking they'd gone blind (in "Hare Tonic"), when Mel Blanc got to imitate Daffy Duck imitating Danny Kaye imitating an old Russian man and a scat singer ("Book Revue"), and when Porky ran a farm where eggs are mass-produced by hens on conveyor belts, only to nearly face ruin when they are all distracted from their work by a rooster who looks and sounds like Frank Sinatra ("Swooner Crooner").

This same period in the 1940s was also when Warner Bros. cartoons got extremely violent. They got that way, and they stayed that way. By 1942, extreme violence was the basis of something like half of the gags, and the percentage would only rise from there. But before we get to the anvils and the dynamite and Bugs sticking sharp swords into a trunk where a gangster is hidden, and Elmer trying to shoot Bugs in the back at point-blank range (he misses, of course), and that time a cartoon ended by dropping a plane on Hitler and then hitting him with a mallet after he rises from his own grave—before we get to all that, we should talk a bit more about the people.

Schlesinger's biggest strength was his judgment about who to place in charge of a directorial unit, and this period was exceptional because the studio's four units collectively were at their strongest. Bob Clampett, Chuck Jones, and Friz Freleng were all doing consistently fine work. There was a fourth unit, not quite equal in power to those others: it was a utility team, charged with working on the few remaining black-and-white cartoons, or cartoons with lesser stars, and weird one-shots. Frank Tashlin directed this unit for several years, making all four units roughly equal in quality, although Tashlin resented the subordinate position of his unit, especially the fact that he usually wasn't allowed to work with Bugs. "Who wants to see the damned pig," he said later of all the Porky cartoons he had turned out, "and I'm stuck with the damned pig. It takes him so long to talk."[2]

It's not really possible to say which of these directors were the best, though judging from how many of his cartoons were mentioned in the media, it seems that Bob Clampett was the top director, or at least the most-promoted director. When a gossip columnist got a tip on a forthcoming Schlesinger cartoon or a cartoon that had some kind of newsworthy or naughty content, it was usually one of Clampett's, like Daffy Duck getting in censor trouble for doing a striptease in "The Wise Quacking Duck."[3]

Enjoying more lavish production values than his black-and-white Porky cartoons had given him,[4] Clampett turned out a series of loud, brash cartoons that thumbed their noses at everything Hollywood had taught movie audiences to consider sacred. With the world at war and every cartoon studio trying to prove it was more patriotic than its competitors, only Clampett would make a cartoon like "Draftee Daffy," which has Daffy, an armchair patriot, freaking out about his draft notice. The rest of the cartoon has him try to escape, and later *kill* the "little man from the Draft Board." The selfish thoughts that few would admit to having, Clampett put on the screen and somehow slipped past the censors.

Something else Clampett had little time for was the idea of a house style, or at least a consistent approach to animation. The two top animators in Clampett's unit in the early 1940s, both inherited from Avery, were Bob McKimson and Rod Scribner, two artists who couldn't have been less alike in style and temperament. McKimson, who animated Bugs's fake death scene in "A Wild Hare," was subtle, or as close to subtle as you can get in cartoons like these. He was great at letting small gestures, a shrug, a pointed finger, a twitch, make big statements about a character and his emotional state. Scribner's characters were the most likely to turn into rubber and contort into hilariously grotesque expressions. Instead of trying to tone down Scribner or make McKimson wackier, Clampett let both men be themselves, and would even get laughs with sudden transitions from one animation style to the other, from extreme calm to just plain extreme.

Clampett's love of extremes can sometimes be too much. Two of his 1940s cartoons, "Tin Pan Alley Cats" and the Bugs Bunny cartoon "The Big Snooze," are about surreal, probably drug-induced nightmares (in "The Big Snooze" Bugs actually takes an overdose of sleeping pills that somehow manages to allow him to invade Elmer's dreams), and they're so dedicated to the proposition that anything can happen as long as it's loud and well-animated that they can leave an audience numb. Clampett could also be sloppy. A classical-music cartoon called "A Corny Concerto" suffers from timing that isn't up to Friz Freleng's standards, killing the point of a music cartoon. But for the most part, Clampett's 1940s work is a combination of audacity and technical skill.

* * *

If Clampett was the underground filmmaker, Chuck Jones was the art house director. His experiments with stylized design and movement sometimes seemed a little ornate for a short comedy cartoon. "Wackiki Wabbit" (1943), with Bugs pursued by two castaways on a deserted island, is a riot of stylized backgrounds that don't fit the traditionally designed characters; Bob McKimson complained that you could hardly see the rabbit in all that scenery.[5] In an animation business that tended toward proscenium staging, with characters placed in static foreground shots, Jones preferred unusual angles, or cuts between characters where other directors would have put them in the same shot.

Jones never got along with Clampett, something that fans were aware of even while the two men were alive,[6] and the two directors eventually had their own competing fan bases. Jones fans argue with Clampett fans in the manner of rival *Star Trek* show fandoms. One of Jones's most unusual cartoons from this era, "Fresh Airedale," has sometimes even been interpreted in light of this rivalry. It's about two household pets, a handsome, well-liked dog named Shep who is actually a conniving, murderous thug, and a perpetually mistreated, belittled cat. Shep allows a burglar to ransack the house; the cat stops the burglar and Shep gets the credit. Shep tries to murder a heroic dog for the crime of being more popular than him; the cat foils Shep, and somehow it all ends with Shep making national headlines for selflessly rescuing this other dog. A common theory is that this cartoon is an allegory for the power politics at the Schlesinger studio, with Clampett as Schlesinger's golden boy and Jones the underappreciated pet.

Even without that interpretation, "Fresh Airedale" is unusually grim for a Schlesinger cartoon. In the end, the cat pounds on a statue of justice, railing against his fate, until the statue's scales fall on his head. That's dark even for Jones, although rival animals and tragic themes are also found in his more lighthearted cartoons. One of the series he developed in the early 1940s starred two mice, Hubie and Bertie, who are usually seen defeating a cat by mentally torturing him, convincing him he's insane or dead: Tom and Jerry for the era of psychoanalysis. A 1945 cartoon called "Odorable Kitty" starts with yet another luckless cat, tired of being physically abused by dogs and humans, disguising himself as a skunk to scare his enemies away . . . only to find himself fending off the sexual advances of a French-accented skunk (later to be named Pepe Le Pew[7]) who won't take no for an answer. The cartoon ends with the cat dropping his disguise and rejoicing when he goes back to getting beaten up by everyone in sight. Jones's cartoons were funny, but they were as close to tragedy as you could get without ceasing to be funny.

Friz Freleng, because of his reluctance to try unusual stories, rarely made one-shot cartoons of any impact apart from the musical cartoons. His Daffy and Porky cartoons, too, were usually good rather than great, but he made up for all this by establishing himself as perhaps the best director of Bugs Bunny cartoons.

Although Bugs was the studio's biggest star, he didn't bring out the best in every director. Clampett's Bugs cartoons were more predictable than was usual for him: he would change the identity of the character hunting for Bugs to a dog ("Hare Ribbin'") or a cowboy ("Buckaroo Bugs"), but they would all run through the same stock gags. Jones's Bugs cartoons have more variety in story and setting, but were initially a bit thin on gags.

Freleng, usually working with Mike Maltese's superb gags, moved Bugs into fairy-tale parodies ("Jack-Wabbit and the Beanstalk," "Little Red Riding Rabbit"); sent him to foreign countries, like Germany in "Herr Meets Hare"; pitted him against gangsters ("Racketeer Rabbit"); and had him play all nine positions in a baseball game against an evil ball club ("Baseball Bugs"). Freleng also created Yosemite Sam, the most memorable antagonist for Bugs since Elmer Fudd. His Bugs was not only the funniest, but the most likable version of the rabbit, striking the best balance between beating people up because they deserved it and beating people up for the hell of it.

Tashlin, upon his return to the studio, developed a style that was a combination of Clampett's wildness and Jones's sophistication. He used abstract or heavily simplified backgrounds and odd movements, like a character moving his head directly forward while the rest of his body remains immobile, but where Jones's use of these techniques could seem cute, Tashlin brought the feel of a sophisticated magazine illustration, or a smart children's book like his own classic *The Bear That Wasn't*.

Tashlin shared Clampett's fondness for censor-baiting jokes, like Daffy turning into liquid after a sexy woman kisses him, or hens popping out eggs from their lower halves as though something other than eggs were coming out of there. But Clampett was a big naughty child, while Tashlin was a cynical adult—his best cartoons felt more grown-up than anything else coming out of Warner.

Maybe Tashlin's best cartoon of the era, "Porky Pig's Feat" has Porky and Daffy try to sneak out of a hotel without paying their bill after Daffy loses all their money in a crap game. The piece is famous for the way Tashlin, the only *Looney Tunes* director who made the transition to live-action features, uses techniques that audiences associated with live-action film. There's a particularly impressive unbroken shot where he uses an animated background to mimic the effect of putting a live-action camera on a dolly, following the characters all the way down a hallway to a close shot of an elevator, and then backward as the hotel manager forces the pig and the duck back into their room. But it also puts its characters into a plot that would have worked for live-action comedians, while still taking advantage of animation's freedom to do reality-bending gags, like the bit where Daffy parts a cloud of smoke with his hands and then closes it back up with a zipper.

Tashlin put Daffy and Porky, singly or together, into situations that made them resemble actual adults with normal lives. Daffy becomes a guest who won't leave and annoys the man of the house with endless stories about a great party he went to ("Nasty Quacks"); a working mother convinces Porky to babysit her evil kid ("Brother Brat"). The premises are not far-fetched as cartoon premises go: a radio sitcom or live-action short might have done them. Still, you know "Brother Brat" is a Warner Bros. cartoon because the first thing the kid does is pull an anvil out of nowhere and drop it on Porky's head, sending him through the floor of his own house.

Which brings us back to violence.

* * *

You can't really talk about the development of the Warner Bros. cartoon style without talking about violence. And you can't talk about *that* without noticing how the level of violence rose in the early 1940s. Early sound cartoons, including Disney's, could have characters stretching or hitting each other's bodies in gruesome ways, but by the time *Looney Tunes* started to take off as a series, it was still relatively sedate. Characters could defy gravity by walking off a cliff and not falling immediately; the fact that they didn't fall would be the joke, and they would often run back to safety instead of hitting the ground.

In the early forties, these setups for potential violence increasingly had violent payoffs. Earlier, we saw how many of Tweety's gags were built around violence: the Lou Costello cat gets blown up, shot down, hit with a club, and flattened by an anvil. In the second Tweety cartoon, "Birdy and the Beast" (1944), Tweety is pursued by a big dumb cat who is tricked into trying to fly. And it works for him until Tweety says, "I didn't know you could fly." The cat does the inevitable double take and, instead of scurrying back to a tree branch, plummets, landing so hard that the screen shakes and he leaves an impression of himself in the ground. In the minutes that follow, Tweety will set the cat's insides on fire and then pump him full of gasoline. If you didn't know that the cartoon ends with the cat grabbing a live grenade that he thinks is Tweety, you could probably guess.

Not every 1940s cartoon was that brutal, but a lot were. Violence permeated the atmosphere of a typical Warner Bros. cartoon, and even an atypical one: Chuck Jones's "The Dover Boys" was very different from any other Warner cartoon at the time, with its all-human, no-animals cast and its dry tone, but we still see the villain, Dan Backslide, repeatedly flung across a room, his head battered like a boxer's speed bag. The film ends with all three of the title characters accidentally punching one another and falling to the ground in an unconscious heap.

The world of Warner Bros. in the early 1940s is a menacing world, like the world of a horror picture, or of what would later come to be called "film noir." The plots revolve around characters trying to capture, kill, or eat each other, and even when they're just talking, the sense is that something could blow up any minute. Many cartoons introduce a promise of carnage as early as possible. To take just a few from 1942:

- Clampett's "The Hep Cat," the first color *Looney Tunes* short, begins with the hipster cat of the title strutting along an alley, past a doghouse. In the darkness of the doghouse entrance, two eyes light up. But even before we see the eyes, we know that the familiar shape of that house means trouble for a cat; it's cartoon shorthand: all dogs are assumed to chase cats unless we're told otherwise.
- "A Tale of Two Kitties" also begins in an alley, with the two cats hidden behind a fence. We see objects thrown around, and the fence posts nearly bust from whatever is hitting them. When we finally get a look at the cats, the Abbott cat slaps the Costello cat.
- Freleng's "The Wabbit Who Came to Supper" opens with the sound of barking dogs and hunting horns from off-screen, followed by an unusually nervous Bugs Bunny running into frame, trying to escape. He also falls over while running, a trademark of Freleng, who loved to show characters falling down or dropping things to indicate that they were fallible, and also creating a mildly violent impact where there otherwise wouldn't be one.

Horror movies build up tension about the coming violence, which makes the actual violence a relief as well as a shock. There's a bloodless, consequence-free version of that in prime-era *Looney Tunes*. The laughter is a release from tension built from hints of violence to come.

What happened, between the late 1930s and the early 1940s, to turn the *Looney Tunes* world into one where something is always just about to explode? Some of it may simply be the films being adjusted to emphasize the strengths of the people who made them. The best and most prolific story men at the studio were great at creating violent gags. In this period, the studio had a pool of writers contributing stories, but several stood out, and they shared a fondness for rough, brutal comedy, as well as a regional background. In *Hollywood Cartoons*, Michael Barrier notes that the top *Looney Tunes* writers had their roots on the East Coast.[8]

Warren Foster, a story man at the Fleischer studio in New York, moved to Los Angeles in the late 1930s and became Bob Clampett's most frequent writer. Lloyd Turner, a younger writer who created stories for another unit, recalled: "Warren was a tough monkey, and you just got the feeling you don't fool with Warren."[9] His gags for Clampett often involved characters taking an enormous amount of punishment. In Foster's third Tweety cartoon and Clampett's last, "A Gruesome Twosome," a cat tries to get rid of his romantic rival by hitting him on the head so hard that his head sinks into his body, inch by inch, like a car jack. The cat then pulls out a pistol and shoots, causing his rival's fur to fly off (revealing the red union suit that half of all cartoon animals seem to have under their fur; the other half wear polka-dotted boxer shorts). Then the rival hits the cat over the head with a club. Then they fight using a gun, a knife, and what appears to be a makeshift medieval mace. All of this *before* they try to catch Tweety.

Michael Maltese was another New Yorker who had worked briefly for the Fleischers before joining the Warner Bros. team. According to Barrier, Maltese was "pushed into the story department" in 1939, but he proved to be perhaps the funniest writer at the studio, equally good at creating visual gags and writing stylized dialogue that ranked with the best comic dialogue of live-action writers like Preston Sturges. Maltese came up with Bugs's stock line for whenever he finds he has tunneled to the wrong place: "I knew I should have made that left turn at Albuquerque."

A third writer, Tedd Pierce, had originally been billed as "Ted Pierce." The story went that he added the extra *d* as a joke about the missing *l* in the first name of puppeteer Bil Baird. Pierce had been in California longer than Foster and Maltese but was born on Long Island. He struck up a working relationship with Chuck Jones, and supplied the story for "The Dover Boys," the arch parody cartoon that announced Jones's coming of age as a comedy director. Pierce was not usually viewed as the equal of the other two writers, and he had a habit of basing his stories on whatever happened to be on the radio or TV last night: in 1946 alone he gave Jones one cartoon based on the radio sitcom *Duffy's Tavern* and one with characters lifted from another radio sitcom, *Baby Snooks*. But Jones liked Pierce's wit, and his sensibility was similar enough to Maltese's that they sometimes worked as a team, providing stories for Freleng's and Jones's units at the same time.

Foster, Maltese, and Pierce would end up writing the majority of the studio's cartoons until the late 1950s. All three of them had, or affected, a sort of cynical wise-assery that could be found in the work of New York–based artists like Groucho Marx or Al Capp (creator of the comic strip *Li'l Abner*), and they were all fascinated by the possibilities of characters being shot, blown up, and pummeled for laughs. None of them wanted their humor to be too gentle or cute, and the atmosphere of comedic menace, with the threat of destruction lurking in every scene, fit with that general cynicism. Instead of a happy world threatened by one villain, as in cartoons of the 1930s, the mature Warner style usually gives us a world where everything and everyone is a threat, and anyone who doesn't notice this probably deserves to get hurt.

External competition among cartoon studios also fueled the on-screen violence. Tex Avery's MGM cartoons attempted to outdo his own Warner Bros. work by being faster-paced and including more violent gags, and that not only pushed MGM's *Tom and Jerry* series to find more creative ways of torturing Tom, but also pushed Avery's old Warner Bros. colleagues to prove he couldn't outdo them. A 1941 Columbia cartoon, "The Fox and the Grapes," was also a significant influence. Directed by Frank Tashlin just before he returned to Warner Bros. (and with Mel Blanc providing voices, just before Warner Bros. signed him exclusively), its story was mostly a series of violent blackout gags about the titular fox trying and failing to catch the titular grapes. It helped establish the idea that violent failure was such a strong subject for comedy that a cartoon barely even needed a story to connect these gags.

On top of all this was the whole war thing. Most of the 1940s animated films were made while the United States was either close to being involved in World War II, or actually in the war. Warner theatrical cartoons had the war practically everywhere, even when it had nothing to do with the plot. In "Little Red Riding Rabbit," the wolf doesn't need to eat Red Riding Hood's grandmother because she's busy working the swing shift at Lockheed. Bugs Bunny ends "Super-Rabbit" by declaring, "This looks like a job for a *real* Superman!" and emerges in the uniform of a US Marine, marching off "to Berlin, Tokyo, and points east." And, of course, generations of children learned about gas and food rationing, about victory gardens and government requests to cut back on nonessential traveling, from throwaway jokes in Warner Bros. cartoons.

Many of these cartoons give the impression that the directors had caught the mood of the public and its mixed feelings about the war: patriotism, fear, xenophobia, and slightly forced good feelings about their allies. Above all, the mood is one of high anxiety, of sitting in the theater trying to have a good time, knowing that the world is blowing up and that you, or someone close to you, might die soon. It's a mood that lends itself to gags about bombs, bullets, and pianos falling from the sky.

As Warner Bros. cartoons became more consistently violent, they developed their own particular take on how violence was presented and staged. At MGM, Avery and Hanna-Barbera developed a type of violence that emphasized how much damage a cartoon character's body can take. Bodies would crack up and fall to pieces. Tom would let out his bloodcurdling scream. They made the roughest cartoons in the business. At Schlesinger's, the directors were slightly more circumspect. They often found it was funnier not to show the violence on screen. In "Draftee Daffy," Daffy tries to blow up the little man from the Draft Board with a bomb, a huge round thing with a short fuse, which is what generations of cartoon viewers have imagined all bombs to be. As he walks away, holding his ears to prepare for the explosion, the little man appears behind him and hands the bomb back to him.

> MAN: Did you lose something, son?
> DAFFY: Oh, yeah, thanks, Pops. (Goes back to walking, now holding
> the bomb)

Daffy does a horrified double take, switching from "unaware" to "horribly aware" in as few frames as Clampett can manage, and the screen fills with an explosion effect, used many times in many cartoons, with those puffs of yellow smoke that turn black in a split second. And instead of showing what happens to Daffy, Clampett cuts to the little man, whose eyes follow the off-screen Daffy, high up into the air, then down on the floor, then bouncing around. The next shot has Daffy lying on the floor while the little man kneels down to help him. But Daffy is completely unharmed. He's not even upset. "I'm a little shaken up," is all he says when asked if he's all right.

That was based on another unwritten rule about Warner cartoon violence: the victims needed to react to it in a way that showed they weren't really hurt. At worst, violence is humiliating. Since many of these characters know they're in a cartoon, it can't be fun for them to look like chumps in front of a theater full of moviegoers. When the cat in "Birdy and the Beast" realizes he can't fly, his scream is followed by a shrug, accepting his fate, and indicating that this really isn't going to be that bad for him. Harm is a loss of dignity, not a loss of life or limb.

* * *

The Warner Bros. house style, based on blackout gags, humiliating pseudo-violence, and cynical humor, didn't allow for clear-cut heroes or villains. The predators weren't hateful and the prey were not helpless; they all walked through their preassigned roles in a world where fate is arbitrary and punishment is disproportionate. This approach required a specific type of cartoon antagonist, likable enough that you feel sorry for him when he fails, but unlikable enough that we don't really mind him taking so much punishment. And, because Warner Bros. was building its identity around solo stars like Bugs and Daffy and Tweety, the antagonist had to be someone generic enough to play second banana instead of sharing the spotlight the way Tom did with Jerry. Enter Sylvester the cat.

Sylvester is an odd character in the gallery of Warner Bros. cartoon stars in that he's not really a star at all. Instead he exists as a rotating, all-purpose cat for any director who needed a character to beat up. Friz Freleng introduced him in a cartoon called "Life with Feathers," and Bob Clampett soon began using the character and planning to team him up with his own character, Tweety; after Clampett left, Freleng inherited the idea, and launched a successful series modeled on *Tom and Jerry*.

Sylvester was another utility character, forever changing to fit the needs of a particular story. Sometimes he could talk, in a lisping voice that was just Daffy Duck's voice played at normal speed. Sometimes he was a silent character communicating through pantomime. Sometimes he was an alley cat, or a domesticated animal. Sometimes he was evil, and other times he was a poor wretch starving to death. The only thing consistent about him, once he was a mature character, was his status as a total loser.

The prototypical Sylvester cartoon is the second picture Freleng made with him, "Peck Up Your Troubles," written by Mike Maltese, where Sylvester repeatedly tries and fails to get up a tree to eat a woodpecker. It's a pure example of the clothesline plot, with no story beyond the basic conflict between predator and prey. There's a third character on hand to provide additional comeuppance to Sylvester, a bulldog in a nearby doghouse. The question in every scene is how Sylvester is going to get hurt. The violent gags come in different styles and lengths:[10]

The complicated plan that fails in a simple way. Sylvester tries to walk over to the nest by using a power line as a tightrope; the woodpecker flicks a switch and electrocutes him.

The gag with the sudden payoff. Sylvester catapults himself up to the tree and toward the bird's house, but he's forgotten that the house has a "door" that the bird can slam shut.

The gag with the delayed payoff. Sylvester's attempt to charge the door of the woodpecker's house leads to him getting stuck in a tree branch. The woodpecker produces a safety pin as big as he is, and we get a long, drawn-out buildup. We know Sylvester is going to be stuck with that pin, but we don't know when, and the focus of the scene is the anticipation: Sylvester sweating and praying (do cartoon characters ever pray for any other reason than impending pain?); the woodpecker smugly flexing the pin, and finally a shot where the woodpecker disappears from view and the camera moves back and forth as if looking for him. When the blow arrives, Freleng doesn't show either character, just the result, with Sylvester rocketing into the distance.

The gag where someone mistakenly thinks violence has happened. The cat is tricked into thinking the bird has been crushed into a bloody pulp, due to the fact that cartoon characters are notoriously unable to tell tomatoes from corpses. The woodpecker then dresses up as his own departed spirit to "haunt" the horrified Sylvester. He hands Sylvester a gun and tries to drive him to suicide.

The death gag. For obvious reasons, this turns up almost exclusively at the end of a cartoon. Sylvester, blown up by dynamite, is sent to one of those fluffy clouds that dead characters float away on. The cartoon even calls attention to how little sense it makes for this one little act of violence to be any more lethal than the others, because after the explosion, the camera pans back and forth looking for Sylvester, clearly expecting another gag to follow. The woodpecker points upward, and the camera finally finds Sylvester, looking mildly annoyed in his "angel" outfit.

This isn't one of the *Looney Tunes* all-time classics, and those last two gags help explain why. The suicide scene scrambles the meaning of the cartoon, suggesting that characters actually can die, which means that maybe Sylvester might actually be dead at the end. The gags cross a line between funny and unfunny violence and, even at a studio known for dark humor, that's a problem. Too much darkness, or too many dark gags in succession, undermines what makes *Looney Tunes* great: the ability to portray the maximum amount of comedy violence while still being charming, fun, family entertainment.

CHAPTER 7

Looney on the Page

All children love comics. Make sure the comics they read are good comics. Subscribe to LOONEY TUNES & MERRIE MELODIES and you give them the clean, beneficial comics they should have. And what is more, you'll give them what they want! LOONEY TUNES is one of the very largest selling, most popular comic magazines ever published, ample proof that it is the kid's own favorite. And no wonder! Every month it brings them the delightful adventures of those famous movie characters, Porky Pig, Bugs Bunny, Elmer, Mary Jane and Sniffles, and all the other Leon Schlesinger movie creations. Here is truly the ideal comic magazine — and it makes the perfect Christmas gift.

— Advertisement in *Modern Screen*, June 1943[1]

IN 1944, WARNER BROS. bought Leon Schlesinger Productions and changed its name to Warner Bros. Cartoons Inc.[2] The cartoon studio remained physically separate from the live-action studio, but the cartoons and characters were owned outright by the film company. Schlesinger's producer credit was removed from the beginning of *Looney Tunes* and *Merrie Melodies* shorts, and replaced with the very prosaic "Produced by Warner Bros. Cartoons, Inc." There would be no attempt to elevate any one person as the face of the cartoon studio, like Walt Disney or Walter Lantz or even producer Fred Quimby, whose credit on MGM cartoons was bigger than those of the directors. The identity of the cartoon series was instead bound up with the company and the characters. That may be why people have always thought of them as Warner Bros. characters. Many of the cartoons would change ownership but the Warner Bros. shield would define them in a way that the Universal logo would not define Woody Woodpecker.

From the studio sale until his death in 1949, Schlesinger was not completely retired. One thing he continued to take an interest in was the licensing and marketing of the characters.[3] Disney had figured out long ago something that most of his animation competitors were slow to grasp: an animated cartoon character gets only part of his value from animated cartoons. Licensing and merchandising bring extra money and make the world more aware of the characters. One answer to Rob Long's implicit question—why is unfunny Mickey Mouse more famous than funny Bugs Bunny—is that cartoon characters can have lives outside their home medium. Most people who know Mickey Mouse have never seen his cartoons but they have seen him on merchandise or at the Disney theme parks. A recurring theme in the history of *Looney Tunes* is that most of the characters have little reach beyond their cartoons.

Schlesinger was aware that his characters might be marketable. He made some early merchandising efforts with Bosko and Honey, but became more serious about the practice once he had stars like Porky and Bugs. In 1940 he signed Mitchell J. Hamilburg, described as "the 'dean' of tie-ups," to get Looney Tunes merchandise into toy stores. Hamilburg had previously handled merchandising for movie stars who appealed mostly to children, like the singing cowboy Gene Autry and the child stars Deanna Durbin and Jackie Cooper.[4]

In her essay "Selling Bugs Bunny" in the anthology *Reading the Rabbit*, Linda Simensky mentions "stuffed plush toys, ceramics, windup toys, coloring books, rubber dolls . . . watches and alarm clocks"[5] among the products that resulted from these licensing tie-ins. Inevitably, there were Porky Pig piggy banks. The ones that seem to turn up in auctions most often have him wearing blue overalls and a little red hat, and looking off to one side as if he sees someone coming to steal your money.

A more promising field was newsstand comics, where, before television, cartoon characters could be sent into homes around the world. Schlesinger made a deal with Western Publishing, a company that specialized in creating comic books based on characters licensed from other media. Their comics were distributed as part of the Dell Comics line until 1962, and then by Western's own imprint, Gold Key.[6]

Although the comics would eventually include most of the Warner Bros. characters, they started small, leaving out Daffy Duck and concentrating on Bugs Bunny, Porky Pig, and Elmer Fudd. A few minor *Looney Tunes* characters were given expanded roles to better fit the new medium, including some who were so minor that they might as well have been originals. Western gave Porky's girlfriend, Petunia, a new prominence in Porky's comic stories, and also in tie-in books and merchandise. This was in keeping with Disney cartoons, where Mickey and Donald had girlfriends who looked uncomfortably like them. Later on, still more minor *Looney* characters were imported, often to get more kids into the cast. There was a comic book version of the Road Runner who talked in rhyme, and had three nephews who also talked in rhyme. Bugs Bunny's nephew Clyde appeared a couple of times in the theatrical cartoons to almost universal disdain, but had more of a presence in the comics.

Despite the oversupply of nephews, Western's comics could actually be superior to the bigger-budgeted material on which they were based. Most famously, a series of Donald Duck stories written and drawn for Western by the former Disney story man Carl Barks turned Donald into one of the most enduringly popular comic book characters in the world. Almost as famous are the Little Lulu comics from writer John Stanley. Although based on a series of cartoons in the *Saturday Evening Post*, Stanley's version of the character and her world have come to define her more than her own creator's work.

Where do the Warner Bros. characters fit into this? In *Funnybooks*, the indefatigable Michael Barrier's history of Dell Comics, the *Looney Tunes* comics get only a few pages, saying very little about the quality of the stories. They continued to be published for decades, but never had a Barks or a Stanley who could make the characters their own, with one surprising exception. The most successful and beloved *Looney Tunes* comic book character was Sniffles the mouse.

Early in his directing career, Chuck Jones created a cute little mouse with wide-eyed charm and an apparent sinus condition, the first of many absurdly adorable characters he would introduce over the years. Once Jones adopted the Warner Bros. house style of violent comedy, an innocent like Sniffles didn't fit. Jones tried to take this little fellow, who had once spent an entire cartoon trying not to fall asleep before Santa Claus arrives, and make him funnier and put him in more violent situations: Sniffles by 1946 was being hunted by cats who need to put "mouse knuckles" on their restaurant menu. But it didn't work, and that was Sniffles's last cartoon. To people who only know the animated films, Sniffles is the key character of Jones's early, unfunny period.

But in the comics, Sniffles caught on. Chase Craig, who would edit *Looney Tunes* comics at Western and Dell for many years, created the Sniffles comic book series, pairing him with a human girl named Mary Jane. She could shrink herself down to mouse size using an incantation that varied: at one point it was "Magic sand, magic sand, make me small at my command!" but when parents began complaining that kids might imitate the comic by throwing sand on themselves,[7] the incantation became: "Magic words of poof poof piffles, make me just as small as Sniffles!"[8]

Craig had found a way to make Sniffles work better as a comic book character than he did as a theatrical star, but it only worked for Sniffles. The other *Looney Tunes* characters, and especially Bugs, remained basically comedy characters, and the comics had to try to make them funny without animation, music, or voices. Mickey Mouse had a successful newspaper strip and Donald Duck had one of the world's most popular comics, but Bugs, even when he was the most popular animated cartoon star in the world, was among the worst characters in the early *Looney Tunes and Merrie Melodies* comics. A Bugs comic story often comes off as writers vamping desperately to figure out what to do with him if he can't blow people up or try to seduce them.

One reason for this may simply be that Bugs is hard to draw, or at least easy to draw badly. Porky and Elmer were easier to handle because they had round designs: a round head on a round body was one of the most basic and effective looks. Bugs was sleeker, with a more complicated body and head, but also a more expressive one. Those expressive moments can only be hinted at in a comic book, and the sharper look makes it easy to screw up. "I think I could have drawn Mickey quite well," said Carl Barks. "Mickey was simple. The one I couldn't draw was Bugs Bunny." [9]

Barks drew one *Looney Tunes* story called "Porky of the Mounties," where Porky and Bugs get trapped on a train to Canada while Porky is conveniently wearing an RCMP Halloween costume. Barks felt that he did well with Porky and Petunia, but most of Bugs's faces in the published story had to be drawn by another artist, Carl Buettner, as Barks explained:

The ones [Buettner] couldn't change he drew on another piece of paper and cut it out and pasted it over the faces that I had drawn. Oh, I didn't get any praise out of it, but I was happy that it came out that way because I had no intention of ever being that much of a cartoonist that I could draw Bugs Bunny. It was over my head.[10]

Barks was not alone. Licensed versions of Bugs Bunny always tend to look "off" in some way, either because they don't match the character's standard design, or they make him look too standardized at the expense of his personality. Mickey doesn't have that problem.

Bugs was also afflicted by the change of format because it undermined his cross-generational appeal. Theatrical cartoons tried to make grown-ups and children laugh equally hard.[11] Manny Farber complimented the Schlesinger crew on making cartoons that the adults in the audience didn't use for a smoking break.[12] Talking-animal comics, on the other hand, were almost exclusively marketed to children. Their characters could not be as violent or as mean as they were on-screen. Barks made Donald Duck much less of a jerk in the comics. This was a problem for Bugs Bunny because his iconic image involves a hunter pointing a gun at him, and even the nicest versions of Bugs are violent sociopaths.

* * *

The very first issue of *Looney Tunes and Merrie Melodies Comics* began with an adaptation of Bugs's breakout cartoon, "A Wild Hare," and continued with hunting stories, although most of the sociopathy and cruelty were soon boiled away. While still a brash wise guy with a vaguely big-city accent, comic Bugs comes off as the token naughty kid in a cast of straight arrows. In "Porky of the Mounties" he's the selfish, cowardly friend who encourages Porky to get into mischief. He seems adrift in the more child-friendly, morally upright world of the comic book pages.

Comic book stories also demand more variety than theatrical shorts, and that, too, was bad for Bugs. Because animated characters appeared in only a few cartoons ever year, it was easy to repeat the same plot. A comic book usually had several stories in it, and kids were expected to read all of them. Burning through this much material required the characters to sustain more than one kind of story, and resulted in writers constantly putting Bugs into unlikely story formulas.

The lack of continuity in *Looney Tunes* or *Merrie Melodies* cartoons presented yet another challenge. It's not that Western's comics had actual continuity, in the sense of one story having an impact on the next. But in a Warner Bros. animated cartoon, the characters have never even *met* each other before a cartoon starts. It's rare for Elmer to know who Bugs is, and when he does, it seems wrong. It's typical for Sylvester to meet Tweety for the first time in every cartoon, several times a year. And everything about them, where they live, who they know, can change from short to short. Elmer Fudd can be a vegetarian or a rabbit stew connoisseur depending on what the writer needs him to say this year.

Comics demanded a more stable world than the free-for-all of cartoons. There was a sense that characters should have a supporting cast, maybe a home base, or something to create the sense that they are people. Donald Duck, who in the animated cartoons can live anywhere and do anything, had a hometown in the comics, and a supporting cast including a new character, Scrooge McDuck, who became a star in his own right. To meet these new expectations, *Looney Tunes* comics, too, treated their characters as if they knew one another and had more or less fixed residences. Elmer and Porky both lived in a vaguely suburban setting, and Bugs was a part of that setting. This small but significant change would eventually alter how the world understood *Looney Tunes* characters. The comics introduced the idea that Schlesinger and Warner Bros. had created a family of characters, a "gang" that could be marketed collectively, or in smaller groups.

This was another thing Disney had figured out fairly early, teaming characters like Mickey, Donald, and Goofy together in cartoons. Schlesinger's studio had a lot of characters but it was rare for them to cross over. In the 1940s, Bugs Bunny never appeared with the star of any other series, except in quick cameos. The notion that the characters shared a universe would have limited the way the laughs-first creators told their stories.

In the comics, and in licensed content more generally, Bugs, Porky, Elmer, and Sniffles shared a reality and crossed over all the time. In the Sniffles story from issue 14 (December 1942), Sniffles and Mary Jane's shadows get bored following them around and leave to make mischief on their own. After playing pranks on Bugs, Porky, and Elmer, the shadows are scared back into place when Bugs, Porky, and Elmer team up to frighten them with a much bigger shadow. Even with this small stable of characters, the comic writers were trying to develop something like a world.

This shared world didn't seep into the style of the cartoons but, down the road, movies such as *Space Jam* and *Who Framed Roger Rabbit* are hard to imagine without a "*Looney Tunes* gang." The comics helped to convey that idea, and it eventually turned into the way most people saw the characters, no matter what the cartoon shorts seemed to imply.

Also, for the first time, the characters became bigger than their films. The success of the licensing agreements, although modest compared to what Disney achieved, convinced Warner Bros. to expand its stable of characters. Making more stars became a priority. In fact, Warner Bros.'

frenzy of character creation (more on this in the next chapter) was soon one of the things that set it apart from its competitors like MGM.

It is telling that Eddie Selzer, Warner Bros.' choice as Schlesinger's successor, came from a marketing and promotion background. When he was close to retirement, he brought a reporter to the studio for an interview about what he claimed to be Bugs Bunny's twentieth anniversary. It wasn't Bugs's twentieth anniversary by any measure, but the reporter didn't know. For the article, Selzer spoke rapturously of the studio's merchandising plans: "We've just licensed Bugs Bunny carrot juice, carrots, and waffle and gelatin molds in the shape of the rabbit."[13]

CHAPTER 8

New Directors

ONE OF THE SURPRISING things about the Warner Bros. cartoon studio is how many of its characters owe their popularity to cartoons made after the business of theatrical shorts was in decline. The late 1940s were the start of a tough time for American movie studios and the business model that made these cartoons viable. Yet somehow, through it all, the *Looney Tunes* staff kept developing memorable characters and building a library of cartoons so huge that it was able to survive division into separate libraries. By the time Warner Bros. was finally ready to stop producing animated shorts, it had outlasted even Walt Disney, who had long since stopped making them.

Theatrical cartoons died out because they were created for a movie business model that fell apart after the Second World War. This is known as the collapse of the studio system, a story so familiar that a few words are sufficient to sum it up: the US Supreme Court forced movie studios to divest themselves of the theater chains they owned; movie stars won more freedom from studio contracts and a chunk of the profits from their movies; and television caused many once-loyal moviegoers to stay home in the evening. When Warner Bros. bought out Schlesinger's cartoon studio in 1944, it was part of a confident industry with a business model that had been working for a long time, and was running smoothly even in the middle of a global war. Before the decade was out, *Looney Tunes* was part of a broken business model created for a type of entertainment experience that television was rendering irrelevant.

All the studio's cartoons released after 1948, which would form the core of nearly all *Looney Tunes* compilations to come, are from a period of constant downsizing, occasional layoffs, and a general sense that the theatrical cartoon was on its way out. The tighter budgets are evident in a number of ways. In a Bugs Bunny cartoon from 1948, "A-Lad-In His Lamp," a genie transports Bugs to Baghdad, but some of the planned gags were excised,[1] and the cartoon was padded out with a series of background shots with signs on them ("Used rug lot: Sell your magic carpet to Mad Man Hassan"), allowing for almost a minute of film without animation. A few years later, the length of most cartoons would be cut by a minute, sending them back to the lengths of the lower-budget black-and-white days.

Eddie Selzer, the uncredited producer of most of these cartoons, seems to have been the sort of man a fiction writer would create for a story about corporate downsizing and shrinking hopes. A former director of publicity at Warner Bros., he had become head of the department that created trailers and titles for the studio's live-action movies, and was occasionally spoken of as a candidate for a bigger position at the live-action studio, but instead he wound up running a cartoon department that wasn't even on the main studio lot. He was a company man who made the studio his home until he turned sixty-five and retired, like any other executive in any other business. While Schlesinger had been respected by his employees for his good hiring choices and his willingness to leave them alone, Selzer was seen the way he probably saw himself, as a Warner Bros. man watchdogging a formerly independent team.

Almost every anecdote about Selzer casts him as the company man who didn't understand animation or comedy, and made suggestions that no one took, like telling Jones not to make a bullfighting cartoon. He instituted the practice of bringing the full directing and writing staff in to do "jam sessions" where they would look at a potential story and offer ideas, but what he actually liked to see, or whether he had any impact on the style of the cartoons, is not clear.[2] The atmosphere at the studio became less friendly.

That employees were desperately protective of their jobs contributed to the unfriendliness. The writing staff was whittled down to a few men, and, as comedy writers usually do, they feared being replaced by someone younger, or having their material stolen. "New blood is dangerous around here. We fear new blood," Foster said half-jokingly to a new writer. When Mike Maltese and Tedd Pierce stopped writing as a team, Maltese reportedly told his ex-partner, "I've carried you long enough!"[3]

* * *

This difference in atmosphere from the freewheeling early days hit just before a significant change in personnel. Two major directors left within a few months of each other, and the new management faced the first and, as it turned out, last important test of its ability to choose new directors. Frank Tashlin was the first to depart, successfully moving into live-action film, although he never developed a major following except in France. Bob Clampett quit soon after, first trying to set up his own cartoon production company, and then finding success and even a measure of fame as the creator and producer of the television puppet show *Time for Beany*, which he also adapted into the animated series *Beany and Cecil*, whose closing theme song identified it to kids everywhere as "A Bob Clampett cartoon." This song made Clampett, for many years, the most famous person who had ever directed Warner Bros. cartoons.

To replace these directors, Warner Bros. chose two qualified men. Robert McKimson was not only one of Clampett's best animators, he had created an early Bugs Bunny model sheet that was regarded as definitive, and before he accepted the directing job, he had become the studio's supervising animator, giving other animators notes on how to draw important characters like Bugs.[4] He also had two brothers who were almost on his level: Tom McKimson was a top Warner Bros. animator and layout artist who later became one of the top artists on *Looney Tunes* comics, while Charles McKimson was an animator in Bob's unit for many years.

Arthur Davis got the fourth unit, the utility unit, where he concentrated mostly on Daffy and Porky cartoons and only got to make one with Bugs Bunny. Davis had not been at the studio as long as McKimson, and he was promoted over some other animators who coveted the job, but he had more directing experience than any of them, having been a director at Columbia's Screen Gems studio before arriving at Warner as an animator.

Being a relative newcomer who mostly worked with new writers, Davis created cartoons that are beloved for featuring some memorably bizarre characters that don't appear in anyone else's work. He sent Porky Pig up against a termite lumberjack with a French Canadian accent; a chipmunk from Brooklyn who sounds like Bugs Bunny if he communicated entirely in 1940s hipster slang ("Cease the chop-chop, chubby! Blow, Joe!"); and, in his final cartoon, "Bye Bye, Bluebeard," a serial-killer wolf with blue hair who tries to execute the pig via guillotine. Few of these cartoons are all-time classics, but in a Saturday-morning cartoon package they bring an enjoyable change of pace.

The difference between the new directors, McKimson and Davis, and the ones who got their start under Schlesinger, was that Freleng, Avery, Clampett, and Jones had all been trained to think like producers, to develop their own individual approaches to the studio formula, and to be incredibly competitive in trying to one-up each other. They would all go on to start their own production companies and become animation entrepreneurs. Davis and McKimson ended their careers directing animated TV series produced by other people, where their skill and experience was needed but not their ideas of what made a good story. At Warner Bros., they were house directors, not pioneers. They had to find their way in a world where the house style and a lineup of characters had already been codified.

This could be difficult for both McKimson and Davis, but especially Davis, because he knew that his unit would be the first to go if the studio had to downsize. Lloyd Turner, one of Davis's main writers, liked Davis personally but considered him indecisive about what was funny. At an early story meeting, said Turner, Davis wouldn't commit to saying that he liked a story until Chuck Jones spoke up and said he'd take it if Davis didn't want it.[5]

Davis's unit was shut down after only two years, when the studio decided that the postwar cinematic economy could not support four animation units. Davis went back to animating, doing fine work for Freleng for many years.

McKimson was luckier. His unit lasted until the studio shut down. He was also luckier because his story man, early on, was Warren Foster, who had done many memorable stories for Clampett and Tashlin, and who did as much as any writer to define what a typical *Looney Tunes* gag should be. He and Foster worked well together. McKimson's first cartoon as a director, "Daffy Doodles," takes a fun, inherently visual premise— Porky is a cop pursuing Daffy, a graffiti vandal painting mustaches on every poster and picture in the city—and spins a series of very good gags out of it, including a nice moment when Daffy actually stops Porky from getting hurt as a result of one of the gags ("Very sporting of the little black duck!").

Early histories of Warner Bros. animation tended to ignore or dismiss McKimson, not entirely without reason. McKimson didn't have the gift that every great director has, of motivating people to produce their very best work. Certain stock gestures and expressions were repeated in his cartoons no matter who was animating, as if everyone was sticking too close to the director's drawings. He often repeated points in the physical acting that should be clear from the dialogue—it's called "indicating," and McKimson's characters indicate a lot. McKimson loved to have characters with their eyelids half-closed to indicate sarcasm or skepticism, and he would often have them point an index finger for emphasis. When a McKimson character points *and* has his eyes half-closed, you know he's serious.

Still, McKimson had some individual ideas about characters, and some surprising ones about Bugs Bunny. As an animator, McKimson was famous for his sleek, streamlined, almost beautiful Bugs. When he became a director, he began drawing Bugs differently: stocky, slovenly in posture, more toothy than usual, and prone to frowning or sneering. He looked like he would beat you up for asking when he had put on weight.

The new design was consistent with the way Bugs behaved in McKimson's cartoons. As Freleng and Jones were pushing the rabbit toward being more unambiguously heroic, McKimson ran with Bugs as a street tough. He's not particularly bright: one cartoon depends entirely on him becoming sexually attracted to the mechanical rabbit at a dog track. And he often gets exploited: in "Easter Yeggs," the Easter Bunny (called the "Easter Rabbit" so they won't be accused of denigrating a beloved holiday mascot) swindles Bugs into making his deliveries for him.

McKimson's Bugs still commits his share of violence, however, and in the most famous "asshole Bugs" cartoon, "Rebel Rabbit," he becomes a literal terrorist, sawing the state of Florida off from the USA, and forcing the military to take him out. The original story also had Bugs kicking a cop and slapping the Secretary of the Interior, which Eddie Selzer negotiated down to clubbing a chauffeur and squirting ink on a game commissioner.[6]

In addition to recasting Bugs, McKimson created a number of new characters for the studio, including several that caught on enough to become ongoing series. The most high-concept one of the bunch was Hippety Hopper, a baby kangaroo Sylvester mistakes for a giant mouse. The redeeming feature of some of the Hippety cartoons was the simultaneous creation of Sylvester Jr., who looked exactly like Sylvester at half the size. Pint-size versions of established characters were usually annoying in the *Looney Tunes* world. Nobody much liked Bugs Bunny's nephew Clyde. But giving Sylvester a son opened new dimensions for the biggest loser in all of cartoondom. When they appear together, Sylvester's motivation is not just to catch a mouse, it's to prove to his son that he is the great mouse-chaser and brave pussycat he always claims to be.

McKimson was the creator of Speedy Gonzales, though his version was very different from the one who became famous. His unit also produced a number of those strange *Looney Tunes* creatures who didn't actually become cartoon stars, but got so popular that everyone thinks they were stars, the most famous of these being the Tasmanian Devil. But there's one character who stands above them all as the signature McKimson creation, a genuine star who is still one of the most beloved *Looney Tunes* characters of all time: Foghorn Leghorn, the man-size chicken.

* * *

Most of McKimson's Foghorn cartoons never received the deluxe restored DVD treatment, but audiences love him, and have loved him ever since he first appeared in "Walky Talky Hawky," a film nominated for an Academy Award. McKimson continued to release at least one Foghorn cartoon every year until the studio shut down.

One of the famous factoids about Foghorn is that he talks a lot like Senator Claghorn, the pompous Southern senator played by Kenny Delmar on radio's *The Fred Allen Show*. He's not actually a knockoff of Senator Claghorn. The dialogue track for his first cartoon was recorded in early 1945, several months before Delmar introduced the Claghorn character.[7] McKimson said that both the chicken and the senator were based on an older radio character, a sheriff played by Jack Clifford on the West Coast radio program *Blue Monday Jamboree*, who had a tic of repeating his words and prefacing them with "I say" ("I believe, I say I believe . . .").[8] Because animated cartoons took a long time to complete and be released, "Walky Talky Hawky" didn't debut until 1946 and, by then, he seemed like a Claghorn clone.

McKimson and his team didn't seem to mind the association, and began to make him more like Delmar's character. They took up some of Claghorn's verbal characteristics, like adding "that is" to the end of sentences ("Yes, dreamboat," Foghorn says to his wife in the one cartoon where he has a wife, ". . . tugboat, that is"). The chicken was given the name "Foghorn" to suggest a similarity to the *Fred Allen Show* character, and Mel Blanc shifted toward a Southern accent, which wasn't used in Foghorn's first couple of appearances.

Foghorn was an example of how attempts to create a star don't always lead to predictable results. The star of "Walky Talky Hawky," and the top-billed star for several of the cartoons that followed, was a young New York–accented chicken hawk named Henery, who had been created by

Chuck Jones several years earlier. Warner Bros. seemed to see something marketable in this feisty little guy who keeps picking and winning fights with characters who are many times his size. They were still trying to market Henery as late as 1951, when there was a two-sided comedy record[9] with Henery as the star. But by that time, Foghorn had completely taken over the cartoon series, and Henery was starting to be phased out.

Initially, the series stuck fairly close to the plot of "Walky Talky Hawky," which had introduced the Foghorn/Henery team and Foghorn's rivalry and ongoing prank war with a gravel-voiced barnyard dog. The signature gag of the series is Foghorn hitting the dog's butt with a wooden paddle, followed by the dog chasing Foghorn and accidentally self-strangulating on his tether. Henery plays off the rivalry between Foghorn and the dog, and a typical ending will have Henery dragging Foghorn away to be eaten, or, in one case, just watching while the chicken and dog fight it out: "I don't care who wins, I'll fricassee the loser!"

This isn't quite like any other *Looney Tunes* series setup, but then Foghorn is not quite like any other *Looney Tunes* star. He allowed McKimson to stake out territory that none of the other directors had covered. Most characters fell pretty neatly into the predator/prey dynamic: their behavior could be justified because they were hungry, or because they wanted to save their own hide. Foghorn rarely fights for his survival, and because he's so huge, no one seems like a physical threat to him, although they sometimes turn out to be stronger than he expected. He's not a nice person. He will often encourage other characters to make trouble, either for his own amusement at watching them fail, or to complicate the dog's life. But while not a hero, Foghorn isn't a nihilistic screwball like the early Daffy Duck, either. He's sane and quite mellow. His stock poses have him leaning nonchalantly on something, wordlessly singing the Stephen Foster song "Camptown Races," which became the theme music for most of his later cartoons.

Foghorn also has his own approach to violence. He uses less of it. In the fourth Foghorn cartoon, "Henhouse Henery," the dog is chasing Foghorn in retaliation for another prank, Foghorn chops down a tree, carries it into a conveniently located woodworking workshop, and uses the equipment to turn the tree into a baseball bat, all in about ten seconds of screen time. This is a classic Warner Bros. gag, where the joke is not what happens but the absurdly small amount of time it takes to do it: cartoon characters change costumes, bake cakes, and construct entire buildings in the time it takes for the audience to finish its next laugh. But the baseball bat is the *most* violent weapon Foghorn gets hold of in the cartoon, and he doesn't even actually get a chance to use it. The dog grabs it away from him, and the chase continues.

There are some cartoons, particularly later ones, where dynamite and guns come into play, but those gags often don't feel right for the series. Foghorn is about paddles, baseball bats, and Rube Goldberg contraptions assembled from the junk lying about the farmyard. If most *Looney Tunes* cartoons take place in the modern world, complete with the constant threat of being blown to smithereens, Foghorn Leghorn cartoons feel like they take place in an old-fashioned America. Not urban like Bugs or suburban like Elmer Fudd, Foghorn Leghorn and the dog are from the old America that urbanites and suburbanites love to revisit in their stories and sitcoms, a place where life revolves around the farmyard and the fishing hole.

By *Looney Tunes* standards, there is even a bit of continuity in Foghorn's cartoons, since he and the dog are almost always portrayed as having a preexisting rivalry, and the cartoons rarely take place anywhere but on a farm, or in a yard resembling a farm. But what really separates Foghorn from most of his stablemates is the low-stakes world he lives in. Most *Looney Tunes* characters are driven by the desire to survive or the urge to win. Foghorn is usually driven by boredom: not ours, but his. He gives the impression of being a smart, talkative guy stuck on a farm, where there is no one to talk to except other chickens and a dim-witted dog. He'll troll Henery, who rarely knows what a chicken looks like, by sending him after other animals, telling him that they're chickens. Sometimes he'll let predators loose on the farm, or team up with them, just to stir up trouble and keep himself entertained in this idyllic but dull farm life.

As antiheroes go, Foghorn is more relatable than the early Daffy. He is someone trapped in a mundane world willing to do pretty much anything to occupy his time. If you think of the farmyard as an office and Foghorn and the dog as employees with too much time on their hands, the popularity of the series makes sense. Foghorn is a jerk and mostly a loser, but, like characters on *The Office*, we forgive him because, within the limitations of his world, he's finding ways to have the fun denied so many of us. Another popular feature of Foghorn's cartoons is his dialogue. Most *Looney Tunes* characters have fairly minimal dialogue. Even Bugs will say nothing for long stretches of a cartoon. There was a taboo against having characters stand around and talk for a second longer than the plot required, because that reduced a scene to illustrated radio, carried by words, not drawings. But Foghorn is a radio-derived character and a motormouth. This was, perhaps, a limitation: when Foghorn isn't talking, he doesn't quite seem like himself (even his body language tends to emphasize the rhythm of his words). At least it set him apart from other characters who were clearly rooted in the silent era.

"A Fractured Leghorn" (1950) is a milestone cartoon for the character. It shows him at his best, refusing to stop talking and accusing everyone else of not letting him get a word in edgewise. It is also the first Foghorn cartoon without Henery or the dog, and the first that showed he could exist within a different plot. The setup is one that Warren Foster used in many Tweety cartoons: two big characters are competing to eat a tiny creature, and they alternate between chasing the creature individually, chasing him together, and just beating each other up. Here the big guys are Foghorn and an unnamed black-and-white cat, similar to Sylvester but designed by McKimson's unit. They're both after a worm, although for different reasons: Foghorn wants to eat the worm and the cat needs bait to catch a fish.

This setup allows for variations on predator/prey gags, most of which could probably have been done with other characters. What makes the cartoon distinctively Foghorn is that he will not stop talking at the cat. The worm doesn't talk, and the cat doesn't, either, until the very end, so the dialogue track is a running Foghorn monologue of Claghorn-esque insults ("Boy's got a mouth like a cannon, always shootin' it off"), irrelevancies ("There's no oil five hundred miles of here! Geology of the ground's all wrong! Even if there was oil, you'd need a drill not a tire pump!") and anything else that can keep his opponent distracted. The animation has him constantly in motion, walking while he talks, pushing and slapping the cat, and blaming him for being pushed and slapped, and generally acting like he doesn't care about eating the worm as much as he cares about ruling the conversation.

Foghorn is so in love with the sound of his own voice that at the end of the cartoon, he simply lets the worm get away because he's too busy lecturing the cat on why, by his logic, the worm was not actually there to begin with ("That's mathematics, son! You can argue with me, but you can't argue with figures!"). Finally, driven too far, the cat clobbers Foghorn with a garbage can and speaks his only words of the film: "AH, SHUT UP!" using a Mel Blanc line delivery that was so iconic that directors used it for multiple characters over the years. As the cat walks away, Foghorn embarks on a long monologue about how he always stops talking when asked, and physically holds back the screen from going black just so he can squeeze in a few more lines about how little he talks.

After this, there were a few other cartoons with Henery. The series evolved away from the original formula and was allowed free range. One of the refreshing things about the Foghorn Leghorn series is how un-formulaic it is by the usual Warner standards. Some shorts have Foghorn trying to fend off the advances of Miss Prissy, a spinster hen in a bonnet who rarely says anything but "Yeeeessss," inflecting it differently depending on her mood. Others feature an outside predator, like a fox or a weasel, trying to catch the chickens on the farm, noticing that Foghorn and the dog are the worst henhouse guardians on the planet. And there are cartoons that cross over into sitcom territory, like a visit from Foghorn's obnoxious old college buddy. Not all these stories worked as well as the original setup but Foghorn remained a consistently funny character, even after McKimson lost Foster in a rather humiliating way.

* * *

Friz Freleng was apparently not satisfied with the work Tedd Pierce was doing as his story man. Mike Maltese was working exclusively for Jones at that point, so Freleng arranged a trade: Warren Foster left the McKimson unit and came over to Freleng, while Pierce was sent to McKimson. It was unmistakably a promotion for Foster and a demotion for Pierce, and an indication that McKimson's unit was considered the lowest priority at the studio.

From that point on until the studio was near to shutting down, the pecking order was very clear at Warner Bros. Freleng, who would direct four Oscar-winning shorts, was the senior director and the closest thing the studio had to a star. He was the first choice for special projects like animated sequences in Warner Bros. live-action movies, and when the studio shut down for a few months in 1953, Freleng was the only director not laid off. Chuck Jones was one rung below Freleng but he, too, had his share of prestige. His unit pulled off the feat of winning two Oscars in one year (one for a theatrical cartoon, the other for an educational film). Jones was doing the best work of his career in the late 1940s and early 1950s, and this hot streak would eventually allow him more fame than all his colleagues.

And then there was the McKimson unit, the place where you went if there was no room for you with Freleng or Jones. McKimson got at least two layout artists cast off by Jones, and his top animator through much of the 1950s had been dumped by Freleng. Selzer would flatter McKimson by telling him that he managed problem employees better than Jones or Freleng could,[10] but there wasn't much anyone could say about the writer shuffle, except that Freleng was entitled to a top writer, and the third unit got Pierce, the studio's third best.

Pierce had written many good cartoons, like Jones's "The Dover Boys" and Freleng's "High Diving Hare," where he managed to make a cartoon story that consists almost entirely of variations on one gag: Yosemite Sam tries to make Bugs jump off a high-diving platform and winds up falling himself, a bit that happens in a slightly different and equally funny way every time, until finally the camera just shows Sam falling without any explanation as to how he got tricked. And Pierce's first cartoon with McKimson was one of the best either man was ever involved with: "Hillbilly Hare," famous for ending with a three-minute square dance sequence where two bearded hillbillies follow Bugs's sadistic rhymed instructions ("Hit him in the shin, hit him in the head / Hit him again, the critter ain't dead"). But it soon became apparent that the Pierce-McKimson team was not a good match of writer and director.

Pierce was good at finding ways to sustain viewer interest during the early part of a cartoon, the setup, where cartoons are often slow. And he was good at dialogue, with Foghorn's one-liners coming easy to him. But

Animation drawing of Bugs Bunny in "Bully for Bugs," looking out and slightly down into the audience.

An early model sheet for Tweety. It doesn't mention that he was pink at the time.

The first Looney Tunes cartoon: the song "Singin' in the Bathtub" would last longer at the studio than Bosko.

Schlesinger with directors and associates (L to R): Frank Tashlin, Tex Avery, Henry Binder, Schlesinger, Ray Katz, Friz Freleng.

Tex Avery takes charge at a story meeting in the 1930s.

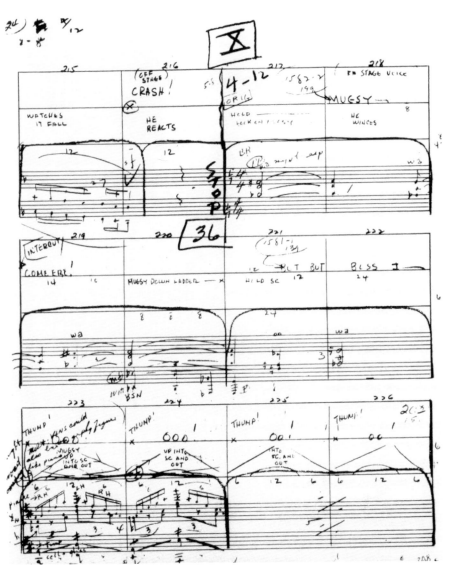

Bar sheet for the cartoon "Bugsy and Mugsy" by Friz Freleng, who continued to plan his timing out on music paper for maximum precision.

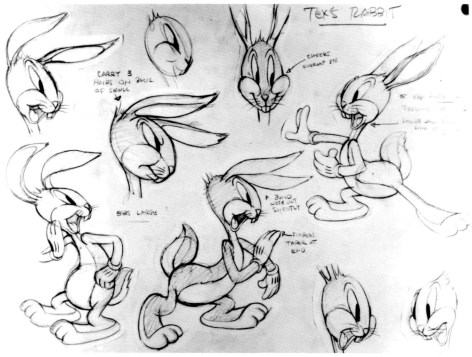

Model sheet for Bugs Bunny in "A Wild Hare," identifying him only as "Tex's Rabbit."

The finalized, classic version of Bugs, alongside Bob Clampett, in a pose that makes it seem like this is his drawing.

Chuck Jones, in his would-be Disney phase, in front of a storyboard for the 1939 cartoon "Sniffles and the Bookworm."

Storyboard for a Bugs Bunny comic book; unlike in the cartoons, he and Elmer know each other and are somewhat friendly.

Michael Maltese presents his "Duck Dodgers in the 24 1/2 Century" story to the key staff members, including Foghorn Leghorn creator Bob McKimson (second row, second from left).

Bugs and Daffy pretend to be each other in "Rabbit Fire," their first team-up cartoon.

Bob Clampett in the 1970s, when Looney Tunes nostalgia made him a sought-after speaker at colleges.

Some minor characters found unexpected popularity on TV, including Chuck Jones's Martian character, later named "Marvin."

Lobby card for a 1941 Chuck Jones cartoon set in Africa. "These depictions were wrong then and are wrong today," as the official Warner Bros. disclaimer correctly states.

Animation drawings by animator Nancy Beiman for the Greg Ford/Terry Lennon cartoon "Invasion of the Bunny Snatchers."

In *Space Jam*, Michael Jordan towers over the Looney Tunes characters, both literally and figuratively.

Mel Blanc, the first person to become famous from cartoon voice acting, in a publicity pose with a character and a carrot.

Official Warner Bros. stationary for a 1959 letter from Chuck Jones, who wrote: "I believe, if I believe anything in this world, that full animation will come back."

Well, how else would you expect this to end?

as a creator of gags, he was weak, which may explain why some of his best stories were single-gag cartoons like "High Diving Hare." Faced with the need to come up with six minutes' worth of material, he and McKimson often fell back on overfamiliar stock bits: characters crashing through a wall and leaving an outline of themselves; women hitting men on the head with rolling pins. Pierce was also what used to be known as a "colorful character," which meant that he had a drinking problem, got into fights in his spare time, and once got bit on the ear by a monkey at the bar across the street from the studio.[11]

Along with the change in writing, the changing art styles of the period had their effect on Foghorn. It was no longer fashionable to have characters overact physically the way Foghorn did in "A Fractured Leghorn," and McKimson started to guide his animators toward a more subtle style that resembled his own. This, in turn, affected Foghorn's dialogue. In keeping with his more restrained movements, Foghorn stopped being a motormouth and became more of a snarker, known for one-liners like "She reminds me of Paul Revere's ride—a little light in the belfry" and "This is gonna cause more confusion than a mouse at a burlesque show." Even when Foster came back to write a cartoon, 1953's "Of Rice and Hen," his Foghorn is much more laid-back than the version he had been writing a few years earlier. Instead of talking a mile a minute, he makes his entrance singing the most early-1950s thing imaginable, an original calypso song: "Now that old hound dog is an awful pest / He barks so much I get no rest."

The new, more sitcom-ish Foghorn worked best when he had a situation that could rattle him and give him opportunities for good one-liners. One of the best of the period was 1954's "Little Boy Boo," written by Pierce, where Foghorn is trying to romance Prissy by ingratiating himself with her nerdy son. The cartoon is unforgettable first for the amazing design of the son: a chick with an enormous round head, two beady black eyes, gigantic glasses that don't seem to have any lenses in them, and a hat that belongs to a schoolchild of an earlier era. He never talks, he walks rigidly, and rarely changes expression. He's like Tweety after a growth spurt and too many science classes.

Most of the gags in the film proceed from a basic premise: Foghorn tries to get the kid to play, whether at baseball, paper planes, or hide-and-seek. The boy participates, but does so by making complicated mathematical calculations that teach him how to hit, throw, and, in one scene, build a paper plane that literally shoots Foghorn's plane out of the sky. This plays to Pierce's strengths at writing variations on a single gag, and it also works for the animators. Rod Scribner, the king of bizarre squash-and-stretch animation, has mostly toned down his style for the new Foghorn, but here he gets to go wild when a baseball is hit down Foghorn's throat.

The most famous gag in the picture, and one of the most famous in the entire *Looney Tunes* canon, has Foghorn and the boy playing hide-and-seek. Foghorn hides in a feed box, commenting that the kid "will need a slide rule to find me in here." Of course, the kid uses a slide rule to calculate Foghorn's location (confounding generations of children raised on digital technology). Based on his calculations, the boy walks over to a spot nowhere near where Foghorn is hiding, digs into the ground, and pulls Foghorn out. A dumbfounded Foghorn is about to check in the feed box, but stops, saying, "No, I better not look. I just *might* be in there." It's a bit of deadpan surrealism that works especially well in the less-loony world of Foghorn Leghorn, a place where someone might actually be surprised and confused to discover that absolutely anything can happen.

"Little Boy Boo" and its sequel, "Feather Dusted," came during a notable upsurge in McKimson's work, where he was getting back some of the vigor of his early work. His layout artist at the time, Robert Givens, was doing a good job finding a middle ground between the old realistic look and the new stylized approach, and the writing and gags were improving. McKimson replaced Pierce as his main story man with a veteran writer-director, Sid Marcus. The Marcus/McKimson team came up with the Tasmanian Devil, as well as some memorable one-shots like "The Hole Idea," a UPA-style story of a scientist who invents "portable holes," and "The Oily American," which may have the most bizarre premise for a chase cartoon ever: Moe Hican, the last of the Mohicans, and his British butler hunt a tiny, screwy moose in a forest specially constructed inside a mansion.

With McKimson's usual luck, the studio shutdown put an end to this upsurge. Fans call this the "3D shutdown," because the first coming of 3D projection was ostensibly the reason for it. Jack Warner thought there was a possibility that 3D would become the industry standard, and the animation department needed to be shuttered until they knew whether their cartoons would be converting to that format.

When it became apparent that 3D was just a passing fad (one that would pass several other times), McKimson, who had been the first director laid off, was the last director to come back, and he couldn't get back any of the animators he had worked with before the shutdown, not even his brother Charles. Marcus was gone, and Tedd Pierce once again wound up as McKimson's sole writer, leading to a lot of lackluster stories, many of them recycled from TV shows of the period. We may know what "The Honey-Mousers" was based on *The Honeymooners*, but how many people remember that "Boston Quackie" was a takeoff on a show called *Boston Blackie?*

McKimson nevertheless managed to make some memorable cartoons, including the best Speedy Gonzales cartoon, "Tabasco Road," which earned his unit its second and last Oscar nomination. Another cartoon with the unusual combination of Daffy Duck and the Tasmanian Devil became one of the brightest Daffy cartoons of a period when the character was going downhill. One of the TV parodies, *The Jack Benny Program* with mice, got the actual cast of Benny's radio and TV show to come into the studio to do their own voices. It was the only moment of his career when McKimson's unit was getting the most publicity and media coverage. Not that most of the media reports mentioned his name.

CHAPTER 9

Daffy, 2.0

I T'S DIFFICULT TO FIND measurements of Daffy Duck's popularity. He must have been popular to have all the Warner Bros. animation units making cartoons with him every year. He was also one of only three major characters, along with Porky and Bugs, to get a special version of the *Looney Tunes* opening with his face in it,[1] and he got a novelty record, "Daffy Duck's Rhapsody," with new lyrics set to yet another rendition of Liszt's Hungarian Rhapsody. But his pop culture footprint was never large, and he seemed to be viewed by theater owners and audiences as just another character from the *Looney Tunes* and *Merrie Melodies* series, not a star who could transcend them the way Bugs did.[2] Bugs and Porky were stars of the *Looney Tunes* comic books, which didn't get around to adding Daffy for many years. Daffy cartoons didn't get nominated for Academy Awards, either. One of the most famous Daffy cartoons today is "Duck Amuck," where Daffy is tormented by an unseen animator who is constantly erasing and re-drawing his entire world. But while Warner Bros. submitted it for Oscar consideration, it wasn't nominated; the fifth nominee that year was a National Film Board of Canada short titled "The Romance of Transportation in Canada."[3]

The lack of Daffy Duck documentation has created a mystery around his famous personality change. As late as 1950, the studio was still releasing cartoons where he was "daffy" in personality, but two years later, that was all over. He changed, and nobody seemed to notice at the time, so it's hard to know why he changed.

The explanation you hear most often is that Chuck Jones adjusted the character. Jones was the director most closely associated with bitter loser Daffy. He was also the first director to make Daffy a foil for Bugs. And his version of Daffy was successful enough that the other two directors began cribbing from Jones when they worked with the duck. Jones had Daffy say, "You're despicable!" and get his beak shot off, so McKimson also made films where Daffy says, "You're despicable!" and gets his beak shot off. Jones made some cartoons where Daffy constantly loses to an unflappable Bugs, so Freleng made a few cartoons with the same idea.

It's unlikely, though, that anyone would have changed the character if he'd been fine as he was. Jones seems to have been reacting to a sense at the studio that "daffy" Daffy had become stale and desperately needed a new approach to keep him going. Again, it's hard to quantify Daffy's popularity, but the studio output seems to tell the tale: he was increasingly rare in solo cartoons. Screwball characters, once the new and fresh alternatives to everyman characters like Porky (who was also on the wane), were becoming old-fashioned. Woody Woodpecker, the most famous Daffy imitator, was making a similar journey away from screwiness. Maybe it was a chance in public mood after the Second World War. Or maybe it was just the problem of finding stories for characters who are too crazy to follow normal story logic.

Even Bob Clampett, the director most associated with screwball Daffy, was moving away from that characterization before he left the studio. In Clampett's last and perhaps best Daffy Duck cartoon, "The Great Piggy

Bank Robbery," Warren Foster's story has Daffy living a humdrum life enlivened only by the arrival of his Dick Tracy comic books. Wishing he could be an exciting crime-fighter like Dick Tracy, he accidentally puts himself to sleep and dreams that he is "Duck Twacy," who fights villains like Snake Eyes, 88 Teeth, Neon Noodle, and Batman (an anthropomorphic baseball bat). In or out of his dream, Daffy is no longer crazy, and Duck Twacy spends as much time running in terror from the bad guys as he spends defeating them.

Other Daffy cartoons of the late 1940s continued this trend of toning down Daffy and making him, more or less, a regular humdrum guy who happens to be an obnoxious duck. "A Pest in the House" (Jones) has Daffy as a hotel bellboy, repeatedly ruining the day of a guest who just wants to get some rest after a long trip. "Daffy Duck Slept Here" (McKimson) continues the hotel theme, but this time he and Porky are sharing a hotel room, and most of the gags are about how bad it would be to share a bed with Daffy Duck. "The Stupor Salesman" (Davis) is the first of a number of cartoons where Daffy is a door-to-door salesman, probably the first profession that came to mind when people tried to think of what someone like Daffy could do for a living. In "Mexican Joyride" (Davis), he's a tourist in Mexico, and in "The Up-Standing Sitter" (McKimson) he's an employee of the ACME Baby-Sitting Agency, sent out on the babysitting job from hell.

Most of these cartoons are funny, because most Warner Bros. cartoons in this period were funny. But they're weak as a group compared to Bugs Bunny cartoons of the same period. Daffy doesn't *do* much in many of them. In "The Stupor Salesman," most of the gags involve him pulling out wacky products from his bottomless sample case, and while some of these products hurt the villain by accident, Daffy has no interest in hurting the villain, only in selling him something. "A Pest in the House" has an oddly

143

complicated gag setup where every time Daffy bothers the hotel guest, the guest goes downstairs and punches out the manager, Elmer Fudd. In a 1949 McKimson cartoon called "Daffy Duck Hunt," despite the title, Daffy barely does anything except talk. The impression you get is that once Daffy could no longer be a total screwball, he became a guest in his own cartoons.

* * *

If this trend had continued, Daffy could have wound up like Porky Pig, whose solo cartoons were quietly canceled in the early 1950s. Chuck Jones saved Daffy by going where "The Great Piggy Bank Robbery" was pointing. In 1950, he released a cartoon called "The Scarlet Pumpernickel," which also uses the framing device of Daffy imagining himself as a famous hero of fiction. In this film, he's trying to move out of cartoon comedy into drama, and he's pitching an unseen Jack L. Warner (called "J.L." by Daffy) on a swashbuckling adventure script that he wants to star in.

As he narrates the story, we see him as a masked hero who tries to do all the things he's seen Errol Flynn do in movies, but they always go a little differently than in the movies: Daffy jumps out a window and misses his horse; he shows up to rescue his beloved from a forced marriage and *she* grabs *him* and throws him out of the church; he swings on a rope to rescue his beloved from a villain with dastardly intentions, and hits the wall instead of the window. Meanwhile, the real Daffy is having trouble coming up with story twists that will satisfy his boss. He finally shoots himself in the head, in one of the last examples of creators throwing in a suicide gag when they're stuck for an ending.

Jones was in the middle of one of the greatest hot streaks of any animation director, which eventually turned out to be fortunately timed. It began during the 1948 release period and lasted into the early 1950s.

After Warner Bros. sold the rights to most of its pre-1948 cartoons, most of the Saturday-morning cartoon packages and compilation films would draw on the period of *Looney Tunes* history when Chuck Jones directed most of the standouts. So Jones directed most of the cartoons people loved best growing up.

Compared to even his finest early 1940s cartoons, Jones's pacing was improved, and he'd learned to put pauses in the right places. His design, later notorious for giving everyone enormous eyes and puffy faces, was under control. He was comfortable working with the increasingly tight budgets of the period. Whereas Freleng suffered when the films were cut back from seven to six minutes, no longer able to carefully establish the patterns on which his humor relied,[4] Jones still had time to create character moments because he had always placed a lot of emphasis on fleeting facial expressions and quick movements to make larger points. If he had Bugs wriggle his eyebrow, or a character shoot a puzzled glance at the camera, this would tell us in a split second what they thought of the situation.

But it's not a criticism of Jones to say that the biggest factor in his hot streak was finding the right writer. During the 1948 release period, Michael Maltese stopped writing jointly for the Freleng and Jones units and became Jones's full-time writer, a position he would hold for about a decade (except for a few months after the 3D shutdown). Maltese was the funniest writer in the business.

In dialogue cartoons, Maltese was a consummate American wise guy who built his comedic style out of wordplay and half-remembered bits of learning. He loved to have characters use big words in inaccurate ways ("Mayhap perchance, foppish that I am . . ." Daffy remarks in "The Scarlet Pumpernickel"), or make garbled references to half-remembered American schoolboy learning like the poems of Henry Wadsworth Longfellow: in one Jones/Maltese cartoon, Daffy describes himself as "brown as a nut," which only people who read Longfellow's "The Courtship of Miles Standish" would get.

When it came to visual gags, a cartoon like "Peck Up Your Troubles" had already demonstrated that Maltese could come up with seemingly endless variations on the simple theme of one character trying and failing to eat another. Soon after he went exclusive to Jones, the two of them came up with a cartoon called "Fast and Furry-ous" that was a series of these try/fail gags and *nothing* else—no dialogue, only the barest excuse for a story. "Fast and Furry-ous" takes place in a desert with paved roads that a "Road Runner" runs along at a speed much greater than real roadrunners can manage. A coyote wants to eat the bird, but realizes that he can't run fast enough to catch him. So for the rest of the cartoon, he sets up traps to catch the Road Runner, and every trap backfires and hurts the coyote instead. There is no further story development, and there are no other characters. The ending comes when the coyote gets run over by a bus.

This cartoon was almost certainly not expected to affect the portrayal of Daffy Duck, or to lead to a series. While the blackout-gag structure was inspired by Frank Tashlin's "The Fox and the Grapes," it was also a parody of the typical Warner Bros. or MGM cartoon. Jones and Maltese wanted to see what would happen if you stripped that type of cartoon down to its barest essentials, took away the houses and owners and other signposts of normal life, and just had predator and prey. The Road Runner doesn't even have the ability to change emotions; he is always happy and smiling no matter what is going on around him, and he rarely does anything except run, eat, and say, "Beep beep!" Instead of finding this boring, audiences loved it, and a series was launched, with each cartoon consisting almost entirely of the predator's failed schemes to catch his prey. It proved that a cartoon could work with almost nothing but the joy of a perfectly timed gag. Structure was created through the alternation of long and short gags, or the occasional running gag within a short.

Later in life, Jones published a list of rules that the Road Runner cartoons were expected to adhere to, which almost certainly were created after the fact. Maltese claimed he had never heard of these rules. Nevertheless, the rules fit the series. "Fast and Furry-ous" has a gag where the Road Runner hits the Coyote with a boomerang, but when the series was launched, the Road Runner was almost never allowed to harm the Coyote directly except by startling him with his "beep beep!" The Coyote could only get hurt as a result of his own plans backfiring on him, so the structure of almost every gag was that the Coyote sets up a trap (usually a gadget made by ACME, which these cartoons turned from a generic company name to the official supplier of gadgets that never work right) and it backfires on him in some violent way. Sometimes it blows up as soon as he tries to use it, sometimes he gets hurt trying to fix it, and sometimes it goes wrong in ways that defy the laws of physics, but the end is always that he gets hurt, the scene blacks out, and we fade in again on the same character, now unhurt, trying a different plan.

The reason this never gets boring is that we never know quite how the gag will end, or how the Coyote will react. While the Road Runner has absolutely no emotional range, the Coyote has the widest range of virtually any cartoon character. Sometimes he's enraged at his failure; sometimes he's crying; sometimes he's laughing at what he thinks is a narrow escape. He will look directly at the audience to wave goodbye just before he falls into a ravine, or look smugly at the camera if he momentarily thinks his plan is succeeding. The Coyote became a showcase for Jones's ability to convey a lot of emotion very quickly with a single pose, often looking directly at us, influenced by live-action comedians like Oliver Hardy who played to the camera without necessarily breaking the fourth wall.[5] This allows us to study his face, making the audience a partner to his emotions. The one thing the Coyote never expresses is genuine pain—it wouldn't be funny if we thought he was hurt.

Although the cartoons of course have no continuity, the consistent setting makes them feel more like a single story than any other Warner Bros. series. They add up to a portrait of someone who keeps trying to catch the Road Runner for reasons that have very little to do with being hungry. Maltese originally wanted to call him "Don Coyote,"[6] because of his quixotic quest to achieve a goal no matter how many times he fails, while Jones liked to say that the character was explained by George Santayana's definition of a fanatic as someone who redoubles his efforts after he has forgotten his aim.

* * *

The new Jones and Maltese understanding of how much comedy could be mined out of failure and frustration was soon bleeding into Daffy's character. In 1951, Jones released "Drip-Along Daffy," which has Daffy spend the entire film as the hero in a typical low-budget Western movie. There is no framing device here, and while the Scarlet Pumpernickel usually won his fights, Daffy never manages to do anything right in this one. And the Don Quixote motif is even clearer than it was with the Coyote, because a Western hero is the closest thing America has to a knight-errant and, like Quixote, Daffy gets laughs from the disconnect between what he wants to be, and what he actually is.

Daffy begins the picture as a white-suited good guy wearing improbably long chaps, riding on a tall horse whose mane and tail are so magnificent that they drag on the ground: everything is beautiful but ridiculously so. Behind him rides his sidekick, Porky, with stubble and a ragged hat, on a tiny burro (in Western parody cartoons, everyone rides a horse that matches their appearance). Captions identify Daffy as the "WESTERN-TYPE HERO" and Porky as the "COMEDY RELIEF." They ride into what the captions identify as a "LAWLESS WESTERN TOWN," where signs advertise "The Old Girdle Saloon: Come in and get tight," and a masked horse is holding up a blacksmith at gunpoint to steal all his horseshoes.

The main body of the cartoon, like "The Scarlet Pumpernickel," has Daffy try to be the typical hero of his genre, but he does everything slightly wrong. Not just physically wrong, as when he pulls out his guns and takes his pants off with them ("Slight pause," he tells us, "whilst I adjust my accoutrements"), but also verbally. Maltese writes his dialogue as a jumble of Western movie clichés that have no relationship to the situations he finds himself in. "Let justice be done! Tear up that mortgage! Unhand that rancher's daughter!" Daffy yells as he strides into a saloon. (Later, when he meets the hulking, slow-moving bad guy, Nasty Canasta, Daffy keeps calling him "hombre" but pronouncing it "hawm-ber," like someone who read the word in a magazine story and never had occasion to use it.)

Things continue to go wrong for Daffy in the saloon. No one pays attention to him. His guns discharge spontaneously as a result of a stiff drink (the only time they are fired in the picture). Tension builds towards a shoot-out with the bad guy but it never happens because Porky, the sidekick, has already defeated the villain with a cheesy cartoon gag: a toy soldier with real ammunition. The crowd rushes past Daffy, who is still walking slowly toward the canceled shoot-out, and rushes back carrying Porky on its shoulders.

It's as if the cartoon is making the case for the superiority of cheesy gag cartoons over the "respectable" genres that Daffy is trying to break into. He *wants* to be in a Western or a swashbuckling epic so people will look up to him and take him seriously, but nobody's buying it. In Warner Bros. cartoons, silliest is best.

Jones and Maltese returned several times to the idea of Daffy as the failed hero. In "Duck Dodgers in the 24½th Century," he's every child's favorite icon of the early television age, the spaceman. In "Deduce, You Say," he's Sherlock Holmes. Arguably their most famous Daffy cartoon, "Duck Amuck," begins with Daffy as a character from *The Three Musketeers*, until the animator draws in a new background, and Daffy has to change clothes to become whatever type of hero fits the scenery behind him.

In each case, Daffy has the costume right, and the accessories (the ray gun, the magnifying glass) but he never gets the one thing a hero needs above everything: the respect of his adversaries. It's not that he's incompetent in the Jones/Maltese cartoons, it's that villains *know* he's incompetent and simply dismiss him. Their last Daffy cartoon together, 1958's "Robin Hood Daffy," put this in the simplest way possible: Porky refuses to believe that someone like Daffy could be Robin Hood, and Daffy spends six minutes trying and failing to prove that he is.

Jones fell in love with this new version of Daffy, and settled, surprisingly quickly, on a new definition of the character. While working on a "Drip-Along Daffy" sequel, he wrote to his daughter: "I love Daffy dearly, he is so completely and foolishly human. I think he serves to accent all the human frailties and vanities and conceits and is funny doing it."[7]

A bonus of this approach to Daffy was that it revitalized Porky, with Jones expressing his surprise that "old Porky" had become a pleasure to work on. The pig was able to parody all the clichés of fictional sidekicks ("What is it, Sheriff Friend? Prairie Pal? B-Butte B—" and Daffy cuts him off before he can say "Butte Buddy"), the number two who is saner and more competent than number one.

* * *

A minor counterfactual exercise is to wonder how different Daffy's history would have been if this version of Daffy, the wannabe hero, had defined him for the next few decades. Instead, he went in yet another direction introduced by Jones and Maltese. He became the guy who constantly loses out to Bugs Bunny, and is furious about it.

Exactly why the Jones unit began to team Bugs with Daffy is not documented, but the Jones/Maltese team had earlier experimented with unusual character combinations, pairing Porky Pig with Sylvester in a comedy/horror cartoon called "Scaredy Cat," which led to two sequels. And in Daffy's "The Scarlet Pumpernickel," they made a very rare gesture toward the idea of a "shared universe" by having most of the parts in Daffy's movie played by Warner Bros. characters like Sylvester, Henery Hawk, and Elmer Fudd. Bugs wasn't in that one, but it did establish that Daffy's personality was flexible enough to interact with any character. And since there weren't a lot of Daffy cartoons being made, why not pair him with the flagship character and see what happened?

The setup of the first Bugs/Daffy cartoon, "Rabbit Fire," might also have derived from a desire to shake up and deconstruct the Bugs Bunny formula, which creators had been faithful to ever since "A Wild Hare." Even though there were no television reruns to familiarize the audience with Bugs Bunny's breakout cartoon, Jones and Maltese elected to open "Rabbit Fire" exactly the way "A Wild Hare" opened. The animation is new, but the action is the same: we start with Elmer tiptoeing through the woods telling us, "Be vewwy, vewwy quiet, I'm hunting wabbits"; and then he follows "wabbit twacks" to Bugs's hole. Even Carl Stalling's opening music is from "A Wild Hare."

The twist is that the tracks aren't actually Bugs's. They're made by Daffy, who is creating a line of footprints that will lead Elmer to Bugs's hole. "Survival of the fittest," Daffy tells the audience, "and besides, it's fun!" He lets out his trademark wacky laugh and hides behind a rock, waiting for the carnage to begin.

This is new: a third character who meddles in the Bugs/Elmer dynamic, turning the cartoon into a series of three-way gags. Daffy tries to get Elmer to shoot Bugs, only to be shot himself. Elmer tries to shoot both of them. Elmer watches as Bugs and Daffy argue about who's going to get shot. It was a new way to use Daffy, but maybe more important at that time, it was a new way to use Bugs. The core of "Rabbit Fire" is that Bugs keeps tricking Daffy into asking Elmer to shoot ducks, and Elmer keeps obliging, with Daffy's beak usually getting detached in a different way. Bugs is calm, collected, and even more smug than usual: before tricking Daffy for the first time, he looks to the audience and wiggles his eyebrow for half a second, just to let us know that *he* knows that *we* know what's going to happen. Daffy isn't an idiot, but he's impulsive and emotional, and points up how much smarter and more composed Bugs is than the typical cartoon hero.

Most people, even those who haven't seen "Rabbit Fire," are familiar with the main device that Bugs uses to trick Daffy:

Bugs: "Duck Season!"
Daffy: "Rabbit season!"
Bugs: "Duck season!"
Daffy: "Rabbit season!"
Bugs: . . . "Rabbit season!"
Daffy: "Duck season! FIRE!"

It's the simplest version of a gag structure that all Warner Bros. writers loved, but Maltese loved most of all. He used variations on it every year. Each time, Bugs and his antagonist establish a pattern, and Bugs takes advantage of the fact that the antagonist will follow the pattern without thinking. My favorite variation is a wordless one in the 1949 Jones/Maltese cartoon "Mississippi Hare." Bugs is being chased by a thinly disguised bootleg of Yosemite Sam across a Mississippi steamboat and, with good Southern manners, each one keeps opening a door to let the other into the next room. The last door Bugs opens is the door to the furnace.

Even the "Rabbit Fire" version of this routine was not new to Daffy: Freleng had used it in a cartoon called "Duck Soup to Nuts," written by Maltese, where the Bugs Bunny role was filled by Daffy, who tricks Porky into claiming to be an eagle rather than a pig. This example is often mentioned as a trivia point about how much Daffy had changed, and sometimes leads to the argument that Daffy is out of character in "Rabbit Fire," that he shouldn't be such an idiot as to fall for Bugs's trick. But it gets more laughs here than in any other version of the gag *because* Daffy isn't an idiot, like Elmer, or an innocent, like Porky. He says the opposite of whatever Bugs says because he's caught up in the moment, so locked into the pattern of contradicting Bugs, that he keeps doing it even when he's aware of the mistake.

The contrast between hyperemotional Daffy and calm, cool Bugs wound up defining not only Daffy, but Bugs as well. This was partly because most of their films together were memorable. Jones and Maltese made two more cartoons with the exact same setup as "Rabbit Fire," and the same gag of Daffy getting his beak shot off, and all of them are good, so much so that people talk about the Bugs/Daffy "hunting trilogy" rather than individual films.

What keeps the sequels fresh is that Maltese and Jones built each one around a different type of gag, a different trigger that gets Daffy shot. In the original, it was the famous reversal gag. In "Rabbit Seasoning," we get the variant where Daffy keeps getting mixed up about whether he's telling Elmer to shoot "you" or "me," leading to the theater-shaking line, "Pronoun trouble." The third is mostly sign gags: Bugs gets Daffy to compare himself to some animal, Bugs holds up a sign declaring that animal in season, and Elmer shoots Daffy.

Over the course of the trilogy, Daffy subtly loses elements of his old personality and is pushed closer to being a pure antagonist for Bugs. In "Rabbit Fire," he still has his classic "hoo hoo!" laugh, the last time Jones would use it. Elmer refers to Daffy as "that screwball duck," and a few seconds later, Daffy teams up with Bugs for the mandatory disguise gag: Bugs is a beautiful woman who seduces Elmer, so Daffy becomes her dog, and bites Elmer in the leg. In the end, they discover it's not duck season or rabbit season, but "Elmer Season," and Bugs and Daffy both don Elmer Fudd outfits and team up to hunt Elmer down. Daffy is no match for Bugs in a battle of wits, but they're willing to work together if it suits them.

When the creators follow up with "Rabbit Seasoning," Daffy never teams up with Bugs. Instead of helping Bugs with his drag act, Daffy is enraged that Bugs can get away with such a corny old gag and that Elmer is falling for it. Finally, in "Duck! Rabbit, Duck!," Daffy spends virtually the entire cartoon trying to convince Elmer to shoot Bugs. He's now Bugs's enemy, pure and simple.

"Duck, Rabbit, Duck!" may be the meanest Daffy of the trilogy, and it's arguably the funniest, climaxing with a long speech from Daffy where he finally snaps after getting shot in the head one too many times: "Shoot me again! I enjoy it! I love the smell of burnt feathers and gunpowder and cordite! I'm an elk! Shoot me! Go on! It's elk season! I'm a fiddler crab! Why don't you shoot me? It's fiddler crab season!" Maltese, with the ear of a born comedy writer, knows that "fiddler crab" is somehow funny where "crab" would not be.

When the studio started making more Bugs/Daffy cartoons, Daffy's antagonism toward Bugs pushed him closer to being a villain who deserves his comeuppance. In Friz Freleng's first original Bugs/Daffy picture,[8] "A Star Is Bored," Bugs is a beloved but humble movie star and Daffy is a janitor, jealous of Bugs's stardom; he gets assigned to be the rabbit's stunt double and gets hurt in his place. In Freleng's most popular Bugs/ Daffy cartoon, Show Biz Bugs, the two characters are vaudevillians, and the audience cheers for everything Bugs does while greeting Daffy's knockout tap dance routine with crickets. In both of these films, Daffy is angry all the time, while Bugs is a rather bland character offering Daffy no provocation beyond his popularity. Daffy has also graduated from encouraging someone else to kill Bugs to trying to murder Bugs himself.

This is part of the normal process of "Flanderization," the term *TV Tropes* popularized to describe how a single trait can gradually take over a character completely. Warner Bros. discovered that it was funny to watch Daffy get angry and frustrated about Bugs's invincibility, so he got angrier and angrier, and there was less and less thought given to Daffy's likability or having Bugs do anything besides making Daffy angry.

In Jones and Maltese's last joint Bugs/Daffy cartoon, "Ali Baba Bunny," Daffy doesn't cross over into outright villainy, but he's now so greedy that he almost never smiles unless he's looking at or thinking about money, and he gets moralistically punished for his greed when a genie shrinks him to the size of a pearl (which Daffy then attempts to claim as his own). It wasn't far from this to the last Bugs/Daffy cartoon the studio made, "The Iceman Ducketh," where Daffy is actually hunting Bugs with a gun. Probably the story was written for another antagonist and rewritten to feature Daffy, but it was no longer a stretch to see him act like a nastier Elmer Fudd.

Fortunately, after making "Ali Baba Bunny," Jones and Maltese teamed up for one more Daffy cartoon. "Robin Hood Daffy" turned out to be the last Daffy solo vehicle Jones directed at the studio, and the last Daffy solo cartoon Maltese wrote before leaving Warner Bros. to join Hanna-Barbera's TV animation operation, where he would write characters like Quick Draw McGraw in very much the same way he wrote Daffy. It's a summing-up of their approach to Daffy as a star, as the comically frustrated swashbuckler, as the clown who wants to be a hero. The plot is simple (running times had been cut back by another half minute, so plots had to be even simpler than before): Daffy is Robin Hood. Porky is Friar Tuck, who wants to join up with Robin Hood, but thinks Daffy is just a clown in a Robin Hood suit. Daffy tries to prove he's Robin Hood by robbing an amusingly foppish medieval gentleman bouncing up and down on a tiny horse.

Again, Daffy is not villainous, although he clearly thinks it's stupid to give money to "some poor, unworthy slob." He's still going to do it, because that's what heroes do. Or, he would do it, if he could ever succeed in robbing anyone. The gags are mostly built around Daffy trying to do what he's seen Robin Hood and similar characters do in the movies, especially Warner Bros.' own *Adventures of Robin Hood* starring Errol Flynn. We know everything that works for Errol won't work for Daffy, but there are little add-ons that make the gags take flight. Like Porky waving to Daffy from a distance, in time with the music, the most sarcastic and mocking wave imaginable. And a recurring gag that finds one last thing to do with Daffy's beak that the Bugs/Elmer cartoons hadn't already done: it repeatedly pops up like a car hood, and he has to snap it back into place. There's also a long sequence where Porky laughs at Daffy's misfortunes, his belly wobbling up and down with mirth (Abe Levitow, who directed some cartoons for Jones's unit when he wasn't available, animated his stomach), stopping only to look at Daffy with those huge eyes wide open, as if he can't believe how amusing it all is. The animation and Mel Blanc's vocal performance make the laughter even funnier than the disasters Porky is laughing at, and the scene gets hysterical when Daffy absentmindedly joins in the laughter. This is the kind of thing that makes the character more than a gag machine, which he might have become in another director's hands.

In the cartoon's most famous gag, Daffy tries to imitate Flynn swinging from a rope tied to a tree, shouting "Yoicks and away!"—his approximation of how Merrie England characters are supposed to talk. He swings right into a nearby tree, and yells his catchphrase again, and hits another tree. Somehow it gets funnier every time it happens, because of Blanc's increasingly punch-drunk vocals, Treg Brown's dull "thud" sound effect, and, once the camera cuts to Porky, his wordless glance at the camera. This is what Warner Bros. cartoons are at their best: animation, music, dialogue, acting (vocal and animated), sound effects, design, and color all working together to make good gags much better.

Cartoon characters can suffer from bad characterization, but they also suffer when their characterization is frozen. If Daffy's characterization had been as tightly controlled by executives as it later became, if Jones had been prohibited from changing his personality or making him anything but a crazy laughing duck, he would probably be a near-forgotten character today. He had to evolve to be a viable character, and he did.

CHAPTER 10

Transitioning to TV

"**F**OR DECADES, ONE OF the greatest names in the most popular medium of entertainment has been WARNER BROS.," says a 1957 publication from Associated Artists Productions (AAP), the company that owned most of the films Warner Bros. released before 1948, and all the color cartoons with a copyright date of 1947 or earlier. The pamphlet is called *Movies from AAP: Programs of Quality from Quality Studios*, and its goal is to sell television station owners on the idea of paying for the rights to show movies with outdated hairstyles and references.[1]

One of AAP's selling points was that the production values of movies far exceeded those of TV shows, with their limited budgets and the need to make a new episode every week. "Television once or twice has spent a month and $300,000 on a possibly successful program," the pamphlet explains. "Movies *regularly* devote months, even years, and a million dollars or more to the production of *each* picture." That value proposition was enhanced where cartoons were concerned. Animation produced on a regular basis for television used a variant of the Hanna-Barbera method, with as few drawings as possible and more emphasis on voices, dialogue, and backgrounds. *Looney Tunes* never had the most lavish budgets in the business, but on TV they looked better than anything new.

In addition to the production values, the AAP tried to sell broadcasters on characters. The pamphlet included a two-page spread showing "all the favorite characters" available to the highest bidder in each local market: Bugs, Porky, Daffy, Elmer, Tweety, Pepe Le Pew, Sylvester, and Sniffles. Like a lot of advertising, this was misleading without being false, because several of those characters had very few cartoons in the AAP package. The 1948 cutoff date meant that AAP only had the first two Tweety/Sylvester cartoons, plus those three where Tweety was pink and chased by different cats. They had two Pepe Le Pew cartoons, but not the one where he won an Oscar and became popular. They had only one Sylvester/Hippety Hopper cartoon, and two Foghorn Leghorns, which happened to be the two where he hadn't yet developed a Southern accent. They did have the complete Sniffles catalog, but because the majority of Warner Bros. black-and-white cartoons were not part of the sale, most Porky Pig shorts were unavailable.

Still, the package had a ton of Bugs Bunny cartoons, almost all of it prime material, enough to ensure against endless repeats. Bugs and Daffy Duck were the heart of the AAP lineup, which would enjoy a lot of ratings success and be one of the company's prime assets when it collapsed a year after this pamphlet was published. The company was bought out by United Artists,[2] which would control the pre-1948 cartoons until it, too, was sold. The cartoons nevertheless kept on airing on local kids' television. They were the perfect kids' TV material: complete, satisfying, well-produced comedy that could rerun endlessly.

AAP went under at a time when most of the movie studios were shuttering their in-house cartoon productions. *Popeye* was canceled by

Paramount Pictures in 1957. MGM released its last *Tom and Jerry* in 1958, and Walt Disney had already discontinued short cartoons for anything but educational or promotional purposes. It was a measure of the popularity of the *Looney Tunes* cartoons and their characters that Warner Bros. was among the very last studios to close, but the shutdown order finally came in 1962. Its last theatrical cartoons came out in 1964.

The theatrical cartoon business had not exactly ended. Some movie studios still wanted them, but they needed to be supplied by independent or semi-independent production companies. The senior *Looney Tunes* director, Friz Freleng, teamed with producer David DePatie to create DePatie-Freleng Enterprises, which operated out of the old Warner Bros. facilities and used many of the same people, including Bob McKimson as a staff director. The studio soon had a major success by creating the animated title character for the movie *The Pink Panther*, which spun off a series of theatrical cartoons.[3]

Chuck Jones, who had been fired from the Warner Bros. studio shortly before it closed (he was discovered to have been moonlighting as the writer of the UPA animated musical *Gay Purr-ee*[4]), signed with MGM to produce a series of Tom and Jerry cartoons, which were less successful: while Freleng was able to make the Pink Panther unique and distinct from his Warner Bros. characters (even while sometimes recycling gags and stories), Jones simply made Tom into Wile E. Coyote.

Warner Bros. also commissioned DePatie-Freleng to make some new, lower-budgeted shorts starring the old characters, but no Bugs Bunny cartoons, probably because they would have cut into his booming value as a television character. Speedy Gonzales was the mainstay of the new era but, weirdly, Daffy Duck usually replaced Sylvester as Speedy's antagonist, making this the first and last attempt to replace the "cat and mouse" formula with "duck and mouse." They also made low-budget

Road Runner cartoons that only proved that these cartoons don't work without carefully thought-out gags and well-animated expressions on Wile E. Coyote's face.

* * *

The new theatrical series didn't last. By the end of the 1960s, Warner Bros. dropped all the famous characters from its theatrical cartoons and tried to launch some new series better suited for low-budget animation (including "Bunny and Claude," with the movie gangsters as rabbits who rob carrot patches). Bugs and Daffy and Tweety settled into their new home on television. Six- or seven-minute cartoons were perfect for the rigid schedules of TV, where they fit easily into a half-hour block of time. The basic format was to have three cartoons take up about twenty minutes, leaving time for commercials, and a brief appearance by a host who gave the illusion that this was a new show.

The nature of the linking material depended on the market and the station. Young performers and executives often used these shows to make a name for themselves. Chicago's WGN-TV assigned a new hire named Fred Silverman to write and produce their *Bugs Bunny and Friends* package, which was renamed *Breakfast with Bugs Bunny* to emphasize that you didn't have to stop eating while watching cartoons in the morning.[5]

As for its post-1948 cartoons, Warner Bros. brought them into national broadcast television with *The Bugs Bunny Show*, a three-short series where the host was Bugs, in short linking segments newly produced by the original cartoon studio. It debuted in 1960 on the ABC network, not in a children's programming slot, but at 7:30 p.m. ABC had noticed the success of animation, original and recycled, in local syndication, and was interested in seeing if cartoons could work in prime time. A month before, the network had introduced *The Flintstones*, an all-new prime-time cartoon. It lasted, but *The Bugs Bunny Show* was moved after two years to Saturday mornings, the designated time for shows that children could watch while their parents slept.

The prime-time effort failed in part because of a problem that would come back to bite the *Looney Tunes* crew again and again. All-new material was required for big-time success in television, but it was impossible to produce all-new weekly episodes to the level of animation Bugs Bunny required. And reruns couldn't command the audiences and advertising rates of original content. *The Flintstones* was all-new, and it didn't matter to prime-time viewers that the animation quality was not up to the level of Bugs Bunny's, any more than it mattered that a weekly TV Western didn't look as good as a John Wayne movie.

The most memorable piece of new animation for *The Bugs Bunny Show*, and probably the most famous *Looney Tunes* animation ever produced for television, was the opening, directed by Friz Freleng. Bugs and Daffy, on a vaudeville stage similar to the one from "Show Biz Bugs," dressed as old-timey vaudevillians with matching outfits and canes, singing the theme song (written by Jerry Livingston and Mack David, who wrote a number of themes for Warner Bros. TV productions), which announces that the characters are professional entertainers and this half hour is their grand opening:

> *Overture, curtain, lights*
> *This is it, the night of nights*
> *No more rehearsing and nursing a part*
> *We know every part by heart . . .*

Downstage, other major Warner Bros. characters march out of the wings and across the stage, arranged roughly though not absolutely in ascending order of height: Tweety, Speedy Gonzales, Hippety Hopper, Yosemite Sam, Sylvester, Elmer Fudd, Pepe Le Pew, Wile E. Coyote, and Foghorn Leghorn. (Porky Pig is absent.) Then Bugs and Daffy sing a little tag, and pose together, eyes closed, waiting for applause.

Tonight, what heights we'll hit!
On with the show! This is it!

The world of vaudeville and old-timey show business had always played an outsize role in the world of cartoons, but especially in *Looney Tunes*, where characters were constantly running into vaudeville theaters and getting pulled offstage by hooks. Used here, it sums up exactly what they want us to take from this show: these characters are vaudevillians, each with a stock role to play that can adapt itself to different stories and different circumstances. The title sequence of an original-to-TV cartoon usually tries to sell you on the idea that the characters inhabit a fixed setting: Yogi Bear lives in Jellystone Park, the Flintstones live in Bedrock, the Simpsons live in Springfield. The opening of *The Bugs Bunny Show* tells us that we're seeing not characters, but performers.

Each of the three shorts on a typical episode of *The Bugs Bunny Show* would feature a different recurring character. The selection was sometimes random and sometimes followed a theme, like fairy tales, or birds, or cats. The linking material usually had Bugs either introducing the cartoons or introducing another character to act as host. Occasionally the choice of host would be someone unexpected, and give the impression that someone at the studio was trying to push them. The Goofy Gophers, a pair of affectedly polite woodland creatures who had been launched on several short-lived cartoon series by at least four different directors, appeared to host two different episodes in three weeks.

The links usually took place in the same world as the main title: Bugs is a vaudeville star introducing the acts, Daffy is the second-billed character who covets the starring role, and the plots, such as they were, revolved around Bugs trying to do his hosting job while characters made trouble backstage or tried to stop the show. This format is probably most famous today from *The Muppet Show*, although that was a more ironic take on the vaudeville format.

Occasional attempts were made to have the links tied to the cartoons. An episode from the second season, which was later turned into a "cheater" theatrical cartoon (a cartoon that uses old clips to save money) and eventually even a feature film, had Yosemite Sam dying and going to hell, where he is informed that he can get out if he manages to kill Bugs Bunny, leading into three cartoons where he tries and fails.

Both approaches to the links had difficulties. Unlike Mickey Mouse or Kermit the Frog, Bugs is not inherently suited to playing the affable everyman in a stable of wilder personalities. It was sometimes strange to see Bugs as the straight man to characters who are usually less funny than he is. But trying to build an actual plot into a three-short episode could damage the short cartoons by removing them from their context: a short that is supposed to be whole and satisfying in itself can be less effective when the beginning or ending is cut off to blend in with new animation.

Once ABC moved *The Bugs Bunny Show* out of prime time, it was no longer affordable to create new linking material. Instead, it reused old links, and eventually dropped them altogether as shorter episode running times (and longer commercial breaks) made them unnecessary. They did well enough for ABC in this form that Warner Bros. created two other compilation shows: *The Porky Pig Show* for ABC, where only the opening and closing were new, and *The Road Runner Show* for CBS, which used quick Road Runner/Coyote gags as interstitial segments. Even while it was distributing its cartoon library to two different broadcast networks,

Warner Bros. held back some of its post-1948 catalog, including several dozen prime Bugs Bunny shorts, to distribute to local stations under the title of *Bugs Bunny and Friends*.[6] This meant a single market could have two, three, or even more distinct packages of *Looney Tunes* playing.

And kids couldn't get enough. Not one generation of kids, but several.

ABC and CBS routinely fought each other over the rights to a third of the cartoon library. CBS took *The Bugs Bunny Show* away from ABC in 1968, but a few years later, Michael Eisner, a young executive at ABC, scored a major coup by getting it back. Two years later, it was CBS's turn to triumph due to Eisner's refusal to keep *Bugs Bunny* as a package deal with the less popular *Road Runner Show*.[7] CBS aired both shows in *The Bugs Bunny/Road Runner Hour*. At one point they were airing two hours of *Looney Tunes*, then ninety minutes. In the mid-1980s the package went back to ABC, which renamed it *The Bugs Bunny and Tweety Show*, the final form until Warner Bros. moved all its cartoons to cable in 2000.

While this was going on, the AAP packages continued to be popular on local stations before also shifting to cable. Ted Turner acquired the pre-1948 film libraries that had been sold off by Warner Bros. and MGM, and used them on his cable channels, making *Looney Tunes* part of the foundation of Turner's (almost) all-animated Cartoon Network.

When home video came in, *Looney Tunes* was there, too. To celebrate the fiftieth anniversary of the creation of Porky Pig, Warner Bros. released a series of "Golden Jubilee" VHS tapes highlighting most of the major characters. They competed in video rental stores with the pre-1948 compilations released by Turner. By the time both companies put out *Looney Tunes* material on the laser-disc format in the 1990s, the old cartoons had proved almost endlessly recyclable in every home-viewing format in five different decades. They finally ended their run on free ad-supported television in the first year of a new century.

* * *

Why were *Looney Tunes* so consistently popular in the home? Mostly because they were the best, and even on Saturday mornings or school-day mornings and afternoons, it helps to be good. The studio also had a deep enough bench of characters, especially in the post-1948 era, that it could create a half-hour or one-hour package with real variety, mixing and matching characters in many different ways. Even stations with the pre-1948 cartoons, a thinner assortment than the post-1948 package, still had sufficient material to create a satisfying program of shorts: Bugs or Daffy to anchor the lineup; a funny one-shot or wartime cartoon like the one where a bunch of Russian gremlins destroy Hitler's plane while Hitler himself is flying it; maybe one of the small but precious supply of Tweety, Sylvester, or Foghorn shorts; and, if necessary, one of those cutesy *Merrie Melodies* musicals from the 1930s, although even those were occasionally brilliant. "I Love to Singa" went from forgotten to all-time classic based solely on the AAP broadcasts. Again, there were *options* for how to structure a Warner Bros. cartoon compilation on television, thanks to an almost endless supply.

The cartoons became a dominant force on television. Bugs Bunny's star turn in the 1940s and 1950s turned out to be a warm-up act. On TV, he was *the* star of his own programming blocks. In Paddy Chayefsky's Oscar-winning script for the 1976 film *Network*, a young television executive is described as having "learned the world from Bugs Bunny." This was supposed to be a complaint about superficial young people who don't know anything they haven't seen on television. To people who actually were raised on Bugs cartoons, it seemed like an acknowledgment of her good taste.

Chayefsky was hardly the only person slow to realize that old Bugs Bunny cartoons had enduring artistic value. Warner Bros. showed little interest in rereleasing cartoons to theaters or even making theatrical prints for art houses, which were assumed to be mostly interested in real classic cinema, not whatever *Looney Tunes* were. When Larry Jackson, a young filmmaker working on a compilation of *Looney Tunes* cartoons for theatrical release, met with the president of Warner Bros. to ask if he could use some of the post-1948 cartoons, he was told that no one would pay to see cartoons that were free on television every Saturday.[8]

One of the first high-profile figures to notice the potential of grown-up *Looney Tunes* fandom was Bob Clampett, the director who had left the studio in the mid-1940s and did most of his successful work for television after that. He began to do public appearances on university campuses, talking to young people who were starting to become aware that Bugs Bunny held up better than most other TV cartoons. Clampett also adopted a public persona that he thought would help him connect with young people: he wore a jacket festooned with patches of *Looney Tunes* characters and sported a mop-top Beatles haircut long after the Beatles had abandoned it.

Clampett developed a habit of putting himself at the center of the creation of all the characters he worked on (he unquestionably created Tweety). None of the animation directors owned the *Looney Tunes* characters or got creator credit on them, so it was only through media reports that they received notice for their contributions at all. The result was that almost anyone could claim to have come up with anything, and there was no way to fact-check them. Clampett could claim to have come up with Bugs Bunny, or anyone else, and it would become fact: after one of his campus appearances, a local newspaper[9] informed its readers that Clampett created Porky and that Daffy was created "after Clampett and fellow cartoonist Tex Avery made a cartoon called 'Porky's Duck Hunt.'"

Other creators weren't happy with this, and it had the effect of stirring longstanding resentments between some very competitive people.

Chuck Jones wrote a letter to Tex Avery quoting the claims Clampett had madeabout his role in the creation of Bugs, Daffy, and Porky. Avery wrote comments in the margins like "Unadulterated hogwash," and "Oh, brother!!" In response to Clampett saying that he had helped Avery on the story of a film called "The Isle of Pingo-Pongo," Avery wrote, "He's a little 'dingo-dongo' on this."[10]

Jones, however, may have hurt his own reputation by refusing to let go of the issue. When he created new animation of Bugs Bunny for a celebration of his old cartoons, released under the title *The Bugs Bunny/Road Runner Movie*, he had Bugs show a list of his "fathers," which includes all the major Warner directors *except* Bob Clampett, a move that made Jones seem unpleasantly petty, whatever the provocation.

Friz Freleng, whose interviews were usually much less self-aggrandizing than those of Clampett or Jones, was mellow about Clampett's tall tales. But Freleng expressed some public disapproval of the way Mel Blanc used *his* interviews to claim credit for things beyond his scope. "He's getting all the glory all over the world," Freleng said. "The writers, creators and directors did most of the work. We told him what to say."[11]

Freleng was not sentimental about his old work. He considered the Pink Panther his favorite creation, and when a reporter asked him about some *Looney Tunes* anniversary the company was promoting,[12] he bluntly said that while he loved knowing that people loved his work, he wasn't making any money off any of it, and was depending on the Panther for his financial future. But while these men weren't sentimental, they were proud, and once the old cartoons endured longer than they expected, it became important to each of them to make sure they weren't written out of a history starting to become codified.

These conflicts over history and credit created some subtext for Larry Jackson's film *Bugs Bunny Superstar*. It was the first and the best of a number of movies the *Looney Tunes* characters would appear in for over a decade: compilation films, with bits of new material surrounding a lot of old cartoons.

Jackson built *Bugs Bunny Superstar* around a selection of pre-1948 Warner Bros. cartoons, mostly starring Bugs, but with Daffy, Tweety, and Foghorn Leghorn getting one cartoon apiece. Knowing that audiences get exhausted and stop laughing if they see too many short cartoons in a row, he decided to include some documentary material between the shorts, to explain how the *Looney Tunes* style came to be and who made it happen. It was the first real attempt to introduce the Warner Bros. cartoons to a nonspecialist audience as important contributions to cinematic art instead of low-budget TV filler. The narration by Orson Welles, who had nothing to do with the cartoons, helped to drive home the idea that *Looney Tunes* deserved to be a full part of the classic Hollywood nostalgia boom.

Bob Clampett, who kept a collection of *Looney Tunes* memorabilia, offered to give Jackson access to it on condition that he could have approval over the final cut.[13] Jackson was hoping to set up interviews with both Clampett and Jones to get some of their rivalry into the film, but was informed that Jones was out of town. Bob McKimson was supposed to be interviewed, but backed out, saying that he was not comfortable appearing on camera. Jackson did get interviews with Tex Avery and Friz Freleng, but they didn't produce much usable material, and there was no opportunity to reshoot. That left Clampett as the undisputed star of the film, and wound up hurting it. What had been intended as the first full-length celebration of *Looney Tunes* and their greatness wound up inspiring a lot of fan and historian arguments over the legacy of one director.

Because Warner Bros. wouldn't allow Jackson any access to post-1948 shorts, *Bugs Bunny Superstar* also became one of the focal points of a split emerging among fans—even the majority of fans, who had no idea who had directed what. The existence of two different catalogs of *Looney Tunes* cartoons, owned by different companies and made available to different broadcasters and filmmakers, had resulted in two different viewing experiences.[14] Everyone liked some cartoons from both packages, of course, but depending on which package you preferred watching (or even just which one you were raised on), you might have very different ideas about who Bugs and Daffy were, or what the format of a typical cartoon was supposed to be, or even what a typical background looked like. If television kept the cartoons popular, the ownership split was responsible for creating almost two different *Looney Tunes* fandoms.

One difference has been noted already, that the post-1948 package was richer. But there were obvious stylistic differences, too. Viewers of the pre-1948s were more likely to see Bugs acting unprovoked (in one Chuck Jones cartoon from 1945, he escapes from Elmer, only to tell us, "I can't leave! I gotta go back and heckle that character!"). Or characters like Tweety portrayed as violent sociopaths. The post-1948s were more likely to show them acting in self-defense, or having villains bring harm on themselves.

A lot of the pre-1948s, and maybe a majority of the great ones, were made during World War II, and reminders of the war pop up all the time in the form of ration cards, warnings against nonessential traveling, air-raid drills. The post-1948 world is one of postwar prosperity, where every human lives either in a suburban home with a garage or in an architecturally flashy "home of the future."

The pre-1948s also have more overt racism, including eleven cartoons that were withdrawn from syndication when viewers complained about malicious Black stereotypes (more about this in the next chapter), and a bunch of other equally malicious stereotypes that stayed on TV for a longer time. The post-1948s weren't a lot more sensitive, but they were made in a time when activists had finally reached the movie studios and convinced them that open racism (or some forms of it, anyway) was bad for business. Blackface gags and the like were rarer in the post-1948 lineup.

The pre-1948 cartoons also dealt more heavily in topical references: caricatures of movie stars, and what would later be called memes about celebrities. Without pre-1948 *Looney Tunes*, most children would never have known that Bing Crosby had a reputation for betting on losing horses, or that Greta Garbo supposedly had large feet), to say nothing of life on the World War II home front. There were topical references in the ABC and CBS packages—for a couple of years writers couldn't get enough of Liberace jokes—but not nearly as many. The reissue programs and the sale of the cartoons to television may have made the creators more aware that their work was going to last, and that it might not be a good idea to date their films with jokes about presidential candidates and union bosses.

Because the pre-1948s included many cartoons where the formula hadn't yet crystallized, they were more likely to have unusual gag payoffs, at least compared to what you would expect if you started out watching only the post-1948s. One of the most famous gags in the post-1948 package was variously known as the "piano gag" or the "xylophone gag" depending on which version you liked best. It appeared in Friz Freleng's "Ballot Box Bunny" and "Show Biz Bugs," and in each one, the antagonist (Yosemite Sam, Daffy) rigs a musical instrument (piano, xylophone) so it'll explode when Bugs plays a certain note. Bugs tries to play the old parlor song "Those Endearing Young Charms," but keeps missing the note. Finally, the antagonist has had enough, pushes Bugs out of the way, shouting, "You stupid rabbit! Like this!," and plays the right version. The Daffy version loses points for being out of character, but wins points for the extra touch of having a few unexploded keys fall to the ground and sound a coda to the song.

A lot of the pre-1948 cartoons are violent and formulaic, yes, but they don't have quite as many repeated gags. The 1950s are typified by the Road Runner cartoons: a sequence of setups and payoffs, most of them violent. The decreasing budgets and running times of the 1950s and early 1960s caused the plots, never substantial, to fall away until many cartoons could only be distinguished by their locations. After watching a lot of these back-to-back, it can be a relief to turn from the relatively standardized style of the 1950s to the free-for-all approach of the war years.

If Warner Bros. had retained ownership of all the cartoons, there might still have been several different packages available, but likely they would have had a balance of characters, eras, and approaches. Different kids watching different stations at different times would have had similar experiences. Instead, the two sets of cartoons were out there (in addition to the black-and-white cartoons, which Warner Bros. still owned and sometimes distributed separately), emphasizing that there was no single *Looney Tunes* approach. Kids chose sides. Some preferred the zany anarchy of the pre-1948s, when Bob Clampett could encourage his animators to distort bodies for the sake of a laugh. Others preferred the more refined characterization and higher explosions-per-minute count of the post-1948s, with Chuck Jones as the star of this period.

The rivalry was good for the health of the franchise. Warner Bros. couldn't control the image and appearances of Bugs, Daffy, and Porky the way it might have had it owned all of their appearances. They were saved from the blandness of official, studio-approved characterizations. Television made these characters into headlining, top-of-the-bill stars, but the ownership split gave them something even rarer for cartoon characters. It gave them competition . . . from themselves.

CHAPTER 11

The Censored Eleven
(and Counting)

THE MIGRATION OF HOLLYWOOD animation to television created a vetting problem. Thousands of short cartoons, hundreds of hours, were released to television stations that couldn't be expected to know what was in every film. Most of the cartoons had been passed for release by the Motion Picture Association of America, so in theory they had already gone through the censorship process. But knowing that a cartoon was fit for theatrical release in the 1930s, 1940s, and 1950s didn't necessarily tell you whether parents would consider it appropriate for kids to watch in the 1960s and beyond. Parents, with their calls and letters about things they had seen while watching cartoons with their children, became unofficial volunteers in helping TV stations identify inappropriate content.

There were two elements in old *Looney Tunes* that caused the most trouble in their TV careers, and, conveniently, they're also divided rather neatly between the pre-1948 and post-1948 packages. With the post-1948s, the trouble was violence. Cartoons would be edited and re-edited in different ways to remove anything that was thought to cross the line between harmless comedy violence and violence that kids could potentially imitate. Gun violence, in particular, came under more and more scrutiny as the years went by, so that the many scenes where characters accidentally shoot themselves in the face would be quietly removed, even if it left scenes with no ending.

Pre-1948 cartoons, taken as a whole, did not have as much brutality as the later ones: you would get anvils, mallets, and dynamite, yes, but not in every cartoon, and even gun violence was uncommon apart from the occasional suicide gag. What the pre-1948s had more of was racism. Old cartoons coming to television had been passed for release in a time when all Black characters in Hollywood cartoons looked, sounded, and acted like characters from blackface minstrel shows. The calls and letters came, and many cartoons went, or had scenes cut.

There's no denying the abundance of racism in old Hollywood entertainment. Most of the things that could be interpreted as racist probably are, with one exception: when Bugs Bunny says, "What a maroon!" he is mispronouncing the word "moron" (much like he pronounces "imbecile" as "embezzle") and not, as is sometimes asserted, using a then-obscure term for runaway slaves in the eighteenth century. But otherwise, the minstrel-show tradition looms so large in US entertainment that many things in animation trace back to it, even if they evolved into something else. The white gloves that many cartoon characters wear are there so their hands are easier for the audience to follow, but so were the white gloves that minstrels often wore. Mickey Mouse is famous for his minstrel-show influences, and Bosko, the first *Looney Tunes* star, is inseparable from them.

While every medium dealt in stock caricatures of minority groups, Hollywood animation went beyond what was possible in more realistic media. Every stock stereotype was taken as far as it could go. Many cartoon caricatures, like the one in "Angel Puss," were influenced by Stepin Fetchit, the slow-moving, "laziest man in the world" character created and portrayed by actor Lincoln Perry. But animated versions would make him much worse than Perry did, and without even the excuse of giving work to an African American actor.

One thing that makes racism in cartoons tricky to discuss is that the cartoons themselves are often not available to see. For public-domain works, frank discussions of racism can actually help and make it possible to appreciate them better. Rudyard Kipling is understood as more than just a popular storyteller due to postcolonial analysis of his work, and any good discussion of him will illuminate his strong points along with his blind spots. But everything Kipling wrote can be published or downloaded legally. When Disney pulled the movie *Song of the South*, discussion became almost impossible: it's just gone.

When it came to television, and especially the electronic babysitter known as children's television, withdrawal of cartoons was the only option: to say that their caricatures influenced impressionable children is a cliché, but it's a cliché because it's true. In 1968, United Artists removed from the market eleven cartoons from the pre-1948 Warner Bros. package it controlled. These were cartoons where racist stereotypes were so completely central to the story that no amount of editing could save them. Known as the "Censored Eleven," they became semi-legendary because only collectors, or people with memories of theatrical screenings and early television airings, could see them.

Others were in the public domain and therefore couldn't be withdrawn, especially once home video came in, and cheap tapes began circulating of the few Warner Bros. cartoons that never had their copyrights renewed. One of Bugs Bunny's public domain cartoons, "Fresh Hare," ends with a group of Mounties transforming into blackface minstrels playing banjos, and in another, "All This and Rabbit Stew," director Tex Avery replaces Elmer Fudd with a grotesque caricature based on Stepin Fetchit. So even if copyright owners try to prevent all illegal sharing of the infamous wartime adventure "Bugs Bunny Nips the Nips," there are still reminders out there that Bugs Bunny is, as the euphemism goes, a product of his time.

When racist cartoon images come to public attention, executives usually attempt to control the damage. With *Looney Tunes*, this goes all the way back to 1944, when an African American weekly, *The Pittsburgh Courier*, got in touch with the Hollywood Screen Cartoon Producers association about "Angel Puss."[1]

* * *

"Angel Puss" is a slow, unfunny Chuck Jones one-shot about a guy who is hired to drown a cat in a sack, but the cat fakes his death and proceeds to disguise himself as a harp-playing angel, harassing and haunting the person who "killed" him. The only thing that distinguishes it from any another bottom-tier Warner Bros. cartoon is that the main character is Black, and he is portrayed the way Black characters had been portrayed in Hollywood cartoons for years. He is shown to be a gambling addict sent into a literal trance by the sound of dice (the Fetchit character in "All This and Rabbit Stew" is also unable to resist a dice game). He speaks in minstrel-show dialect, and is generally dehumanized from beginning to end.

None of this would have surprised any of the producers contacted by the *Courier*, but the reporter, Herman Hill, made a point that got their attention. He noted in his story the unintentional irony of putting this cartoon on the same bill as the March of Time's "Americans All," a short film that tried to convey the message that Black and white Americans had an equal stake in the Second World War. It was a nice message, said Hill, but wasn't it contradicted by a cartoon like "Angel Puss," which suggested that Black people were in some way different from—or alien to—other Americans? How was this supposed to convince Black viewers that the war was also a fight for *their* freedom and equality?

Eddie Selzer, who had just taken over as producer of the Warner Bros. cartoons, answered the situation with a response straight out of the entertainment executive handbook: he deflected blame to his predecessor. Selzer told the *Courier* that "Angel Puss" had been produced by Leon Schlesinger Productions, before Warner Bros. bought the studio and made him the producer. This was true, but allowed him to avoid saying what he thought of the cartoon, or why Warner Bros. was distributing it.

A month after "Angel Puss" was released, UPA unveiled its Franklin Roosevelt campaign promo "Hell-Bent for Election," which Chuck Jones also directed. Jones, a Roosevelt supporter who liked to troll the politically conservative Carl Stalling by saying things like "Roosevelt declared himself king today,"[2] portrayed FDR as a sleek and modern train and the Republicans as a rickety old locomotive that included a "Jim Crow Car." It was a dishonest gag, since the Democrats were still the Jim Crow party in the South, but dishonesty in a campaign commercial is not surprising. What is important to understand about the white liberal of 1944 is that Jones could use anti-racism as a talking point and then go back to his day job and make a film like "Angel Puss." Ten years later, he would probably have felt a need to excuse or justify the contradiction. In 1944, it was just the way he automatically designed a Black character.

While "Angel Puss" is one of the worst cartoons Jones made by any standard, the technically good work can't always be neatly separated from the morally bad work. Some of Jones's best early efforts had gone into

Inki, the little African lion hunter who first appeared in a cartoon called, helpfully, "Little Lion Hunter." It was one of the first cartoons where Jones showed promise as something more than a Disney imitator. Jones himself wasn't entirely sure what to make of Inki, or why the series was successful enough to last to 1950. While the premise of the series is clear enough—Inki is a kid perpetually trying to prove himself as a hunter by bagging his first lion—the actual cartoons go off in surreal directions that Jones admitted made no sense; Walt Disney ran them for his staff to try to figure out what people were laughing at, but he didn't know and neither did Jones. "They were really fourth dimensional pictures, and I don't understand the fourth dimension," Jones said,[3] but Inki kept doing well enough in theaters for theater owners to ask for more.

What people responded to in the series, and the main memory almost any TV viewer had of them, was a bizarre running gag involving a mynah bird who appears at random times during Inki's hunts. The bird doesn't say anything, never even looks at anyone directly, and is always seen with his head hunched over, doing a strange, hopping walk to the tune of Mendelssohn's "Hebrides" overture (one of Carl Stalling's most inspired arrangements of classical music). All the animals in the jungle are terrified of the mynah bird, who usually shows why: he can defeat any huge creature, whether a lion or a dinosaur, with no effort at all. Sometimes he saves Inki from danger, but if Inki tries to reach out to the bird and be his friend, he gets thrown aside like anyone else who crosses the bird's path. There aren't a lot of mysterious characters in the relatively straightforward comedy of Warner Bros. animation. The mynah bird is appealing because his appeal is so inexplicable.

The Inki cartoons actually had a longer life on TV than the Censored Eleven, and some of them even made it onto VHS and laser disc. This was because Inki himself is not quite as offensive as the guy from "Angel

Puss" or characters in other Censored Eleven cartoons, mostly due to omission. He's silent, so there is no dialect, and he doesn't behave in a stereotypical way. His physical acting establishes him as a curious, plucky boy who goes out hunting and gets into trouble. If he'd been designed differently, he might have lasted even longer on TV and video, but while Inki *acts* like a plucky young hero, what we *see* is what the *Atlanta Journal-Constitution* accurately described as "a barefoot, spear-throwing black Pygmy with large eyes and lips."[4]

That description was part of a two-page article in the *Journal-Constitution* in the early 1990s, at the height of the VHS era, about racism in old cartoons, and it began with Earl Shinhoster, a Black civil rights activist and NAACP executive who described watching a tape of old Warner Brothers releases with his son, until it got to a cartoon with Inki: "You talk about a parent being upset. I saw some of this same stuff as a kid, and I didn't like it then. I pulled that bad boy out of the VCR immediately."

Bob Clampett didn't have a series like Inki and the mynah bird, but he put some of his hardest work into the most famous of the Censored Eleven cartoons. This was "Coal Black and de Sebben Dwarfs," an all-Black jazz fairy tale in half-spoken, half-sung rhyming couplets. "So White" is a laundress (which, as Christopher P. Lehman notes, "was one of the most common occupations for African American women at the time, especially in the Jim Crow South"[5]), and after she escapes an assassination attempt by the wicked queen, she meets up with the dwarfs, who have all signed up to serve in World War II. So White becomes their camp cook ("Didn't join up 'cause I'm good-lookin'/But to answer the boys when they say, 'what's cookin'?'") and the rest of the story of Snow White proceeds more or less as normal, until the twist ending. It came out in early 1943, and the National Association of Colored People soon made a public statement calling for its withdrawal.

"Every established stereotype ever concocted to depict the Negro has been used in the picture,"[6] said the statement from NAACP leader Walter White. The NAACP used a similar argument to the one that Warner Bros. would soon hear against "Angel Puss": the use of degrading stereotypes was not only wrong, but potentially damaging to the war effort. White also protested directly to Warner Bros. executive Harry Warner, and NAACP member Odette Harper organized telephone call-in campaigns to protest directly to theaters showing the film in New York City.[7]

Clampett shouldn't have been surprised by any of this, but he probably was. As far as he was concerned, "Coal Black" was a special project for his unit, one that needed extra care and preparation because it had an all-human cast except for one gag involving a talking worm in the poisoned apple. Virgil Ross, who was one of the top animators for Tex Avery and Friz Freleng, didn't have happy memories of his short stint in Clampett's unit, but he made an exception for "Coal Black," which he called one of the best pictures he ever worked on in his thirty years at the studio. Clampett took his animators around LA nightclubs to see the latest dances and incorporate them into the film, which was to be his celebration of jazz.[8]

As his film became harder and harder to see, Clampett tried to argue that it was not the animated equivalent of *Birth of a Nation*. His origin story for the film, which, like many of his stories, is hard to double-check, was that black artists asked him to make it.[9] In 1941, he went to see *Jump for Joy*, the Los Angeles musical revue created by Duke Ellington. The show reinvented a familiar genre, the all-Black revue, with a new assertiveness and political awareness that Ellington said would "take Uncle Tom out of the theatre."[10] As Clampett told it, he met cast members of the show, local performers who asked why animation soundtracks never used any of them. As the hero in his own story, Clampett promised to come up with something.[11]

* * *

And so came "Coal Black and de Sebben Dwarfs," a jazz musical in the vein of *Jump for Joy*, plus a bit of the all-Black hit play (and Warner Bros. movie) *The Green Pastures*, which reimagined Bible stories as a white writer imagined Black Southerners might have imagined them. Although most of the musical score was by Carl Stalling, as usual, Clampett brought in some Black jazz musicians to play on the soundtrack, and the voice cast included Vivian Dandridge and Ruby Dandridge, the older sister and mother, respectively, of *Jump for Joy* performer Dorothy Dandridge. One of the most famous songs from *Jump for Joy*, "I Got It Bad (And That Ain't Good)" is paraphrased by one of the dwarfs when they're standing over So White's lifeless body.

If you see "Coal Black," which has never been that hard to do, you can tell it's a passion project by the number of unusual directorial choices it contains. In a standard *Looney Tunes* cartoon, the staging is uncomplicated, with straight-ahead angles and static shots. "Coal Black" is full of shots that call attention to themselves. When the queen decides to have So White killed, she yells into the telephone: "BLACKOUT SO WHITE!" and the letters pop out of her mouth and appear, hovering, above her head as she proceeds to bite off the telephone. An establishing shot of the prince's name on his car, which in any other cartoon would be a static shot, instead has the prince exit the car in the middle of the shot at a strange angle, as if the camera accidentally caught him at the wrong moment. Just before he tries to wake So White[12] from her sleep, the prince does a completely out-of-nowhere parody of Orson Welles's cry of "Rosebud!" in the opening of *Citizen Kane*, with a sudden switch from a medium shot to an extreme close-up of his mouth.

As for the theme of the film, it's one of many Warner cartoons that is in part a commentary on Disney, and specifically the sweet, sexless, self-consciously timeless world he created in *Snow White and the Seven Dwarfs*. Clampett decided to respond with a sexy, jazzy, contemporary take on the fairy tale, something to make Disney look out of touch.

"Coal Black" constantly reminds us that it takes place in the here and now, not in Disney's generic fairyland. The queen's wealth is established by showing us that she's hoarding rationed items like tires, sugar, and coffee. The murderers hired to rub out So White display a neon sign reading: "WE RUB OUT ANYBODY, $1.00 – MIDGETS ½ PRICE – JAPS FREE," in case we felt this cartoon needed an extra bit of defamation.

So White meets her prince the way Disney's Snow White does, seeing him as a reflection in a well, but instead of running away and hiding like her timid Disney counterpart, she begins to dance with him, first as an elegantly old-fashioned ballroom dance, and then as an up-to-date jazz dance with interjections of 1940s hipster slang ("All reet!"). When the dance begins, both characters are animated in a way that parodies the non-cartoony, rotoscoped (traced from live-action models) animation of the prince and princess in Disney's film. When they switch to dancing like they actually enjoy it, the animation style switches back to the normal Warner Bros. style.

A lot of sequences in the film are based on this idea of switching from the Disney style to the Warner Bros. style in a way that makes Disney look stodgy by comparison. There's a nice Disney-esque shot of So White tiptoeing through a forest, the innocent in a frightening natural setting. A pair of eyes appear in the dim light. Trembling with fear, she lights a match, and reveals one of the dwarfs, in his military uniform and carrying a bayonet (which has a broken barber's razor where the blade should be, one of a number of jokes that imply the dwarfs are not getting first-class equipment). So White asks where all seven of the dwarfs are, and the other six dwarfs immediately pop up from behind the first one, in sync with the six-note main theme of the classic Warner movie song "Blues in the Night."

Even the comeuppance of the wicked queen is done in a way that moves from Disney to Warner Bros. An arty shot of the queen in the distance, laughing triumphantly, is followed by the dwarfs using their military equipment to fire a shell at her. The shell opens to reveal the smallest dwarf, who hits the queen with a mallet.

Defenders of "Coal Black" sometimes make the leap from enjoying it to absolving it. "Everybody, including blacks, had a good time when these cartoons first came out," Clampett insisted.[13] All the controversy, he said, "has developed in later years merely because of changing attitudes toward black civil rights that have happened since then."

Clampett is not the only one to argue that "Coal Black" is being mistakenly judged by the standards of a different time, but it's a stretch, and not just because there were already public complaints against the film when it was in theaters. If audiences flinch when this cartoon gets shown, or prefer not to let their children watch it unsupervised, they're reacting to something that is certainly less mean-spirited than in "Angel Puss" or "All This and Rabbit Stew," but still meaner than its creator admits. It's an unwritten rule of Warner Bros. animation that cartoons stop being funny when they become cruel. "Coal Black" has considerable cruelty in it, starting with the dehumanizing designs.

The zoot-suit-wearing "Prince Chawmin'" seems to be inspired by Cab Calloway in his movements, but his actual design not only makes him look less than human, his teeth are all gold except for the two front teeth, which have been replaced by dice. Two stock stereotypes in Hollywood cartoons were that African Americans had gold teeth and gambled a lot, and Clampett was forever taking stock cartoon bits and pushing them to the next level.

Most of the dwarfs are drawn to resemble the great jazz composer/ performer Fats Waller,[14] whom Clampett deeply admired (he was also caricatured as the main character of Clampett's other Censored Eleven cartoon of the same year, "Tin Pan Alley Cats"), but there's one who is based on Stepin Fetchit. So White, the sexpot, embodies a bunch of other stereotypes. When she first appears, she's bending down over the well, wearing a short skirt and with her rear end on prominent display, gyrating back and forth to the music. To emphasize her status as the sexy, available alternative to Disney's Snow White, she escapes from her kidnappers by kissing all of them.

"Coal Black" is about the link between jazz and sex, and the contrast between its characters and their Disney counterparts, but it's also about the idea that Black Americans are more uninhibited in sex, in dance, and in music than "respectable" white people. This is arguably one of the defining stereotypes of American popular culture: the minstrel show traded on the idea that by playing a Black character, a white performer could say and do things that he could never get away with as himself. Eddie Cantor, the famous singer-comedian who was caricatured in Warner cartoons several times, usually played a nebbish character intimidated by women, and in keeping with this, he almost never sang songs where he expressed love or sexual attraction except when he was in blackface. Then he would sing songs like "If You Knew Susie (Like I Know Susie)" and "My Baby Just Cares for Me," as if blackface was an outlet for the feelings he repressed.

So "Coal Black" isn't just about paying tribute to jazz or thumbing a nose at Disney. Every character in the cartoon is from a particular tradition of stereotyping that implies Black people need to be kept separate from white society because of their supposed lack of inhibition, and that they are actually happier that way because white people are boringly inhibited—an example of deprecation disguised as self-deprecation. As the NAACP's statement implies, it was a stereotype that could be used to justify the existence of separate military units for Black soldiers.

That may be one of the reasons why the Black stereotypes in old cartoons cause so much more discomfort, even among children too young to know exactly what they signify, than the seven minutes' worth of Italian stereotypes Italian American writer Mike Maltese unleashed in Jones's "A Hound for Trouble" (featuring the original song "Atsa matta, atsa matta, hey! atsa matta for you?"). People everywhere in the world have caricatured the customs and languages of people in other countries. It's childish, but it's a kind of childish urge that everyone recognizes. The caricatures in "Coal Black" or "Angel Puss," however, imply that some people are just happier being second-class citizens in their own country.

* * *

It's difficult to talk about these issues without making the people of a particular time sound in some way inferior to the people of today, blind to truths that we are smart enough to see.[15] Of course, it's not like that, and particularly not with a franchise like *Looney Tunes*, which runs on instinct. Like Steven Spielberg or George Lucas or many other entertainers who were influenced by *Looney Tunes*, the creators made entertainment out of a set of basic assumptions remembered from childhood, and which most of their viewers were presumed to share. Every cartoon about US history draws on the same few facts or legends: Columbus and Queen Isabella's jewels, George Washington and the cherry tree, Paul Revere's ride. Every cartoon about show business takes place in a vaudeville theater; every literary reference is to the same few poems by Longfellow; and every character is based on a collection of stock traits and stereotypes. The creators were overgrown schoolboys, and what we see in their films is a world where schoolboy assumptions are always assumed to be right.

Not that they would never change with the times. In the case of racist stereotypes, some of them (not all) began to disappear after the war, as more and more white Americans began to see racism as a serious problem. In his article on "Angel Puss," Herman Hill mentioned that he had talked to a representative of the Screen Cartoonists' Guild who mentioned not only that some of the membership had complained about the "racial caricature material" in cartoons, but also that the matter "was brought to the attention of the Office of War Information for correction." Nothing frightened Hollywood producers more than the possibility that the government might begin "correcting" them. Ben Washam, a top animator in the Chuck Jones unit, knew that Selzer did not want the company to be accused of racism, so when Washam wanted to hire the studio's first Black animator, Frank Braxton, as his assistant, he opened the conversation with Selzer by saying, "I hear Warner Bros. has a racist policy and refuses to hire Negroes,"[16] knowing that this would make Selzer anxious to disprove this rumor.

"Angel Puss" was the last of the Censored Eleven. One of Clampett's last cartoons, "Bacall to Arms," would be one of the last to end with the stock gag of something exploding in a white person's face and turning him Black. The very last blackface gag at the studio was done by Bugs in Freleng's 1953 release "Southern Fried Rabbit" (originally announced as "John Brown's Bunny").

Although some aspects of the old minstrel tradition were inseparable from the cartoons (and from popular culture in general), there was increased scrutiny of things the filmmakers might have remembered from their childhoods. In Jones's "Long-Haired Hare," Bugs annoys an opera singer by singing and playing a number of decidedly non-operatic songs, and one of the songs chosen was a turn-of-the-century hit called "My Gal Is a High-Born Lady." But we don't hear Bugs sing the actual lyrics:

> *My gal is a high-born lady*
> *She's black, but not too shady*

Someone must have looked at the sheet music and realized those words would not fly in 1949, so Bugs sings an entirely new set of lyrics.

This does not mean the people who made the 1950s cartoons suddenly became better people than they were in the 1940s or, for that matter, that the people making Hollywood entertainment today are better people than those from the earlier era. Hollywood is driven by caution and risk assessment. In the post–World War II era, a lot of stereotypes turned out to be financially risky and a source of bad nationwide publicity, and that's when the creators and producers began to retire them. The acceptable limits of stereotyping in Hollywood are defined by who the creators and producers are willing to listen to, and whose pressure they fear, which are pretty much the same things. And nothing makes them listen like fear of losing money.

Stereotypes, then, were retired only when creators or their bosses began to notice negative reactions. This could be years, decades, even centuries after the negative reactions begin. There was a stereotype lag where some racial or national caricatures remained in *Looney Tunes* and other cartoons long after others had become taboo. Black stereotypes and blackface gags were out, but a 1957 Tweety cartoon ends with the old gag of a character being knocked from one end of the earth to the other and emerging in China, where he meets a Chinese Tweety who shows just how many negative stereotypes a character can embody in only ten seconds of screen time. This gag is replayed with the Road Runner in his last cartoon from the original WB cartoon studio, released in 1964.

Producers and broadcasters were so unconcerned about Asian stereotypes that "Bugs Bunny Nips the Nips" was not one of the Censored Eleven. It's not that the cartoon was *less* racist than the Censored Eleven. It was more vicious than any of them. It's just that the copyright owners took longer to become aware of how many people were hurt by the stereotypes.

* * *

Since most (but not all) of the obviously racist cartoons had been made before 1948, Warner Bros. didn't have as much to worry about when it came to the post-1948 cartoons it still controlled in the television era. In 1990, a Warner Bros. executive was asked for a statement about racism in cartoons and replied, a bit smugly, "Since we have the later cartoons, we don't run into too many problems."[17] The biggest exception was Speedy Gonzales, who is a Mexican stereotype. Speedy Gonzales cartoons were the only ones that ever made headlines for being dropped from TV.

Speedy became Warner Bros.' biggest cartoon star in the 1960s, if only because, after the original studio shut down, cheaply produced Speedy cartoons made up much of the *Looney Tunes* output. His was the only post-1948 series inseparable from racial caricature, but the character was popular in Mexico, something that became internationally known in the late 1990s when people complained that his cartoons weren't on TV anymore. The subsequent news stories all mentioned or talked to Speedy's Mexican fans,[18] and that helped restore the character's profile, maybe more than he deserved, since most of his cartoons weren't very good.

Speedy's popularity was slow to develop but not accidental. On first appearance in 1953, he embodied almost every negative stereotype imaginable, including another prominent gold tooth. In the mid-1950s, he was taken up by Friz Freleng, who had already demonstrated with Tweety his gift for softening an abrasive character. In Freleng's pilot for a new series, simply titled "Speedy Gonzales," the director and his longtime layout man Hawley Pratt made the mouse elegant and attractive. He wore an expensive-looking white suit that seems impervious to damage. Most of his stereotypical attributes except the heavy accent and fake Spanish (*"El gringo pussycat problemente?"*) were omitted. The other mice, who Speedy rushes to save, are more stereotypical, however. Portraying one character who is seemingly superior to everyone else in his group is itself a negative stereotype, one increasingly common in Hollywood in the 1950s. But the cartoon won the Academy Award, and turned Speedy into a star.

Freleng also chose to feature Sylvester as Speedy's antagonist in this cartoon and most that followed, probably because Freleng loved Sylvester and used him in almost any cartoon that required a cat. This usually worked out, but when paired with Speedy, Sylvester was boring. He's obviously outmatched against Speedy. He can't catch a regular mouse, let alone a mouse with superpowers. (It would have been funnier to watch Speedy go up against a "super genius" like Wile E. Coyote.) As a result, most of the Speedy series, shared between Freleng and McKimson, suffers from extreme predictability.

But the choice probably helped Speedy's popularity in Mexico, because he is almost always fighting an American cat who is oppressing Mexican mice. McKimson and Freleng both made a few Speedy cartoons with new antagonists, and these are mostly funnier because the villains aren't as obviously doomed as poor Sylvester (or Daffy, when he replaced Sylvester in the 1960s). But those antagonists were Mexican, and the dynamic was different. The heroic quality of Speedy saving his people from an American cat was lost, and with it, the popularity that helped keep his cartoons on TV.

If you watch *Looney Tunes* in chronological order, such changes in sensibility and sensitivity are evident, with some elements becoming more acceptable, others less. Certain stereotypes were avoided or downplayed, others not so much. Armed with the knowledge of what these caricatures mean, how they shifted, and what people thought of them at the time— and not just the people the creators listened to—we can see in these films what Hollywood considered acceptable at a particular moment in time.

Hopefully the Censored Eleven, Inki, and other cartoons will eventually be made available in that spirit, rather than being treated as harmless filler for children.

If they ever are, you can safely skip "Angel Puss."

CHAPTER 12

New Cartoons,
Old Characters

I
N THE 1970S AND 1980S, *Looney Tunes* cartoons became a bigger pop
culture phenomenon than they had ever been when they were new.
The continued success of both TV packages made the cartoons
unavoidable if you were a TV-watching child. *Bugs Bunny Superstar* and the
Warner Bros. compilation films proved that people would go to theaters
to see the cartoons that they'd been watching on TV for free. Critics,
too, were paying attention, particularly adult critics who remembered
watching the cartoons in their youth. *Film Comment* magazine, one of
America's leading serious film journals, devoted an entire 1975 issue to
classic Hollywood animation, which was heavily skewed toward Warner
Bros. cartoons and Chuck Jones and Tex Avery in particular. What's more,
the influence of *Looney Tunes* began to pop up unexpectedly in live-action
movies.

Hollywood directors also remembered loving Bugs Bunny and the
Warner Bros. style when they were younger. Nothing in the premise of
Mel Brooks's *Blazing Saddles*, a comedy Western about a Black sheriff,

didn't seem to demand cartoon references. But in one of the movie's most famous bits, the hero, Bart (Cleavon Little) defeats a superstrong villainous henchman (Alex Karras) by dressing up in a delivery uniform and handing his foe a booby-trapped box of candy. After the explosion, Little exits to the tune of "Merrily We Roll Along," just in case we didn't get that he's a real-life Bugs Bunny, using cheesy disguises and explosives to defeat stronger opponents.

There's another scene in *Blazing Saddles* that has the feel of a Bugs Bunny homage, although without direct shout-outs. When Bart arrives in town, the locals are ready to kill him on the spot. He gets out of it by pointing *his own gun* at himself and taking himself hostage, and the people who wanted to kill him a few seconds ago are crying out for help as Bart walks himself to safety in the town jail. This isn't an actual Bugs Bunny routine, but it has a lot of the elements of one: escaping through a sudden distraction, fooling people through the most transparently phony means possible, and playing on the willingness of idiots (namely, everyone except him) to react in a certain way instead of thinking about what they're seeing. *Blazing Saddles* was the closest thing to a Bugs Bunny feature film that had ever been made, and maybe still is.

The cartoons were cultural reference points for directors like Steven Spielberg and George Lucas, as well. They weren't ashamed to love things that had once been considered disposable entertainment, and especially loved what they'd seen as boys in the late 1950s, when *Looney Tunes* were the funniest short cartoons in US theaters. Spielberg, who would influence the future of the characters when he arranged to borrow them for *Who Framed Roger Rabbit*, included a Road Runner cartoon clip in his first theatrical feature, *The Sugarland Express*, as an ironic juxtaposition with the movie's much more serious chase story. When George Lucas, who had once tried to get an internship at the Warner Bros. animation department,[1] hit it big with *Star Wars*, he arranged for Chuck Jones's science-fiction parody "Duck Dodgers in the $24^{1/2st}$ Century" to be shown before screenings of *Star Wars* in his hometown of San Francisco.[2]

The post–*Star Wars* advances in special effects technology made it easier to do cartoon gags in live-action, which led to more specific *Looney Tunes* homages like the scene in *Spaceballs* (Brooks again) where the singing frog from "One Froggy Evening" bursts out of a human stomach, *Alien*-style. Joe Dante, a protégé of Spielberg who enjoyed his greatest success in the 1980s, established himself as the most *Looney Tunes*–influenced live-action director since Frank Tashlin died. In a Dante film called *Explorers*, kids meet aliens who have learned everything they know from Earth TV reruns: the kids say, "We come in peace," and one of the aliens replies, "What's up, Doc?"

Gremlins, a dark comedy take on the basic premise of Spielberg's *E.T.* (kids discover an adorable, marketable creature who turns out to spawn an invasion of ugly, mean-spirited creatures), interested Dante because of the parallels to two Bob Clampett cartoons about gremlins who sabotage planes during World War II. He wasn't able to include clips from the cartoons in the film, but the creatures were played more for comedy than for horror, doing a series of visual gags that paid homage to classic cartoons, and the sequel, *Gremlins 2: The New Batch*, was an out-and-out live-action cartoon that began with Bugs Bunny riding the Warner Bros. shield and ended with Daffy Duck commenting on the credits. These sequences were directed by Chuck Jones, one of Dante's personal heroes (Jones was given small acting parts in two of his films). Dante would eventually make an entire *Looney Tunes* movie, against his better judgment, as an act of reverence for Jones.

Looney Tunes almost had it all: success, prestige, influence. What didn't it have? New material. TV reruns of old cartoons were not going to keep the characters at the top forever. Television was changing, and not in ways favorable to the filler programming blocks that had kept *Looney Tunes* in the public eye.

* * *

People in the entertainment business knew that cable and pay TV were going to fragment the TV audience, and that kids would no longer watch local *Looney Tunes* broadcasts because there wasn't anything to watch on other channels. There was more competition, not only from other programming but from infomercials, which were even better for a TV station's finances than old Bugs Bunny cartoons. Old cartoons didn't cost much, but infomercial owners would actually pay the station for airtime. Some of the filler packages migrated to cable but the trend was unmistakable. The *Looney Tunes* characters were almost guaranteed to lose value unless Warner Bros. started producing new cartoons that could represent them in the TV world of the future.

There was no artistic reason why there needed to be a new Bugs Bunny or Daffy Duck cartoon, no hidden depths to the characters unexplored before 1964. The imperatives were commercial and technological. New material, whether a new Bugs Bunny cartoon, a new James Bond film, or a new Spider-Man comic book, keeps the characters commercially relevant. And while the imperfect prints and tinny sound of Looney Tunes material was good enough for older TVs, they wouldn't compete in the coming world of high-definition television.

One of the first attempts to create an up-to-date *Looney Tunes* cartoon happened, like so much in modern entertainment, because of *Star Wars*. The publicity around George Lucas's "Duck Dodgers" screening impressed Warner Bros. enough that it commissioned Chuck Jones to create a sequel. Jones and Friz Freleng were also doing some original material for television, but the idea behind "Duck Dodgers and the Return of the 24½th Century" was that it would be released theatrically, and perhaps get a screening with the *Star Wars* sequel. The mentions of this cartoon in "Of Mice and Magic," Leonard Maltin's groundbreaking history of Hollywood animation, provide a sad little portrait of raised and shattered expectations. The first edition refers to the "Duck Dodgers" sequel with great excitement, noting that Jones had hired Mike Maltese, the writer of the original and many more classics. A later edition adds: "Unfortunately, Maltese's script wasn't used, and the finished cartoon turned out to be a disappointment."[3] Maltin's reaction was everyone's. The sequel was incorporated into a television special, and there would be no further "Duck Dodgers" adventures until the new millennium.

There had been a lot of classic animators working on the "Duck Dodgers" sequel, and if you don't mind Jones's late drawing style (characters' smiles are always a little sloppy and their bodies are a little lumpy), it looked good. But they never got the story right. Maltese's original storyboard[4] had some nice moments, most of them involving Marvin the Martian and his dog sidekick K-9, but it was too reliant on old gags, like Daffy getting repeatedly shot. Instead of reworking the story, Jones wrote a new story that included almost no gags at all and cut K-9 from the film. The short goes through various expected plot points: Daffy gets his mission, Daffy meets Marvin the Martian again, Porky solves everything while Daffy runs away. But pretty much nothing happens.

There is still some charm in the cartoon if you don't go in expecting it to be up to the classics. It hints at what *Looney Tunes* might have been like if the original series had continued into the 1970s: an occasional hint of disco in the soundtrack, an occasional hint of design influence from the space vistas in *Star Wars* and the light show in *2001: A Space Odyssey*. Daffy, thankfully, is not evil and not outrageously incompetent. At its best, the cartoon is a window into what Jones valued about his old work: proud of what he had done with Daffy, happy about his influence on modern sci-fi blockbusters, but maybe too anxious to prove he'd moved beyond the surefire violent gags of his youth.

Warner Bros. continued to do other *Looney Tunes* projects, mostly compilation movies and compilation TV specials using the *Bugs Bunny Show* formula of linking a themed selection of cartoons, edited here and there to make them seem a little less old, like redubbing "radio company" into "television network." What the company was reluctant to do was to make completely new material. The budget for a fully-animated cartoon would be difficult to recoup, while doing limited animation in *The Simpsons* or *South Park* style would devalue the characters. It took a long time for Daffy Duck to recover from the shame of chasing Speedy Gonzales in low-budget 1960s cartoons.

This started to change around the time when the studio gave in to Steven Spielberg's request to loan out its characters to Disney for *Who Framed Roger Rabbit*. Spielberg was immensely powerful in Hollywood and personally friendly with Warner Bros.' top executives, so the gesture might have been mostly to keep him happy. But as *Roger Rabbit* began its multiyear production process, Warner Bros. began, cautiously, to embrace the idea that their cartoons had adult appeal.

A 1986 prime-time special for the anniversary of Tex Avery's debut (and therefore the creation of what we think of as the *Looney Tunes* style) was executive-produced by *Saturday Night Live*'s Lorne Michaels, and directly aimed at adults, with celebrities showing up to deliver dry parodies of traditional anniversary testimonials (Bill Murray on Elmer Fudd: "I just don't have any respect for him intellectually"). Michaels assigned two of his comedy writers to create the jokes, while Warner Bros. was represented in the process by Greg Ford, a writer and animation historian who had guest-edited the *Film Comment* classic animation tribute issue. Ford's relationship with Warner Bros. went back to the 1970s when he'd written an unproduced script for the studio's first *Looney Tunes* compilation feature; his version was called "Hareport," and had all the characters stuck on a plane together, hallucinating their past adventures when they thought the plane would crash.

The next step was a push for new cartoons by new talent. Terry Lennon, who had worked as an animator on the new material for Friz Freleng's compilation features, teamed with Ford and the two received joint credit as writers and directors on two new cartoons starring Daffy Duck, both monster-themed: "The Duxorcist," where Daffy meets a cute demonically possessed female duck, and "Night of the Living Duck," where he dreams he's in a nightclub trying to entertain a tough crowd of monsters.

Both of these shorts became part of the next and last compilation film, a selection of horror comedies called *Daffy Duck's Quackbusters*. But "The Duxorcist" was also released to theaters as a stand-alone short, partly at the instigation of a TV executive who wanted to get more theatrical film credits.[5] It was produced by a new animation department, usually called the "Classic Animation" division, with Kathleen Helppie-Shipley, who had gotten her start as Freleng's secretary,[6] as the producer. The mandate of this department was to create fully animated segments with the famous characters, produced mostly in-house (or by freelance animators in the US) without outsourcing the animation overseas, as most TV animation was doing by that time. Having a staff that specialized in this type of animation would allow Warner Bros. to meet the demand for its characters in advertising and promotion, without the off-model or erratic drawing that outside studios produced. Meeting the promotional demand would help to finance a series of new shorts, which could make back money through the many distribution methods now open to them: theaters, television specials, and home video.

That, at least, was the plan, but only one of the subsequent cartoons made it to theaters. This was "Box Office Bunny," directed by Darrell Van Citters, who was also directing commercials and approving licensed images with the classic characters. The cartoon wasn't up to expectations, despite a decent premise: a modern multi-theatre cineplex is built over Bugs's rabbit hole (one of those cartoon construction companies where an entire prefabricated building can be put up in seconds), and Elmer Fudd is the usher trying to throw Bugs out for being there without a ticket. But then Daffy Duck shows up, and what should be a good, simple Bugs/Elmer cartoon turns into a cartoon with one antagonist too many. Bugs comes off as unbearably smug when he can outwit two people at once without breaking a sweat. Daffy, once again, is too much a villain.

It was still the first new Bugs Bunny short in a quarter-century, and that should have made it a big deal, only the studio didn't know how to distribute a theatrical short. It kept trying to find an appropriate movie to release it in front of: something family-friendly, something popular, something that would get the short some attention. For months, executives kept proposing different films, and rejecting each one because it didn't seem likely to be a hit. In the end, they attached it to the sequel to *The NeverEnding Story*, a children's fantasy movie that didn't do great business either, and that Van Citters felt didn't fit his cartoon.[7] Not long after that, Warner Bros. cut back its investment in classic-style animation, eventually folding it into the television unit. Several new Van Citters shorts were shut down in various stages of production.

Fine, so it didn't completely work out. But how were the cartoons?

* * *

In general, it's best to approach post-1964 *Looney Tunes* on their own terms, not closely comparing them to the originals. Even a weak or middling original selection has the advantage of being comfortable in its own skin, of a style that is organically part of the time and place when it was made. Once the studio formula was established, the rules of comedy and animation came so naturally that they may not have even needed discussion: a gag was funny or unfunny, smart or dumb, and that was that. Making a modern *Looney Tunes* cartoon meant thinking everything out, deciding, at every step, whether they should do what the original cartoons would have done at a particular spot, or if it would be more appropriate to try something that they *wouldn't* have done. The results could be good, but they were always a little self-conscious. Reconstructing a style is not the same as inhabiting it. So the fair question to ask is not whether a new cartoon measures up to some past masterpiece, but whether it is entertaining and funny and distinctive on its own.

The distinctive thing about the "Quackbusters" material, and all the Ford/Lennon cartoons, is that it is self-aware about *Looney Tunes* history. The classic directors rarely assumed that we had seen their older cartoons, and considering how often they recycled gags or whole scenes, they probably hoped we hadn't. Just as the characters before 1964 have no continuity, they have no history. The "Quackbusters" release "Night of the Living Duck" begins with a scene that is an homage to the opening of Bob Clampett's "The Great Piggy Bank Robbery." In 1946, Daffy is reading a Dick Tracy comic book and excitedly turning the pages to see what happens next; in 1988, he's reading *Hideous Tales* comics. In 1946, he accidentally knocks himself out and dreams he's "Duck Twacy"; in 1988, he accidentally knocks himself out and dreams he's a lounge singer in a monster bar. Much of the cartoon is then taken up by Daffy singing (in the voice of Mel Tormé) a song called "Monsters Lead Such

Interesting Lives," a paraphrase of a Bugs Bunny line from Chuck Jones's "Hair-Raising Hare."

This historical approach also resulted in a well-meaning use of music that didn't pan out. Instead of trying to commission a new score in the Carl Stalling style, the producers used samples of actual Stalling music, taken from the many soundtracks that had survived without voice tracks. This was supposed to re-create the original style with a larger orchestra than the new cartoons had at their disposal, but the older recordings didn't fit seamlessly with the newly recorded voices, and the echoes of old familiar cartoons were distracting.

Probably the best thing about the "Quackbusters" cartoons is the characterization of Daffy, who is nicely balanced between the greedy antihero and the wackier antihero he used to be. He doesn't always lose, but he takes a lot more punishment while winning than Bugs Bunny usually does. Younger creators, like those who rejected Chuck Jones's ideas for Daffy in *Roger Rabbit*, were familiar with all eras of *Looney Tunes* and wanted to honor them all at the same time, and though Daffy would fall back into his bad old habits whenever he was teamed with Bugs, "Quackbusters" at least demonstrated that there were other ways to portray him.

One blow to further attempts to revive *Looney Tunes* was the death of Mel Blanc, shortly after the release of the "Quackbusters" material. In truth, he wasn't heard to best advantage in those cartoons. In *Who Framed Roger Rabbit*, his characters sounded much more like their old selves, or at least like they had been more aggressively sped up. Whether it was the voice direction or the postproduction, his characters don't sound right in the Ford/Lennon cartoons. Still, Blanc was the closest thing *Looney Tunes* had to a public face, and his death was almost as traumatic as that of a live-action performer.

Warner Bros. acknowledged this in one of the most memorable trade ads ever created for a celebrity death: a spotlight on an empty chair, with all Blanc's characters downstage, bowing their heads, saying nothing. "SPEECHLESS" was the only word in the ad.[8] The animation team carried on with new voice actors, although the company tended to rotate actors in and out instead of settling on permanent replacements.

The two other Ford and Lennon shorts produced before their unit was shut down are both bitter about a parent company that was gradually losing interest in quality animation. "(Blooper) Bunny" and "Invasion of the Bunny Snatchers," both starring Bugs, are meta-cartoons that comment on the franchise and the way the characters have been watered down through their status as corporate symbols and advertising pitchmen. They play with the inherent conflict between the anarchic, violent *Looney Tunes* style and the needs of a modern giant entertainment corporation.

"(Blooper) Bunny" was inspired by another round of anniversary celebrations that Warner Bros. rolled out in 1990, this time for the fiftieth anniversary of Bugs Bunny's official debut. Bugs and other characters are shown rehearsing for Bugs's "51st and ½ anniversary spectacular," and the script they're rehearsing has drained all the conflict from their relationships. After a happy dance, Daffy, Elmer, and Yosemite Sam all congratulate the rabbit on his birthday. Elmer's gun isn't loaded, and what looks like dynamite turns out to be just decorations on Bugs's birthday cake. After that bland "official" celebration, the rest of the cartoon is presented as a series of outtakes and behind-the-scenes footage with the characters blowing their lines, fighting with each other, and grumbling about what Warner Bros. is forcing them to do. Daffy's most famous line in the picture has him worry that the company will stick him with "three snot-nosed nephews" to make him more like Donald Duck, and the final credits roll over Yosemite Sam screaming about how much he hates rabbits. The characters have become so imprisoned by WB's organizational goals that they can only be themselves when no one is supposed to be watching.

"Invasion of the Bunny Snatchers" is even bleaker. Apart from being an *Invasion of the Body Snatchers* takeoff, it's a roast of Bugs's parent company and the history of Hollywood animation since the 1960s. It begins with a bored, jaded Bugs physically traveling back and forth between the "locations" of three different cartoons, like a movie actor who's been overbooked. He goes through the motions of performing old gags with his three main antagonists, Elmer Fudd, Yosemite Sam, and Daffy Duck. But the sameness of those routines is nothing compared to what follows, when aliens replace all three of those characters with pod-people versions of themselves, poorly drawn, inconsistently designed (Elmer keeps changing his design from shot to shot), with only their mouths animated. Worse, all of them are nice to Bugs and want to be his friend. Bugs gets rid of the alien impostors and returns to his usual schtick.

"(Blooper) Bunny" is one of the most satisfying of the post-1964 shorts. It gets some of its individuality from the particular style of meta-humor the filmmakers use, which is typical of the 1990s. They assume not only that the audience is familiar with the *Looney Tunes* formula, but also that we're cynical about show business and entertainment corporations, and that we will enjoy hearing Daffy complain about Warner Bros.' lack of originality. This style of humor was everywhere in the pop culture of the period, starting from the comedy clubs, moving to David Letterman's NBC show, and shows like *The Simpsons* and *Seinfeld*, all of which were aimed at people who had watched way too much TV growing up and were bored yet fascinated by show business clichés. That tone makes "(Blooper) Bunny" feel different from *The Bugs Bunny Show* and all the other cartoons set backstage in a theater: it's *Looney Tunes* humor that has been allowed to evolve with the times.

But the best thing about "(Blooper) Bunny" is the animation, which calls back to the classics while also trying new and slightly risky things.

The dance sequence, animated by Doug Compton, is in the style of classic animators like Chuck Jones's favorite animator, Ken Harris, and it's a strong enough piece that we can enjoy seeing it over and over. (There are also some bits that showcase how small movements are sometimes funnier than broad ones, like when Bugs shows his frustration by letting his right ear droop down just a little, a technique that Chuck Jones would have recognized.) The fake behind-the-scenes footage begins with a shot that would never have been in the old cartoons: a minute-and-a-half sequence without a cut, simulating a handheld camera as it travels around the backstage area, taking in things like Elmer Fudd trying to grow hair in his dressing room, Bugs rehearsing his tap dance in the background, and Daffy pacing in front of his beat-up trailer. The illusion of camera movement is hard to pull off in traditional animation because the characters have to be drawn differently every time the camera gets closer; in the classic cartoons, this kind of tracking shot was impossible. And that instantly gives the new film its own identity. We're seeing the characters in ways we've never seen them before.

Neither of the shorts found glory. "Invasion of the Bunny Snatchers" was tossed into a half-hour compilation special with Ford and Lennon's Daffy shorts, while "(Blooper) Bunny" remained unreleased for many years, developing a mildly legendary status online until Cartoon Network finally aired it in the late 1990s.

This wasn't quite the end of original theatrical cartoons, as the studio made a few here and there. A *Casablanca* spoof ("Carrotblanca") has achieved some fame by being included as an extra on DVDs of the classic movie, though it mostly proves that these characters don't seem like themselves when they're forced into a beat-for-beat movie parody. A series of cartoons were outsourced to Chuck Jones's production company. They started with a well-received Road Runner cartoon, but mostly disappointed with the larger challenges of Bugs, Daffy, and Foghorn Leghorn. The director of those shorts, Douglas McCarthy, then made another "Duck Dodgers" film, the 3D "Marvin the Martian in the 3rd Dimension," for Warner Bros. to use at its theme parks. The last short appeared in 2000: "Little Go Beep," about the Coyote and Road Runner as children.

The characters were luckier in the world of advertising, although no one knew it at the time. In the early 1990s, while their theatrical projects were either unreleased or incomplete, the Classic Animation department was asked by an advertising agency to create a spot for Nike's Air Jordan sneakers, which would co-star Bugs Bunny and the shoes' namesake, Michael Jordan. The commercial, a minute-long Super Bowl entry, begins with a classic Bugs setup: big, mean athletes are disturbing his sleep by playing basketball above his rabbit hole. After taking some abuse from them, he declares war and teaches them a lesson. Only this time, he doesn't do it alone. Michael Jordan shows up ("Who'd you expect? Elmer Fudd?") as Bugs straps on his "Hare Jordan" sneakers, and the two of them beat the four mean players with a combination of basketball moves and cartoon gags: sometimes they're dunking the ball, and sometimes they're using anvils, pies, and the irresistible lure of Bugs dressed as a woman. At the end, Bugs strolls toward the exit next to Jordan, saying, "This could be the beginning of a beautiful friendship."

A long article on the Classic Animation division in 1992, around the time the commercial aired, mentions only that Bugs acts too much like Roger Rabbit in the commercial (he screams frantically, like Roger does, when the evil players are tossing him around at the beginning). Other than that, the article treated the Nike spot as an insignificant side project. No one guessed that it would be the most successful of the *Looney Tunes* revivals, a new formula that would finally allow the characters to be stars of an all-new feature film.

CHAPTER 13

Space Back in Jam Action

Today, kids yawn when I tell them that I worked on Beauty and the Beast, *but their eyes light up when I mention* Space Jam. *Go figure.*

—Bruce Woodside, supervising animator, *Space Jam*[1]

THE 1996 WARNER BROS. movie *Space Jam* is the most successful *Looney Tunes* project since the original studio shut down. This is not easy for a *Looney Tunes* fan to admit, or at least this *Looney Tunes* fan. All the attempts to revive the characters, all the hard work and talent and love, all the modern reimaginings to make the characters live again for a new era, and the only smash hit is a film based on a commercial, credited to a commercial director who never made another feature film after it was done, and where all the characters play supporting roles to a great basketball player who isn't an actor. Its popularity eventually became so great that Warner Bros. made a sequel starring a *different* great basketball player who isn't an actor, cementing the idea that the *Looney Tunes* characters are at their most commercially viable when they're involved in something basketball-related.

Looney Tunes: Back in Action, the 2003 movie also released by Warner Bros., was an even bigger failure than *Space Jam* was a success. This, again, is difficult for a *Looney Tunes* purist to admit, because that movie was made by *Looney Tunes* purists who were determined to rescue the characters from being a basketball star's sidekick. The director was Joe Dante, director of *Gremlins* and *Explorers* and possibly the biggest *Looney Tunes* fan among successful directors. To direct the animation, the studio hired Eric Goldberg, best known as supervising animator for the Genie in *Aladdin*, Disney's most successful attempt at creating a wacky character in the Warner Bros. vein. Dante accepted the offer to make *Back in Action* in part because he disliked *Space Jam*, which he considered a Michael Jordan movie that happened to have the *Looney Tunes* characters in it.[2] He wanted to make a better movie that would do justice to the classics.

The failure of *Back in Action* was a turning point in the history of *Looney Tunes*. When the movie, the first feature that ever had *Looney Tunes* in the title, recouped only a fraction of its big budget, it became conventional wisdom that the characters had not survived the dawn of a new century. Warner Bros. canceled a series of theatrical shorts that the primary writer of *Back in Action*, Larry Doyle, had produced. It also pulled back on creating *Looney Tunes* merchandise, and began to treat the characters as problems to be solved. For the next decade, *Looney Tunes* projects would mostly be attempts to rethink the characters and introduce them to young people who didn't know who they were. A movie intended to save *Looney Tunes* purism instead wound up dooming it.

Although *Back in Action* was not a sequel to *Space Jam*, the movies have enough in common that they're easy to compare. Above all, they are both inspired by the live action/hand-drawn animation hybrid that was *Who Framed Roger Rabbit*, but this time with the *Looney Tunes* characters as the stars. The animation in both movies is inspired by *Roger Rabbit*'s solutions to the problem of putting cartoon characters in a live-action setting. The characters look, for want of a better word, glossy; they always seem to have real-world light bouncing off them. Their designs are the same standard versions that the studio had been marketing since the 1960s but reworked so they could be photographed from any angle on the 360-degree axis, instead of the limited number of angles a short cartoon needed to use.

Both movies have large parts for human actors, giving the (mostly) human audience someone to identify with the way they identified with Bob Hoskins in *Roger Rabbit*. In *Space Jam*, it's Michael Jordan, the most famous athlete in the world at the time. In *Back in Action* there are two: a Warner Bros. studio security guard and the son of a famous movie star (played by Brendan Fraser) who winds up going to Las Vegas with Daffy Duck; and a studio executive (Jenna Elfman, from the then-recently canceled sitcom *Dharma & Greg*) who fires Daffy, is ordered to rehire him, and winds up accompanying Fraser, Daffy Duck, and Bugs Bunny to Vegas and elsewhere for reasons it's even harder to explain.

Both movies have a similar approach to Daffy Duck. The creators seemed to recognize that he'd been portrayed as a jealous, angry jerk for too long, but can't let go of that aspect of his character, especially when he's sharing the screen with Bugs. So they split the difference by having Daffy be jealous and grouchy when Bugs is around, and letting him occasionally break out his old-school crazy laughter and troublemaking when he's interacting with humans.

Both movies were intended to revitalize a brand and sell a lot of merchandise with the characters' images, although *Space Jam* was more blatant about this, and more successful at it. So much merchandise was produced and sold that Gerald Levin, the CEO of Warner Bros.' parent company, was quoted as saying, "*Space Jam* isn't a movie, it's a marketing event."[3]

The producer of *Space Jam*, Ivan Reitman (director of *Ghostbusters*), supervised most of the production after "Hare Jordan" director Joe Pytka delivered the live-action footage. Reitman was told by executives that these characters were their crown jewels and needed to be handled with special care,[4] and it was made clear throughout the company that Bugs Bunny needed to become the studio's equivalent of Mickey Mouse,[5] someone who could anchor a merchandise empire. The hope was that by pairing Bugs with Michael Jordan, he could get some of Michael's power to sell people things they didn't need. And it worked well enough.

Only seven years separated *Space Jam* from *Back in Action*, but the gap was critical. The success of *Space Jam* had faded and the characters were increasingly in danger of becoming something for older nostalgists by the time of *Back in Action*. Worse for the latter film, hand-drawn, two-dimensional animation was being abandoned by Hollywood studios. Executives had decided that the success of Pixar movies and *Shrek* had rendered analog techniques obsolete. Before *Back in Action* was released, Dante and Goldberg appeared in a BBC documentary about the displacement of traditional animation, with Goldberg arguing unconvincingly that things would turn around as soon as someone made a great hand-drawn film.[6] *Back in Action* was being asked to save a franchise and an entire medium. Even a great film wasn't going to do that.

This helps explain why *Back in Action* is suffused with the sense that the whole franchise is about to become obsolete. A startlingly high percentage of the jokes, and most of the best ones, are based on the idea that the old *Looney Tunes* comedy style is out of date and no one knows what should replace it: Bugs is informed that cross-dressing used to be funny but is now "disturbing"; Wile E. Coyote's mishaps have become so predictable that they can all happen offscreen ("Be careful of the fireworks," a character calls to him, just before the explosion); Yosemite Sam tries to get a couple of other characters to throw dynamite, but they're worried that it will send a bad message to children.

* * *

Space Jam wasn't being asked to save the franchise, just pep it up a bit. If it missed the opportunity to make the characters more popular, it's largely because it had almost nothing to do with the actual personalities of most of the characters it was supposedly showcasing. Few of them get to do anything of interest, and when they do, it's usually an attempt to make them more "nineties," like Tweety using martial arts, or Daffy using the word "screwed." Bill Murray pops up randomly in the film as himself ("The producer's a friend of mine," he replies when asked why he suddenly joined the climactic basketball game), barely even bothering to make eye contact with other live-action characters, let alone with the animated characters. So although the movie was successful, the cartoon characters didn't benefit much from its success, except as merchandise: even kids who enjoyed the movie didn't really know who these talking animals were, or what they did.

And then there's the premise, which guaranteed that even if *Space Jam* had been a much better movie, it could never have been a satisfying *Looney Tunes* movie. The premise is that evil aliens want to kidnap the *Looney Tunes* gang for a theme park called Moron Mountain (one of several rather toothless Disney jokes in a movie that only exists because of Disney's *Who Framed Roger Rabbit*). Unable to beat the aliens on his own, Bugs challenges them to a basketball game to decide his fate and the fate of the other characters in what the movie calls "Looney Tune Land." The aliens then cheat by stealing the abilities of the greatest active basketball players, becoming a team of hulking basketball-playing dynamos called the "Monstars." The only person who can save the *Looney Tunes* characters is Michael Jordan, whose abilities the aliens didn't bother to steal because the movie takes place during the period when Jordan was trying to play professional baseball. So Bugs gets Jordan to come out of retirement and join the team as a ringer.

Let's repeat that slowly. Bugs Bunny. Needs help. Defeating five aliens.

It's inherent in the premise of *Space Jam* that Bugs is a shadow of himself. There have been many different takes on the character since "A Wild Hare," but not one of them had Bugs so weak and powerless that he'd need a professional athlete to save him. Nevertheless, the Bugs/Jordan team was the basis for the project, and a story was created to fit it. Michael is the star, and all the *Looney Tunes* characters suck up to him.

As a student with too much time on my hands, even by the standards of a student in the 1990s, I was upset enough by this premise that I wrote to Roger Ebert explaining why Bugs Bunny shouldn't need help from anyone. Ebert printed my note online but my objections didn't cause Warner Bros. executives any stress because most moviegoers weren't *Looney Tunes* purists. *Space Jam* wasn't one of the very biggest hits of 1996, but it made enough money at home and abroad to be considered a hit, the merchandising went well, and it turned out to have a huge afterlife in home viewing. It was a combination of two things people love watching on TV—cartoons and basketball—so many people grew up with this movie as comfort-food entertainment. Nobody who knew the *Looney Tunes* franchise really thought *Space Jam* was good, however.

Even before *Space Jam* was made, Dante had tried to get Warner Bros. interested in a more ambitious *Looney Tunes*–related project, developing a script for a live-action comedy called "Termite Terrace," a sort of biographical film about the birth of the *Looney Tunes* comedy style, told through the story of the wild young men who worked at Leon Schlesinger's studio in the 1930s. The studio decided not to make the film, in part, Dante recalled, because a nostalgic period piece didn't fit their plan to rebrand the characters as more contemporary.[7] *Back in Action* would be his chance to protect the characters and the *Looney Tunes* style from a studio that had shown over and over again that it didn't know who these characters were.

The movie that resulted isn't better than *Space Jam*. Even the premise isn't better, just less crass. It was one of those movies where people spent years trying to come up with an idea, and finally went into production without one, just so they could make *something*. When a *Space Jam* sequel didn't happen, the studio looked into the idea of replacing Michael Jordan with another international icon, Jackie Chan, where he and Bugs and Daffy would get involved in a spy adventure. The title was *Spy Jam*, and although it didn't happen, the idea of a spy story somehow managed to stay with the project until it finally emerged as *Back in Action*.

Larry Doyle, a writer for *The Simpsons*, pitched the idea that the film should take the characters around the world, with the story broken up into seven-minute segments taking place in different locations.[8] This, in theory, would solve the problem of how to do a feature-length plot with characters who were never meant to sustain one. Although Doyle was the sole credited writer on the picture (there were an estimated twenty-nine writers who worked on it at one point or another), there are only remnants of this idea in the finished film, mostly in a scene in Paris where Elmer Fudd chases Bugs and Daffy around the classic paintings in the Louvre. The problems the movie faced in development can also be deduced from the fact that, although it's called a *Looney Tunes* movie, and theoretically was supposed to revive interest in the studio's entire stable of cartoon stars, most of those characters have small or cameo parts, and only Daffy Duck and Bugs Bunny have a substantial presence in the story.

That story, to the extent that we can follow it, starts with Daffy getting kicked off the Warner Bros. lot and going home with the Brendan Fraser character. We then find out that Fraser is the son of a famous actor who played a James Bond–type spy (he's played by former James Bond actor Timothy Dalton), and then we discover that his father was a *real* spy and he's been kidnapped while on the trail of something called the "gold monkey," so Fraser and Daffy Duck hop in not-James-Bond's secret super-spy car and set out on the trail of a mysterious MacGuffin that turns out to be connected to a sinister plot to turn humans into monkeys.

This is a plot that could be taught as an example of the dangers of piling too many absurd story points on top of one another. It's what is sometimes called "putting a hat on a hat": if a character is wearing a funny hat in a scene, it won't get funnier if you put another funny hat on top of it, because the contrast with the rest of the scene, the thing that makes the hat funny in the first place, is lost. *Roger Rabbit* worked because the cartoon characters were in a semi-serious film noir story, and the film was funny because of that contrast. Once it's revealed in *Back in Action* that the humans live in a world of crazy gadgets, monsters, and quasi-magical artifacts, Bugs and Daffy have nothing to contrast with. One of the funniest bits in the film is that scene where Jenna Elfman's character, seeing cartoon characters with dynamite, wonders aloud, "Who has dynamite!?" and Daffy replies, "Welcome to *my* world." But for most of the movie, that isn't really true.

Dante managed a better balance between cartooniness and human realism when he made the sequel to *Gremlins*, still the closest thing there has ever been to a full-length original *Looney Tunes* movie. Warner Bros. was so desperate for a sequel that they told Dante he could do whatever he wanted; what he came up with was a comedy in which a bunch of gremlins run wild in a television studio, and most of them act like *Looney*

Tunes characters at their most sociopathic. The definitive gag in the picture is when an unusually intelligent gremlin (voiced by Tony Randall) pulls a gun and shoots another gremlin to illustrate his point about how uncivilized gremlins are. *Looney Tunes: Back in Action* wasn't allowed gags like that. Warner Bros. was uncomfortable letting the characters be nasty or hurt anybody.

But the bigger reason *Gremlins 2* succeeded is that the gags are mostly performed by the gremlins, with the humans as their stooges. There are wacky human characters here and there, but the gremlins are wackier. Dante could do what he wanted with them.

As mercenary as *Space Jam* was, it had a simple premise that made it a hit and allowed it to continue being popular: basketball game, with evil aliens vs. *Looney Tunes* characters and their pal Michael Jordan. *Space Jam's* plot is ridiculous, but by using the most basic, uncomplicated story ideas imaginable, the writers (four credited, and many others uncredited) were able to keep working through many rewrites and a frantic production schedule. Hurrying toward a 1996 release date, several different animation units were working simultaneously, taking live-action footage of Michael Jordan bounding around a green studio, and figuring out how to include cartoon characters. But they all knew the premise which, in fact, was similar in approach to the way the classic cartoons approached storytelling. It was a simple clothesline story on which to hang the gags. The gags aren't great, but nothing gets in their way.

The premise of *Space Jam* also solved a problem that pops up in any piece of media that tries to include more than a couple of *Looney Tunes* characters: most of these characters were not intended to appear together, and have no reason to hang out. *Space Jam* introduces the characters (referred to as "The Looney Tunes," a name that stuck, even though it makes as much sense as calling Charlie Brown and his gang "The Peanuts") living together in an animated community inspired by *Roger Rabbit*'s Toontown, with a town hall where they all assemble to hear the announcement of their pending abduction. They are less funny when they're all in the same room together but the premise of the film at least provides a reason for why they're all together. They have to be, because they are either going to win the basketball game together, or get kidnapped together.

The other advantage of this crass premise is that it offers something new for these characters to do, something that hasn't already been done with better animation. The first time we see Bugs Bunny in *Space Jam*, rather late in the film, he's in the most stock Bugs Bunny situation of all: Elmer Fudd is threatening him with a gun. Just at the moment when we're all expecting Bugs to start tying Elmer's gun barrel in a knot, the alien spaceship opens up and crushes Elmer, taking him out of the scene. People who aren't familiar with Bugs and Elmer find the bit funny in itself; people who *are* familiar with them are grateful to see something less predictable. When we first see Bugs Bunny in *Back in Action*, he's replaying the "duck season/rabbit season" routine from Chuck Jones's early 1950s cartoons, the only difference being that the animators have come up with some new ways for Daffy's beak to get shot off. It signals that the characters will never get too far out of their comfort zone.

* * *

Even the most crass, focus-group-driven, executive-mandated element in *Space Jam* helps bring the characters out of their comfort zone. I refer, of course, to Lola Bunny. So obviously created for marketing reasons, she is the film's biggest offense against purism. Bugs Bunny doesn't *need* a romantic interest. Practically none of the characters do. There are a few classic cartoons where we see Bugs wooing a girl rabbit, or Daffy married to a female duck, and it looks awkward, out of step with their usual motivations, which are about revenge, survival, and messing with other people's minds.

But marketing dictated that there should be a girl bunny in *Space Jam*. You had a cartoon franchise where nearly all the characters were male, mashed up with an all-male sports league. The intended audience of the movie was male, but not all male. There had to be at least one girl in the cast. They were thinking of using Honey Bunny,[9] a character who had appeared mostly in comic books and video games whenever Bugs needed his own equivalent to Minnie Mouse, and possibly Daisy Lou, who appeared in a not-very-good cartoon where Bugs was fighting with another rabbit over her affections.[10]

In the end, the animators were ordered to come up with a new girl rabbit, who would look similar to Bugs, but not so similar that they looked like relatives, and also sexy, like Jessica in *Who Framed Roger Rabbit*. And she should get mad when 1940s relic Bugs calls her "doll," so the studio can claim she's a feminist character. And don't bother explaining why she's there: in the middle of the movie, she should just pop up when they need a basketball-playing "Tune," even though all the characters are supposed to live in the same place and no one seems to have ever seen her before. She was so much a creature of marketing that when the sequel, *Space Jam: A New Legacy*, came out, she was simply redesigned and rethought to fit the marketing priorities of 2021: she was given a less sexualized design, and the creators announced this to the world so that they could stir up online controversy over this decision.[11] If there is ever a *Space Jam 3*, you can bet Lola will be back and still reflecting the marketing priorities of a particular time.

Back in Action, again, had more integrity. There's no Lola Bunny, but this also means there isn't an animated character who can elicit new or different reactions from the *Looney Tunes* stars. The most painful thing for a *Looney Tunes* purist to admit is that Dante's love for the characters, his dedication to making them act like themselves, may have hurt *Back in Action* more than it helped.

Dante, who had been dealing with interfering executives for most of his career, found them particularly clueless on *Back in Action*, where they objected to things like Bugs Bunny breaking the fourth wall to talk to the audience ("It takes you out of the movie," they said), and even to Bugs saying, "What's up, Doc?" After finishing the film, he knew he hadn't made a masterpiece, but he could at least take pride in the fact that he had kept Bugs Bunny true to his character, over the objections of executives who pointed out that Bugs doesn't really *do* anything in the finished film, whose plot (such as it is) is driven almost entirely by Daffy. Dante insisted that Bugs should stay true to his persona as "the chairman of the board, the hip character who never loses his cool and is always above everything," even if it meant he didn't get involved much in the story.

> I can't tell you how many times executives said, "We want Bugs to do this," and we said, "No, that's not what Bugs would do, that's what Daffy would do." And they said, "We're sick and tired of hearing what Bugs would do and wouldn't do." There was an idea to have a scene where Bugs reveals his vulnerability—and then we thought: No! We'd be cashing in the whole character after 60 years![12]

But sadly, the studio executives had a point. Not only is Bugs not involved in the plot of *Back in Action*, he barely reacts to what's going on around him. He isn't faced with anything that can disorient him, so he walks through the film calm, unflappable, and kind of boring. Bob McKimson once said that by the time the original studio closed, Bugs had become "too much of a suave character."[13] This is definitely true of the *Back in Action* Bugs.

In the best classic cartoons, Bugs has a fairly wide emotional range: he's smug, yes, but he can also get angry, frightened, excited, scream at the top of his lungs. There were cartoons where he loses, cartoons where he's an idiot, cartoons where he acts unprovoked and cartoons where he's much nicer than usual. *Back in Action* doesn't convey those sides of his character because it is so determined to keep him in-character. At least *Space Jam* makes clear that Bugs can be flustered, even if it's by a studio-mandated female rabbit in gym shorts. And the moment he screams at Michael Jordan for help is, however out of character, a nice moment for the character to show what his voice and face and body are capable of.

Space Jam: A New Legacy, which became one of the first big hit movies of the COVID-19 pandemic era, makes Bugs even more vulnerable by introducing him as a lonely guy who stayed in the classic cartoon world after all the other characters left for other Warner Bros. franchises. This allows him to cry and get drunk (on carrot juice, of course) and remind us that he can do more than look smug. When the film's villain transforms Bugs and his fellow *Looney Tunes* characters from their classic hand-drawn selves into CGI characters—the filmmakers' way of criticizing the death of classic-style animation while still going along with it—Bugs's signature line, "this means war," has some real anger behind it.

The sequel, whose plot (if you can call it that) reverses *Space Jam*'s plot setup by having NBA legend LeBron James seek Bugs Bunny's help rather than vice versa, is no more successful than *Back in Action* in its attempts to bring the characters back to their roots. During the big basketball game when the good guys are inevitably down by 1000 points, James realizes that he's made a mistake by trying to rein in the *Looney Tunes* characters, and encourages them to resort to wacky cartoon silliness instead. It's a nice thought, but the ensuing gags aren't very funny and the idea of the characters doing a rap battle was handled better in an episode of the satirical Cartoon Network show *Robot Chicken*. Still, there's nothing in *Back in Action* as satisfying as seeing Bugs and the other characters get transformed back into their original 2D selves when they win the game, reassuring fans everywhere that this is one franchise that won't get completely overtaken by the latest technology.

Still, Warner Bros. was probably banking more on basketball fans than *Looney Tunes* fans to show up for this movie, just like an earlier generation of basketball fans showed up for the last one. The biggest contributor to *Space Jam*'s success, as Dante and others pointed out, was that it was really a Michael Jordan movie rather than a *Looney Tunes* movie. That helped it survive a curious choice made by both *Space Jam* and *Back in Action*: the assumption that the *Looney Tunes* characters needed no introduction or scenes to establish their identities because everyone was already familiar with them. All the introduction we get in *Back in Action* is that brief scene with Bugs and Daffy doing their 1950s routine, but it doesn't make sense to anyone who hasn't seen those cartoons. In *Space Jam*, we get silent clips of the old cartoons playing on television sets behind the villain, and then most of the characters simply show up without even identifying themselves by name. This is a curious choice for any property that isn't already established in feature films.

When the characters from *The Simpsons* made a movie, the producers and the studio tried to establish everyone's personality and avoided anything that seemed too impenetrable to people who hadn't watched them on TV (several characters from the show were replaced by new characters, just so the creators didn't have to call back to the TV episodes). And that was a show that was still making new episodes every week. For that matter, *Space Jam* offers a fairly elaborate introduction to Michael

Jordan and his career. But Warner Bros. executives seemed to feel that the *Looney Tunes* characters were incredibly popular icons on par with Mickey Mouse or Donald Duck, even as the keys to their popularity, the classic cartoons, were disappearing from TV.

Warner Bros. had a certain complacency about these assets. It accepted the bland characterizations they were given in *Space Jam* and *Back in Action*. When the latter bombed, it became clear even to studio executives that the *Looney Tunes* characters were not as famous as they believed. In an early scene from *Back in Action*, Jenna Elfman tells a boardroom full of executives, "Our latest research shows that Bugs Bunny is a core asset that appeals to male and female, young and old, throughout the known universe." Say what you will about the projects that followed, they at least recognized that that wasn't true.

CHAPTER 14

A New Bunny

ONE DISADVANTAGE *Looney Tunes: Back in Action* had compared to *Space Jam* is that when *Space Jam* came out, it was still possible for children to see the original cartoons on TV and find out who the characters were. Shortly after, Warner Bros. merged with Turner Entertainment, finally uniting all the cartoons under the same ownership. And in 2000, the notorious decision was made to hand exclusive television rights to all of the cartoons, pre-1948 and post-1948, to the Turner-owned Cartoon Network, now the only channel in the United States showing the classic cartoons.

For people who subscribed to Cartoon Network, this resulted in some nice programming, including an annual "June Bugs" marathon that included almost all the Bugs Bunny shorts ever made (subtracting "All This and Rabbit Stew," and a few others too racist to include). But exclusivity becomes a problem when the exclusive license holder decides it's no longer worthwhile to make use of its license. That's what happened with Cartoon Network, and rather rapidly.

The *Looney Tunes* cartoons started to appear less frequently on the network, even with the much larger catalog at its disposal. Despite being part of the same corporate family, Cartoon Network relished its independence and favored its in-house programming, like the surreal late-night "Adult Swim" block. The *Looney Tunes* landed in its lap just when the network had less real estate to give to cartoons than ever before.

After *Back in Action* bombed, Cartoon Network cut the *Looney Tunes* further, to one half hour a week on Saturday mornings, and in 2004 it moved the entire package of cartoons to a spin-off channel, Boomerang.[1] By the time Cartoon Network's exclusive license expired in 2005, the characters had the stigma of a failed movie *and* several years' near absence from television. Maybe this would have happened anyway if Warner had continued to split the shorts between different networks, but to fans, it felt as though the company had bet the entire future of its cartoon library on a network that was free to stop using the catalog whenever it wanted. Cartoon Network couldn't be blamed for pursuing what it considered its best programming options; it was the parent company's fault for not having a backup plan in case this happened.

By the time *Back in Action* came out, barely any *Looney Tunes* material had been released in the then-prevalent DVD format, and parents had nothing to rent for their children from Netflix, which at that time was a mail-order DVD rental service.

Finally, to coincide with *Back in Action*, Warner Bros.' home video department released a four-DVD set called the "Looney Tunes Golden Collection." Nearly all the cartoons were from the post-1948 library, and the discs seemed more like a random sample of cartoons than an attempt to curate the best of them, or to trace the development of characters. But a lot of classics were there, and the DVD producers used special features to add some depth, allowing the original creators to provide audio commentary, creating documentary featurettes about the characters and their creators, and, best of all, offering music-only tracks wherever possible. Sometimes an overfamiliar cartoon comes to life again if watched without dialogue and only Carl Stalling's music to keep viewers company.

While *Back in Action* failed, the " Looney Tunes Golden Collection" sold better than expected,[2] and led to several more sets. These included more pre-1948 cartoons, with new restorations from the original negatives, making them look better than they had in decades of TV showings. It wasn't perfect. There was never an attempt at a complete or nearly complete Bugs or Daffy collection, and the cartoons were haphazardly arranged (often in alphabetical order), but it was still a wonderful feeling, during the DVD boom, to walk into a store and see people gathered around a screen and laughing at "Drip-Along Daffy" or even "The Up-Standing Sitter."

Though the Censored Eleven and other related cartoons like the Inki series were off-limits, the company became more willing to include some cartoons with blackface gags or other racist scenes. They added a disclaimer at the beginning of most video releases, which included a brilliant line written by DVD producer Constantine Nasr,[3] forcefully stating: "These depictions were wrong then and are wrong today," a line that has been imitated in other companies' disclaimers. Instead of trying to engage in relativism, or pretend that no one had a problem with it at the time, it comes down on the side of absolute standards. That lack of special pleading makes it easier to agree with what the disclaimer goes on to say, that pulling these cartoons from circulation "would be the same as pretending these prejudices never existed."

While the "Golden Collection" series did well, lasting six volumes before succumbing to the contracting DVD market, their high price point meant that they were almost entirely aimed at people who already liked the cartoons. (They even added another disclaimer that stated: "The Looney Tunes Golden Collection is intended for the adult collector and may not be suitable for children.") The company released cheaper, bare-bones versions of some of the discs for the family market, but the overall impression was that the characters were now mostly aimed at those aforementioned adult collectors.

* * *

As the classics slowly faded away from television, the future of the franchise and its ability to keep adding new fans increasingly depended on all-new, all-original TV series. From broadcast to cable, and through the rise of online streaming, the big question about *Looney Tunes* characters was whether they could be made to work in television series with no old material and, if so, how much they would have to change to fit the new format.

There had already been a few attempts at this when the characters were still popular. A show called *Taz-Mania* had premiered on the Fox Network in 1992. The Tasmanian Devil, who kept on getting more popular despite the tiny number of cartoons he appeared in, was the only classic character in the regular cast. Creator Art Vitello, a former *Tiny Toons* director, made Taz the black sheep of a comically bland '50s-style suburban family, including a father who talked like Bing Crosby.

The series was often funny, although very talky. Virtually every character talked up a storm except Taz, who was not rethought in any major way because he was a merchandising icon. In his design, in his attitude, and in the things he said and did, he was recognizable as the same character from the Bob McKimson cartoons. To make him a lead character instead of a villain, he was rarely shown trying to eat other characters. He was still a predator, just one who usually seemed to be between meals. Vitello could only change Taz by association, creating new characters who would talk to him differently than Bugs or Daffy did.

By 1995, when Warner Bros. launched its own broadcast network (the now-defunct WB) and moved most of its animated series there, its Saturday-morning lineup included a new show featuring Tweety and Sylvester. The premise: Granny, the dotty old lady who had been Tweety's usual owner since 1950's "Canary Row," becomes a globetrotting investigator modeled on Angela Lansbury from *Murder, She Wrote.* As in many of the old cartoons, she not only owns Tweety but also Sylvester, the cat who is always trying to eat the bird, and Hector, a bulldog who beats the hell out of Sylvester at every opportunity. Now they're all working to solve mysteries: it's *Looney Tunes* meets *Scooby-Doo*, or *The Sylvester and Tweety Mysteries* as it was officially titled.

Most of the characters were unchanged in this new format. Granny, stuck with most of the work of analyzing clues and summarizing the plot, was a little smarter than she was in 1950, but everyone else did what they were doing in the classics: Tweety is a mischievous, sometimes sarcastic little bird; Sylvester tries to eat him and his plans backfire violently, or if they don't, Hector steps in to provide the violence. Every episode was about half a new 1950s-style Tweety cartoon and half a mystery plot, and the longer the show went on, the closer it moved to being a straight-up revival of the old Tweety/Sylvester series; some of the cartoons were funny and imaginatively designed, but the mystery plots always held it back a little.

By the time *The Sylvester and Tweety Mysteries* ended, the franchise's post–*Space Jam* high was over and the lavish budgets of the 1990s, which allowed every episode to be scored for a full orchestra, were over, too. Many of the same people moved on to a different, lower-budget *Looney Tunes* project for WB: *Baby Looney Tunes.* This was an idea that sounded so similar to *Tiny Toons* that people involved with it kept having to explain, no, this isn't a revival of *Tiny Toons.* While *Tiny Toons* featured kids who were similar to the classic characters but technically separate, *Baby Looney Tunes* turned everyone into a baby: Baby Bugs, Baby Daffy, Baby Taz, even Baby Lola.

The show didn't attract much attention (even of the negative variety) since it was so obviously not aimed at anyone over preschool age. It did well enough to last three years and forty episodes on WB, ending its run there just before *Back in Action* came out, and going on for one extra season on Cartoon Network. Its characterizations were traditional, although without anything inappropriate for small children. It aimed to be a gateway drug for *Looney Tunes*, introducing kids to the key characters and some of their basic personality traits, so that they would have some affection for those characters by the time they were old enough to watch stuff with violence in it.

While *Baby Looney Tunes* was winding down, Warner also produced a new show starring Daffy Duck. After other TV pitches for the duck had failed, including one that would have had him as a TV host with a messy personal life, the studio went with a series based on "Duck Dodgers in the 24½th Century." It used some ideas that had originally been developed for a "Duck Dodgers" feature film, and featured a lot of science-fiction parodies, including a *Green Lantern* parody called "Green Loontern." It also added some new characters, like the Queen of Mars (Marvin the Martian's boss), who is romantically interested in Dodgers. The show did a clever job of combining traditional Daffy plots and gags with a slightly greater sense of continuity and consistency: there weren't any story arcs to speak of, but there was an actual status quo, and the second season's finale tried to lead the characters and their relationships to a new place. The third and final season, with different writers, wasn't as good as the first two, but overall it was an enjoyable show for people who had some familiarity with the characters.

There were fewer of those people around, however. When it came time to develop another *Looney Tunes*–related television show, it was clear that something more contemporary was needed. And this is how we got to the most infamous of all *Looney Tunes* original TV shows. Even though most people who knew of it never watched it, and even though the characters were technically not the same as the classic characters, *Loonatics* was the franchise's defining original TV event.

* * *

The year was 2005, and the WB network, then in the last years of its existence, had dumped most of the *Looney Tunes*–influenced comedy shows it had started with. Its most successful original show was *Teen Titans*, adapting the DC Comics superhero group with a more contemporary design approach, and a tone that was somewhere between straight superhero storytelling and comedy. Inevitably, someone asked, what if we did *Looney Tunes* . . . but they're all superheroes . . . and with a more contemporary design approach . . . and a tone that is somewhere between straight superhero storytelling and comedy?

In February of that year, WB announced that *Loonatics* would be one of its new animated series for the upcoming season. It would take place in a postapocalyptic future where six characters gain superpowers and use them to fight evil. Each of the characters would be similar to, and possibly a descendant of, a *Looney Tunes* character: Bugs, Daffy, the Tasmanian Devil, the Coyote, the Road Runner, and Lola. The announcement was accompanied by designs for the new characters, including the lead, Buzz Bunny, a huge rabbit with black fur, a psychotic grin, and an equally psychotic look in his two unevenly sized eyes, which shoot lasers.

Looney Tunes was still considered a significant enough property that Warner Bros. treated the rollout as a big deal, including sending WB's president, David Janollari, to the press to talk it up. "We just said, 'Wow, what a great way to take the classic Looney Tunes franchise that has been huge with audiences for decades and bring it into the new millennium,'" he said, adding that this would not destroy the legacy of the franchise. "If anything, it's an homage to the legacy instead of a destruction of the legacy."[4]

Sander Schwartz, the head of the animation division, told another outlet that this would be "a kids show intended for kids today who are growing up in the Internet age, an age of technology, an age of hip, cool animation, and something that we hope will resonate with that age group."[5]

Probably the executives were ready for some of the mockery these statements would encourage. What they may not have been prepared for was just how much the mockery would hurt them. After all, *Space Jam* had a very mockable premise, too, and it did fine. But *Space Jam* appeared in a world where the Internet was less pervasive. People like me, complaining online about how Bugs Bunny would never need Michael Jordan to help him out of a jam, were barely noticed.

In 2005, the base of purist *Looney Tunes* fans was probably smaller than in 1996, but the Internet gave a voice and a small measure of power to statistically insignificant groups of fans. Message boards erupted, online petitions went up, and one such petition, saveourlooneytunes.com, caught the attention of the media, because the creator was an eleven-year-old boy in Oklahoma who wanted to protest the new designs: "They're evil-looking," he said.[6]

This was also a time when video was easier to share than it had been in the past (YouTube was created in February 2005, the same month *Loonatics* was announced) and programs like Adobe Flash made it relatively easy to take an existing design and put it into a homemade animated cartoon. One such video that got shared a lot that year was "A New Bunny," written by Niraj Shah of the comedy site TLG.com. In the video, two guys are walking down the school hall when they meet "Buzzed Bunny," who talks the way Buzz Bunny's design looks. Almost every line he says is screamed. Every other word he says is bleeped (there's also an uncensored version, for the un-squeamish). His catchphrase is: "*I'm extreme*!!!" with his head wobbling back and forth as he says it. With its ironic-offensive tone and its admitted borrowing of dialogue from the not-safe-for-work webcomic "Sexy Losers," it was more up-to-date and in tune with the zeitgeist than any show on the WB Network could hope to be.

Warner Bros. dealt with the combination of anger and mockery by ordering some design changes, not an easy thing a few months before an animated show is set to premiere. The lead character's eyes were altered from their original scary/psychotic look to friendlier, cartoonier eyes. The producers also changed the name from Buzz Bunny to Ace Bunny, partly because it turned out there was already a Dutch character with the name Buzz Bunny,[7] and partly because it turned out the name was also used for a sex toy. And they amended the title from *Loonatics* to *Loonatics Unleashed*.

The show finally aired and stood revealed as a standard, inoffensive action-comedy that would have been exactly the same if the characters were all different species of talking animals. It resembled other action-comedy cartoons more than it resembled *Looney Tunes*, so if anything, its problem wasn't that it disrespected the franchise, but that it was disconnected from it. There was no way kids were going to watch this and know who Bugs Bunny was, so even if it had been a huge hit, the franchise would have been no closer to a revival. The second season tried to push it closer to being a *Looney Tunes* show by adding futuristic characters like

Pierre Le Pew and Sylth Vester, and then it was gone, and so, for several years, was the *Looney Tunes* franchise.

* * *

By the time Warner Bros. was ready to try again, it had learned from the two main mistakes of *Loonatics Unleashed*. It had been wrong to take the franchise out of the comedy genre, and also to substitute new characters for Bugs, Daffy, and the rest. The next effort, *The Looney Tunes Show*, created for Cartoon Network, featured the actual characters, and it was unmistakably a comedy. It was a paradigm shift in the way the parent company approached the *Looney Tunes* characters, and especially Bugs. As their biggest icon, he had always been held back from TV animation and anything else requiring a low budget. In the 1960s, Daffy was considered unimportant enough to use in poorly animated theatrical cartoons, but Bugs was only allowed to look and move the way he did circa 1959. Even as his popularity fell in the 2000s, he could only appear regularly in TV animation as a baby, or a futuristic descendant, never as himself. With *The Looney Tunes Show*, that was over.

Character designer Jessica Borutski created a shorter, less detailed Bugs, recognizably the same character but also recognizably different from any version that had appeared in the theatrical cartoons. This version of Bugs was more suited to a television budget. Borutski was surprised at the almost personal viciousness of some of the comments she saw about her work.[8] In the early 2010s, it was still just possible to be surprised at how much viciousness someone young and female could experience online.

But it wasn't the designs that provoked the biggest arguments, it was the comedy style. The format of most episodes was to have a single story take up most of the half hour. The story would feature premises like lies that spiral out of control, get-rich-quick schemes, and socially awkward encounters. It was the first *Looney Tunes* animated sitcom. Instead of trying to find a culturally acceptable way to feature violence in a kids' show, or battling with corporate executives about whether Yosemite Sam could have guns or not, *The Looney Tunes Show* mostly did without violence, patterning itself after a mostly nonviolent comedy form.

In *The Looney Tunes Show*, Bugs and Daffy share a house together, and their characterizations are meant to remind us of various sitcom odd couples, but most specifically Jerry Seinfeld (Bugs, the snarky semi-normal one) and George Costanza (Daffy, the wheedling, perpetually unemployed loser). The other characters come into the show the way sitcom characters do: Yosemite Sam is a wacky neighbor; Daffy and Bugs's other roomie, Speedy Gonzales, runs a local pizza parlor; and the Goofy Gophers run an antique store.

The show embraced the idea that this was a sitcom that played by sitcom rules, rather than classic cartoon rules. A recurring joke is that the gags we have come to expect from the classic cartoons are impossible to pull off in a sitcom world. Yosemite Sam doesn't have his guns because open carry isn't permitted. Bugs's cross-dressing act doesn't always work, and even when it does, it gets him into mistaken-identity complications more typical of Tom Hanks in *Bosom Buddies* than anything from the classics.

One advantage of this approach is that it does allow the characters to be used in new ways. This Daffy is not a rehash of the version from the 1950s hunting cartoons, and because he annoys Bugs, the dynamic between them is different than in any previous team-up. As the straight man surrounded by idiots, Bugs isn't as smug as he was in *Back in Action*. And Lola is more tolerable than in *Space Jam*, because she gets to be a comedy character: she's introduced as a woman who goes on a date with

Bugs and becomes obsessed with him, constantly following him around and refusing to admit that he doesn't consider her his girlfriend. She seems vaguely patterned after the character Melanie Lynskey played on the then-popular sitcom *Two and a Half Men*, who spent the series stalking Charlie Sheen. But once she becomes Bugs's actual love interest, she's still a ditz who drives him crazy, and her overdramatic, overreacting style brings a welcome dose of over-the-top broad comedy to a show that was often too mellow.

A show where Lola Bunny is the funny one and Bugs Bunny is the straight man was bound to provoke plenty of backlash even before it started. But the big question around the show was the same question that haunts every *Looney Tunes* project: Should it be judged by comparison to the pre-1964 cartoons, or as something different that happens to star the same characters?

Judged by the second standard, *The Looney Tunes Show* was at least promising. Maybe if they had kept going with these characterizations, tried to refine them, found stories that were less standard sitcom fare and incorporated more physical comedy, it could have evolved into something new. We'll never know, because Warner Bros. changed course again. Cartoon Network canceled *The Looney Tunes Show* after fifty-two episodes, and the studio announced that the next *Looney Tunes* TV show would bring back all the slapstick comedy *The Looney Tunes Show* left out.

Airing on Cartoon Network for a while and then exiled to Boomerang, it was called *Wabbit: A Looney Tunes Production*. The official description practically begged traditionalist fans to come back, while also reassuring nontraditionalists that it wouldn't be the same old thing:

> With *Wabbit—A Looney Tunes Production*, the hilarious, heroic and mischievous Bugs Bunny you love is back. The new 26-episode,

half-hour animated series from Warner Bros. Animation features
Bugs starring in all-new shorts that find the iconic carrot-loving
rabbit matching wits against—and getting the best of—classic
characters like Yosemite Sam and Wile E. Coyote. Along the way,
Bugs will encounter brand-new foes . . . and he'll have some help
from new friends like Bigfoot and Squeaks the Squirrel.[9]

Most of the *Looney Tunes Show* cast was sent packing, the format went
back to short five- or six-minute cartoons, and Bugs went back to putting
on disguises that actually work and playing mind games on characters
who deserve their comeuppance (in one short, he becomes an Apple
Store employee who installs an earthquake-level "vibrate" feature on
Yosemite Sam's phone). As the official description implies, most of the
characters were new: the concept this time was that Bugs would revert to
his old slapstick ways, but with unfamiliar characters, which would help
ward off accusations that they were simply rehashing the classics on a
lower budget.

This concept lasted about one season before being retooled yet
again. The focus on Bugs was dropped and characters like Daffy and
Tweety returned to the mix, along with some fairly obscure classic
characters such as Blacque Jacque Shellaque, the Canadian answer
to Yosemite Sam. It also acquired a new title, *New Looney Tunes*, and
began doing more premises that the old cartoons might have done if
they'd been produced many decades later, with titles like "Daffy Duck:
Motivational Guru" and a bunch of James Bond parodies with Elmer as
"Blofudd."

Another running theme was to put characters back to what they were
when they first appeared, before their characterizations and looks were
standardized. The George Costanza version of Daffy was retired, but

instead of the vainglorious egomaniac from "Duck Dodgers," he went all the way back to being the wild, bounding lunatic from "Porky's Duck Hunt" from 1937. In one of the more effective shorts from this run, Bugs does a modernized version of Daffy's classic "Duck Amuck" short, in which a sadistic off-screen animator keeps changing his reality. In this version, the traditional animation techniques are replaced by computer animation, and the animator turns out to be Daffy, as if to tell the audience that the decades of Bugs always besting Daffy are over.[10]

This version lasted two more seasons, during which it briefly received publicity for featuring Axl Rose as a special guest voice, in a story where a meteor is heading for Earth and Bugs prevails upon Axl to use the power of amplified rock 'n' roll singing to stop it. Then it was retired, and Warner Bros. announced a completely new retool: out with *New Looney Tunes*, and in with *Looney Tunes Cartoons*.

* * *

Looney Tunes Cartoons was announced in 2018, with Pete Browngardt, creator of Cartoon Network's *Uncle Grandpa*, in charge of the project. Warner Bros. didn't originally specify a format, but when the show premiered in 2020, it had settled on a series of eleven-minute episodes, incorporating two five- or six-minute cartoons, usually separated by some standalone gags with characters like the Road Runner.

To contrast with the more heavily scripted style of *The Bugs Bunny Show* or Steven Spielberg's *Animaniacs* (which was also revived in 2020), the company also announced that the cartoons would be "cartoonist-driven," each one written by a team that included the director and storyboard artist. The Canadian actor Eric Bauza, who voiced supporting characters on *The Looney Tunes Show* and *New Looney Tunes*, took over as Bugs, Daffy, and Tweety for this show, while Bob Bergen, who had been voicing Porky Pig in most *Looney Tunes* projects since "Duck Dodgers," returned for this show, making him one of the few actors who had convinced Warner Bros. that a Mel Blanc character was his and no other's.

The premiere of *Looney Tunes Cartoons* was part of the launch of the Warner Bros. streaming service HBO Max. This was one of many services that the big studios launched when they realized, possibly too late, that licensing their content to Netflix had allowed Netflix to turn into their biggest competitor. So AT&T, the new owner of Warner Bros., threw together an all-purpose content farm that included material from HBO, Warner Bros. TV and film, and pretty much every other franchise it owned. Needing new *Looney Tunes* content that would look good in a high-definition wide-screen format, Warner Bros. reversed the trend of declining budgets and declining expectations and put real money into *Looney Tunes Cartoons*, bringing back the kind of fluid animation that *Looney Tunes* slapstick seems to require, and bringing the designs back to something we could recognize from the original theatrical shorts.

HBO Max itself didn't do as well as the company had hoped, despite being launched during a pandemic when everyone was desperate for home entertainment. But the first batch of *Looney Tunes Cartoons* were among the most popular content on the service after it was launched, and it was surrounded by scores of classic shorts, many of them newly remastered for high definition (though the remastering wasn't always up to the best standards). The characters and their cartoons had a home again.

Every *Looney Tunes* reboot seems to start with a concept around the way the characters are designed, and the concept of *Looney Tunes Cartoons* is to get the characters back to an earlier time, before all the previous reboots. This is most obvious in design choices. Almost every character has a design element that makes it look like it did early in its career, even if the original creators dropped that element quickly. Elmer Fudd has a red nose, because he had one in "A Wild Hare" and a few other early appearances. Bugs Bunny's gloves were white in "A Wild Hare" and every cartoon thereafter, but the Bugs Bunny prototype had yellow gloves in one early cartoon, and that's the color of his gloves in this show. It's a way of signaling, almost subliminally, that there is something here that isn't exactly the same as the standardized Bugs and Elmer from most licensing and merchandising. It's a way of going back to basics without looking exactly the same. Daffy has the long beak and screwball attitude he had in the 1930s. One of the few characters who has not reverted in some way is Tweety, possibly because his cuteness makes him one of the most successful Warner Bros. characters in merchandising, and no one was about to change that by making him ugly and pink again.

The initial episodes leaned very heavily on three series, each with a somewhat consistent approach. The Bugs Bunny cartoons recall his 1940s prime, where he is mischievous and sometimes actively malicious, but doesn't usually act unprovoked. Elmer is his most frequent antagonist, but others appear now and then, including Cecil Turtle, the only classic character who consistently beat Bugs. The Tweety and Sylvester cartoons recall the Friz Freleng cartoons of the 1950s, with Tweety more unironically innocent than he was in the Clampett days, and Sylvester often getting hurt by others while Tweety watches. Daffy and Porky are almost always paired together in an odd-couple format, with Porky as the straight man and Daffy as his screwball friend who is constantly getting him into trouble.

When *Looney Tunes Cartoons* appeared, it wound up getting quite a bit of unwanted publicity over the news that Elmer Fudd and Yosemite Sam would not be allowed to threaten Bugs with guns. This wasn't a surprising or particularly new choice. Companies are always worried that a child might imitate something they see in one of their products, and in a country with as many guns in it as the United States, it's not considered a good idea to give kids the idea to try out Dad's pistol or shotgun.

A marketing mistake, perhaps, was that one of the preview clips released in advance of HBO Max's launch was a short musical cartoon called "Dynamite Dance," where Elmer keeps getting blown up while chasing Bugs to the tune of Ponchielli's "Dance of the Hours." It's a normal *Looney Tunes* setting except that Elmer is chasing Bugs with a huge scythe, like the Grim Reaper. This immediately called attention to the fact that Elmer *ought* to be using a shotgun, and that someone wouldn't let him do it. Just as it's sometimes better to avoid a swear word altogether instead of finding a euphemism that can pass the censors, the creators might have avoided negative attention if they'd just allowed Elmer to use improvised weapons, or no weapons at all. Anything but a scythe.

It's unfortunate that weapons got so much of the publicity because "Dynamite Dance" is one of the few shorts that actually suffers for lack of guns. Most of the shorts know enough not to call attention to it, and one of the few that does makes a good joke out of it: Elmer tells us that he no longer hunts with guns, he's switched to "more humane methods" like dynamite. When a cartoon has a problem, it's usually from *too much* violence; the gags that don't work are often the ones that make the characters look like they're in pain, or inflict damage on them that goes into the territory of body horror, like having Daffy crack Porky open like a piggy bank, or letting bugs knead Elmer's head like dough and turn it into a pizza.

Nevertheless, *Looney Tunes Cartoons* is made with care and after serious thought about how to do old-school *Looney Tunes*. They are full of devices that are familiar to any *Looney Tunes* buff. The characters always deliver exposition out loud, half to themselves and half to the audience; with even shorter running times than the originals, there's no time to waste on setting anything up. Stupidity is symbolized with a dunce cap, Bugs literally fastens his mouth with a zipper when told to "zip it," Elmer is forever calling Bugs "Mr. Wabbit" because it would just sound wrong for the characters to act like they know each other, and the closing theme of the show is "What's Up, Doc?" composed by Carl Stalling as Bugs Bunny's theme. The premises rarely attempt to be up-to-date, as previous revivals did, but lean heavily on setups like Bugs burrowing to a distant location. And the premises sometimes mix and match bits of classic setups, like a cartoon where Porky is terrorized by a computerized house (recalling a number of old cartoons about "houses of the future") and goes through a scene of mechanized torture that's a shout-out to Bob Clampett's conveyor-belt-of-doom cartoon "Baby Bottleneck."

While some gags and stories are shout-outs to individual cartoons, many others are *stylistic* shout-outs, an attempt to recapture the spirit of the way cartoons did things. Background elements and props from old cartoons pop up, classic animators' styles are reflected in some of the poses, and not always where you'd expect. In a scene from a Bugs Bunny/ Yosemite Sam cartoon, Sam meets a woman pushing a baby stroller, and the woman is not only designed in the style of Chuck Jones, but the framing pays homage to a particular type of profile shot that Jones constantly used with human characters. Jones never made a Yosemite Sam cartoon, so this isn't a reference specific to the story. It's there because for a hard-core fan, this is a fun thing to spot and for the average viewer, it's an almost subliminal connection to the homey world of classic *Looney Tunes*.

Watching *Looney Tunes Cartoons*, then, is like getting together with a friend to share a mutual love of the *Looney Tunes* characters and the way the original creators used them. The most effective bits almost feel like a dialogue between the classic cartoons and modern creators, trying to figure out how they can put their own spin on gag structures we're all familiar with. In one cartoon, when Elmer sends a robot after Bugs (a buff would recognize, but not mind, that he sent a robot after Bugs in 1953), Bugs becomes distraught that nothing he tries seems to work on his new antagonist, and he has a crisis of confidence in the middle of the cartoon, poring over the pages of a book ("I wrote it") looking for a gag he hasn't tried before, before finally, in desperation, settling on the oldest, corniest gag of telling the villain that his shoelaces are untied and, of course, it works.

The meta-humor, the acknowledgment that Bugs has a past and that he might actually have a memory of what he's done before, is something the classics usually avoided, but it doesn't violate their spirit. And watching Bugs lose his cool is something that happened just often enough in the classics to be recognizably in character for him, while still being rare enough that it hasn't been done to death. *Looney Tunes Cartoons*, at its best, manages to find that sweet spot where they're not rehashing things that worked before, while not doing things the classics would never have done.

The big question that will remain unanswered long after this book appears is whether *Looney Tunes Cartoons* will turn out to be a long-term approach, or just another retool in an endless series of retools. What we can see in the history of *Looney Tunes* in this century is that there is something worse than a bad series, i.e., an inability to commit to an approach. Every failure has been followed by a complete change of course: new designs, characterizations, and target audiences come and go, and we rarely get to see how an approach could be refined and eventually evolve into something really new.

If there's one thing the classics teach us, it's that a style doesn't arrive fully formed overnight, or even in a year. It took the original studio a decade to find the star who would turn them into the top cartoon studio in Hollywood. And if it took ten years to find Bugs Bunny, it may take longer than one or two development cycles to make him a superstar again.

Racketeer Rabbit
(Anatomy of a Cartoon)

A *LOONEY TUNES* OR *Merrie Melodies* cartoon begins before it begins, and it ends after it ends. Other cartoons from other studios just began with the studio logo and then moved on to the credits of the particular short. But the first thing we see in "Racketeer Rabbit," a *Looney Tunes* cartoon released in September 1946, is an opening that flaunts the power of animation, perspective, and sound to give new life to a familiar logo.

We see the copyright information and production number for a cartoon whose title we don't even know yet, displayed against a background of concentric circles, using two basic colors (blue and red) painted to contrast lighter and darker shades as though the rings were real and someone was shining lights on them. Then the Warner Bros. shield logo emerges from the center ring, animated to look as if it's actually moving toward us from a great distance. And we hear the twang of an electric guitar, demonstrating the strange power of sound to suggest a physical action— we know it is music, but we feel that this is the sound a studio logo makes when it pops toward us. This leads into the *Looney Tunes* theme, "The Merry-Go-Round Broke Down" (here in a new arrangement that had only been introduced a few months earlier).

Because Bugs Bunny was the studio's special star, he gets a special opening. Like most Bugs cartoons from the 1940s, this one has Bugs lying on top of the shield as it appears, eating a carrot and seemingly having a fine time until he makes eye contact with us. Annoyed at being interrupted, he reaches up and pulls down a screen by a handle that appears out of nowhere. It says: "LOONEY TUNES—A WARNER BROS. CARTOON—IN TECHNICOLOR." Then, when "The Merry-Go-Round Broke Down" is finished playing, he pulls the screen back up again, revealing himself lying on top of a big "BUGS BUNNY" sign, the cartoon equivalent of a live-action movie star getting his or her name above the title. And then, only then, do we dissolve to the actual title and credits. The *Looney Tunes* title sequence is its own little animated story.

This chapter is about a lot of seemingly little things that add up to a great *Looney Tunes* cartoon, the things we may not think we notice, and yet we can somehow sense—the things a lot of professionals had to dwell upon to make a cartoon that was funnier than the usual Hollywood cartoon.

I've chosen the 1946 *Looney Tunes* Bugs Bunny cartoon "Racketeer Rabbit," directed by Friz Freleng because it's one of the best Bugs Bunny cartoons, even by the high standard of the Bugs cartoons Freleng was making in this period (including the first appearance of Yosemite Sam and the classical music cartoon "Rhapsody Rabbit" that impressed James Agee). I chose it because it was a childhood favorite, one of the cartoons I was always happy to see pop up in the pre-1948 packages. And I chose it because it has a caricature of Edward G. Robinson, and Edward G. Robinson always makes everything better, particularly when he's accompanied by a caricature of Peter Lorre.

Let's start with a quick summary of the plot, the clothesline on which the gags are hung. "Racketeer Rabbit" is a fairly long cartoon, almost eight minutes, and it has a bit more plot than usual, even leaving an important plot point off-screen to save time. Still, the story is simple. On a rainy night, Bugs Bunny takes shelter in a spooky abandoned house. While he's sleeping, two gangsters fleeing the scene of a robbery take refuge in the house: Rocky, the Edward G. Robinson lookalike, and diminutive Hugo, the stand-in for Lorre. After driving away a rival gang, the crooks begin to divide up their cash, but Bugs happens upon them and immediately tricks them into giving him most of the money. Rocky stops Bugs from leaving, but Bugs has already hidden the loot and won't tell them where it is.

Rocky orders Hugo to take Bugs for a ride, but in the next scene, Bugs is back in the house, saying only that he "got rid of" Hugo. How he did this is left up to our imagination, but there is no real need to go to the time and expense of showing it: he's Bugs Bunny and this is his sixth year of cartoon stardom—we know he's going to win.

Now that there are only two characters left, Rocky gives Bugs until the count of ten "to give me the dough," and you can pretty much guess what Bugs is going to do here, too. He returns with a literal bowl of dough, looks at us and wiggles his eyebrows, and then looks at us again before shoving it in Rocky's face, as if to say that he knows we can predict the next payoff, and the predictability is what makes it funny.

Bugs then disguises himself as Mugsy, a rival gangster whose name and appearance are apparently bad news to Rocky. Bugs says, "It's curtains for you, Rocky, curtains!" Theoretically, we should be getting tired of literal takes on gangster slang expressions, but in practice, seeing Bugs stick a set of curtains onto Rocky's head ("Aw, they're adorable") gets the biggest laugh yet.

The final gag sequence is the longest. Bugs pretends to be a cop, knocking on the door and calling for Rocky to come out, then running back to Rocky, who begs Bugs to hide him. (Bugs turns to the audience and calls attention to Rocky's gullibility: "Isn't he a trusting soul?") Then Bugs has fun stuffing Rocky into various uncomfortable hiding places, finally settling on a trunk. Rocky listens as Bugs argues with the "cop," which is Bugs using another voice. Bugs sticks swords into the trunk to prove to the nonexistent cop that Rocky couldn't be in there, leading to that all-time champion Mike Maltese line, a classic of highfalutin language inserted where it doesn't belong: "Would I also have the temerity to do this if my bosom chum was encased therein?"

What makes the whole sequence is that every time Bugs changes from his own voice to the cop voice, he also changes clothes, from regular Bugs to a bowler hat, sheriff's star, and cheap cigar, and back again to Bugs. At no point is this necessary, since Rocky can't see him, but something in Bugs demands he wear a disguise even when no one can see it but him. When he fakes a fight between himself and the cop, we see him punch himself.

After this scene, Rocky runs off into the distance, shouting for the police to come and take him to prison: "Don't leave me with that crazy rabbit! Help! Police!"

Bugs does a quick Edward G. Robinson impression, and we iris out: rabbit triumphant, crime doesn't pay.

* * *

Now let's look at how this plot gets turned into an animated sound cartoon, starting with the first thing that was created specifically for this particular cartoon: the credits.

They actually take up less screen time than that elaborate stock opening, and they are as simple as they need to be to set up a cartoon in only fifteen seconds. They use the format that was standard for most cartoons from 1945 on, just three cards.

First, the title card, over an image that suggests an association with the subject matter of the cartoon: here's it's a smoking tommy gun, the weapon of choice in Warner Bros. gangster movies for two decades running. This is accompanied by Carl Stalling's main title music. It opens with some ominous chords to set the tone, then switches to quoting a song called "Jimmy Valentine" ("A sentimental crook with a touch that lingers / In his sandpaper fingers"), written in 1910 by a composer who had died not long before the cartoon came out. But if we recognize the song and its connection to the subject of crime, great; if we don't, well, it's a catchy tune.

The second card is the most crowded, a quick list of people whose jobs are deemed important enough to get credit:

Story: Michael Maltese. The writer was always credited with "story," although this doesn't mean what it would in a live-action film. A storyboard consisted of both the scenario and the dialogue, and the writer was responsible for both. And while cartoon writers needed to be able to draw a storyboard, they were still writers, who specialized in that craft as much as any live-action writer.

Animation: Virgil Ross, Gerry Chiniquy, Ken Champin, Manuel Perez. These four were longtime regulars in Freleng's unit, with Ross and Chiniquy sticking with him to the end of the studio and beyond. Animators were usually allowed some freedom in how to draw a character. So when Virgil Ross animates Bugs, most prominently in the scenes before and after the mysterious "ride" with Hugo, Bugs looks cuter and even smaller than he does with other animators. Ross's animation is very fluid, with gradual and visible transitions from one key pose to the next, while Chiniquy was the exact opposite, preferring rhythm over fluidity.

Layout: Hawley Pratt. Pratt was even more indispensable to Freleng, working with him practically to the end of his life, and sometimes filling in for him as director. The layout man's job is difficult to describe, in part because each director used his layout man a little differently, but the basic responsibility is that of production designer, laying out how a shot should look, what the backgrounds should be, and where the characters should stand in relation to the backgrounds. Pratt also did much of the character design work. Freleng didn't consider himself much of a draughtsman, so he would create character poses and sample drawings and give them to Pratt, who would refine them into the final reference drawings from which animators worked.

Background: Paul Julian. Cartoons used painted backgrounds, and Julian, Freleng's main background painter from the mid-1940s through 1951, was a serious painter in various modernist styles, who had several well-reviewed exhibitions of his paintings in the Los Angeles area while he worked in cartoons to support himself. (He also provided the "meep meep" sound for the Road Runner, which he thought should be spelled "hmeep hmeep.") He was reportedly not very happy with the art styles and colors that Freleng preferred,[1] but he was a professional, and his backgrounds gave some beauty and class to every cartoon he worked on.

The background painter's job also varied from unit to unit depending on how much influence the layout man had on the design style. Some layout artists, like Maurice Noble, would provide the background artist with sketches that were indistinguishable from the final painted version: Noble was the production designer, and the background man would build what he designed. Pratt seemed to give background people more leeway, and Julian's paintings have a very recognizable style, plus their own trademark running gag of placing Freleng's nickname "Friz" anywhere they could get away with it; here two cars drive by a billboard advertising the "HOTEL FRIZ."

Voice Characterization: Mel Blanc. Blanc's credit was unique in the animation world at the time. He was the first actor to get on-screen credit for doing voices in short cartoons. In addition to Bugs, Blanc performs the Peter Lorre voice, but the Edward G. Robinson impression is done by an actor named Dick Nelson. It's sometimes wrongly assumed that Blanc's contract prevented other actors from getting credited, but other voice actors at Warner Bros. didn't get credit because *no one* got credit at any studio, only Blanc. Originally, he was credited only for Bugs Bunny cartoons, and later for any cartoon he worked on. It was a tribute to how important he had become to Warner Bros. Other voice actors were important for individual voices: no one at Disney could do the voice of Goofy properly except the original, Pinto Colvig, so when he was away from Disney for a few years, they mostly stopped giving Goofy lines. But nearly every important *Looney Tunes* character except Elmer Fudd was dependent on Blanc, and his on-screen credit meant that if he ever left, people would notice it with their eyes and not just their ears.

Freleng, as we've seen before, grumbled about Blanc being so much more famous than the people who told him what to say, but even without creative involvement, he shaped almost all the studio's cartoons, even the few in which he didn't participate. Before Blanc, most cartoon voices were done by anyone available, or someone from around the studio (like Walt Disney, who did the voice of Mickey for many years). With Blanc as the primary voice artist, the studio had someone who could give extra dimensions to characters before the animation even started; this encouraged the animation crew to match the energy of Blanc's line readings.

Musical Direction: Carl Stalling. Stalling was usually credited for musical direction, although the credit changed to just "music" in the late 1950s. Both Stalling and Blanc were billed together at the bottom of the screen, and usually (although not yet in this cartoon) with their names a little bigger than the others on the card, thanks to their stronger unions.

The Uncredited: A lot of names were left off the card. Selzer never took on-screen credit as producer. Treg Brown, the sound effects genius and general sound designer of the cartoons, didn't get a credit until about ten years after this, and even then, it was for film editing, which does seem to have been part of his job although not the biggest part (since the directors tried to produce as little unused footage as possible). Special effects, like explosions, rain, bullets, and falling anvils, were the purview of an effects animator, who would only get credit if there was an exceptional amount of work in a particular film. Stalling's music was orchestrated for most of his career by Milt Franklyn, who eventually took over some of his composing work and succeeded him after he retired. Franklyn would usually only get credit on cartoons not featuring Blanc, when there was an extra bit of space on the card.

Director: Finally the director's name appears alone on a third card. Freleng was credited as "I. Freleng" for many years. He didn't like the name Isadore, and the studio wouldn't let him be billed as Friz, so he just went with his first initial.

The title sequence fades to black, and before we see or hear anything else, we hear Treg Brown. He creates the sound of rain, and then the cartoon proper fades in, and we actually see the rain.

Now comes the setup.

* * *

Most cartoons follow, to the extent possible in a different medium, live-action film grammar, such as the idea of starting from a distance and moving in closer. So here we fade in on an establishing shot of the abandoned, boarded-up house where almost all the action will take place, with the effects animator layering in some rain to let us know that this is the proverbial dark and stormy night. We dissolve to the interior of the house, with the camera panning quickly across the background, showing us the kind of a house it is: full of cracks, things hanging at wrong angles, unlit areas. The camera completes its pan and starts moving in on the door. Now the camera has shown all it can of the static background, and we dissolve into a closer shot of the door. This is a fully animated shot, with the door now separate from the background. It is, if you will, alive.

The door opens with a heavy Treg Brown creaking noise, and we see the top of Bugs Bunny peek out from behind the door, carrying a bindle over his shoulder and looking around the joint. He observes that the creaky door "sounds like *Inner Sanctum*," the now-forgotten radio horror/humor show whose episodes opened and closed with a similar effect. The place is creepy and scary, sure, but that isn't a problem for Bugs, whose second line is: "Not a bad place to spend the night."

A few seconds and two lines of dialogue in, and we know that Bugs has been driven indoors by the rain, and is going to sleep in an old dark house that doesn't frighten him the way it would frighten the average movie comedy character. Freleng and Maltese have been at this a long time, and they know how to keep the exposition to a minimum of words and images. The hobo bindle is all we need to know that this is a character on the road.

But there's something off about the premise. We know *why* Bugs is spending the night in the house, but it still doesn't seem right for him to be in a cartoon without a rabbit hole to climb out of. So the first thing Maltese and Freleng have him do inside the house is pull a huge hand drill out of his bindle and drill a hole in the floor. He then puts on a sleeping cap, takes out a candle, and descends a set of nonexistent stairs into the hole. The trick of a good formula cartoon is catering to the formula in a nonformulaic way. It was already old and boring to have Bugs in a rabbit hole in the forest, but he needs to be a forest creature out of his element in a house, and he needs to live in a hole, even when, or *especially* when, it makes no sense for him to do so.

For a capper, Bugs hangs a "Do Not Disturb" sign on a doorknob that isn't attached to a door. Maltese loved jokes about characters acting as if they're in a house or a hotel, keeping up the formalities and signifiers of those places even when they're in the middle of nowhere.

The actual plot of the cartoon begins a few seconds later, as two gangsters run into the house and start shooting at the cops who have followed them. While the shootout is going on, we get an example of the extra, humanizing details Friz Freleng was particularly good at. Tiny Hugo tries to shoot a tommy gun and finds himself pushed backward by the force of the recoil. Rocky pushes Hugo back to where he was standing, the gun firing off endless rounds all the while, and while he's pushing, Hugo's hat falls off and Rocky puts it back on his head. Freleng liked to have characters do something mundane in the middle of a gag, like dropping something and picking it up, just to show the characters can do things not completely dependent on gags and payoffs.

Freleng also would move the final payoff of a gag to somewhere we wouldn't expect. A few seconds after the hat scene, as Bugs wanders sleepily through the gunfire ("Low bridge!" he says, ducking under the bullets), we see that Rocky has used a board and nails to affix Hugo to the floor while he shoots. It's as if the film has so many gags that it can afford to put a few in the background.

A word about those backgrounds. They are a huge part of the impact of a cartoon, because they create not only the setting, but also the lighting. It's not easy to light an animated character in motion, since the light has to change wherever they move. Bugs and the rest of the bunch would not really be lit that way until their expensive cameos in *Who Framed Roger Rabbit*. So the backgrounds here are painted with a lot of black, a lot of dark colors, a lot of shadows around the edges of the screen, so that we get the feeling of a moodily lit room, without lighting the characters that way.

In Julian's serious work, he showed the influences you would expect from a serious painter of the era, including Surrealism, Cubism, and Abstract Expressionism. And when he left Freleng's unit in the early 1950s and moved to UPA, he was able to experiment with more radical ideas about design and color. But you weren't going to see that in the average Warner Bros. cartoon from the 1940s. Most backgrounds were realistic in appearance, soft in texture, and moderate in their color choices. They hardly ever try to be funny in and of themselves: no matter how goofy the characters look, the paintings always look beautiful. They are like the realistic sets in the classic productions of Gilbert and Sullivan operas:

nothing funny about the setting; rather, it is funny to see comic-opera hijinks and low comedy in front of a background that seems to demand something serious.

There are other, subtler visual choices shared between the director, the layout man, and the background artist. Like the background when the director cuts in for a medium close-up. Freleng didn't use a lot of close-ups, but at one point he needs to give us a really good look at Hugo's creepy Peter Lorre face and his creepy attempts to sound jovial ("They make me laugh . . . UHHH-HAAUH!"). The background for this shot is lighter and brighter than the film noir lighting of the long shot, and it's also mostly blank, to save on the money and time of creating an entirely new background for this one brief shot. But Julian or Pratt or Freleng, or all of them together, makes the choice to put a shadow at the left of the frame. It's not shaped like anything in particular, because that would draw attention from Hugo. Its purpose is to make the character look as though he's part of the same "world" as the main background, not a guy talking in front of nothing. In Freleng's later cartoons, working with background men other than Julian, close shots sometimes look like they're in a different place entirely, which is the difference between having one of the best background artists and one who is merely good.

One of the best bits in Bugs's entire film career comes right after he meets the gangsters. Like many of Maltese's Bugs Bunny gags, it's based on Bugs exploiting a pattern that his opponent will follow without thinking. While splitting up the stolen money, Rocky absentmindedly hands some to Bugs. Bugs then poses as six different gangsters ("How 'bout me, boss? . . . And me, boss?") and Rocky hands money to each of them, until Bugs has all the cash and Rocky realizes he's been conned.

The gag is based on the speed with which Bugs notices the pattern and takes advantage of it, and the speed with which he changes from one persona to another: five gangsters, each distinguished by a different voice and a different hat, and finally, for absolutely no reason except that the gag needs a "capper," in a war bonnet. And you can't say enough good things about Mel Blanc, who does six different voices ranging from a guttural gangster growl to a high falsetto yet somehow all Bugs. One of the voices is a weird, nasal, strangulated thing that Blanc would eventually give to a regular character, Marvin the Martian.

Almost all that scene is in one long shot with no camera movement, a shot back far enough to show the entire round table, Hugo at the left, Rocky at the right, and Bugs popping up on all sides of the table. The only cut occurs when Bugs enters: the closer shot allows Freleng to show us that Bugs is tired and still half asleep (until he gets the money, and instantly wakes up); it also allows him to simply rise up from the bottom of the frame, without needing to show us where he is coming from or how long he's been in the room.

Warner Bros. cartoons usually had a lot of long, static shots. Going back to the silent era, there was a theory that comedy plays better in long shots than close-ups, and creating the effects of camera movement can be difficult in animation: the shot can pan from side to side, and zoom in slightly, but to actually track characters the way live-action movies do, you would have to animate not only the changing perspective on the character, but also the entire background. So you almost never see that kind of movement in *Looney Tunes*. The basic unit of a cartoon is the static tableau, where we watch the characters as if they were on a stage, our eyes following them as they move around the set.

To convey the feeling of Bugs dropping down at one area of the table and popping up at another, animator Ken Champin[2] uses smear lines: very briefly, for a couple of frames, we see lines that are not physically part of the scene. These lines are used as a compression device. Instead of making a smooth, animated transition between poses, which would eat up precious frames and waste time, we just see one drawing of Bugs changing positions, and the smears do the rest of the work in convincing us that we saw him move.

This scene doesn't really involve Hugo, but he's in the shot, so Freleng just has him turn his head toward Bugs each time he pops up. It adds to the effectiveness of the scene that Hugo's and Rocky's reactions are mild throughout. Hugo looks surprised at what Bugs is doing, but it's a look of dull surprise, like there's something strange going on here but he doesn't know what.

When Rocky realizes the money is gone, there's no bug-eyed take or over-the-top shouting, he just looks at his empty hands and his eyes widen a bit. That's it. We think of slapstick cartoons as being hammy, and they certainly don't mind us thinking of them that way, but the directors also knew that overacting could kill a joke, and that characters should never have to sell us on a gag. The bad guys are kept on a leash in this scene, letting Bugs be the ham actor in the shot. Without a certain amount of restraint, a cartoon seems desperate to please us. A common mistake of *Looney Tunes* imitators is to think that louder, faster, and hammier is always better, when even the craziest classic shorts, if you look at them closely, are often visibly holding back and showing us that there are things they *won't* do for a laugh.

The same applies to sound effects. Treg Brown turns them off. Where you might expect lots of wacky sound effects and slide whistles and such, there's nothing; it wouldn't make the scene funnier. And the same applies to the music. Carl Stalling is famous for mimicking every action, but here he shows that he knows when the music should *not* mimic the characters' actions too closely: if we heard a big, loud musical sting every time Bugs moves from one end of the table to the other, it would distract us from the gag, so the score just gives us a puckish little woodwind motif to play under the action, and saves the traditional action cue for when Bugs finally leaps off the table and walks off counting his dough.

Also, at the end of this scene, Rocky winds up pulling a trick normally associated with Bugs. We see Bugs leave the room with the money, and immediately walk back into the room, with Rocky holding a pistol behind him. Bugs's obvious superiority to everyone he goes up against should make him seem like a bully, even against gangsters. One reason he doesn't is that his cartoons often slip in gags like this, where we see that his enemies also have access to the same cartoon "powers" he does, like the ability to be in two places at once. That Bugs is capable of being taken by surprise and having his own tactics turned against him tells us the villain *could* beat Bugs if he would only think straight for a time. Bugs doesn't have superior power, just superior intelligence.

That's a lot of information to pack into a gag that lasts a few seconds, but everything in a short cartoon has to be as compressed as possible, conveying information in an instant. This includes clothes. Bugs doesn't wear them as a rule, but he constantly uses them in disguise, and we have to instantly know what he is supposed to be. So when Rocky opens the door and finds Bugs disguised as the fearsome Mugsy, the costume is loaded up with items that convey that he's a gangster, and a nasty one: a bowler hat tilted over one eye, a carnation in his lapel, a cigarette dangling from his mouth, and a coin in his hand that he keeps flipping. This last bit is a reference to George Raft in the movie *Scarface*, whose character had the coin-flipping tic.

Bugs's outfit, along with the reference to a fourteen-year-old movie, is meant to suggest a gangster of an earlier period, or at least remind the audience of what gangsters looked like in the movies when they were kids. *Looney Tunes* celebrity references were usually up-to-date, but costuming was often out of date. Sometimes this is done because it's funny to see characters wearing old-fashioned clothes. When Bugs is trying to get some sleep, he's wearing a full-body bedtime costume and a cap, like he stepped out of a stage production of *A Christmas Carol*, accompanied by a candle. When he goes out driving with Hugo, he changes into an old-timey turn-of-the-century costume that people used to wear when automobile trips were dustier and dirtier. And his idea of how a cop is supposed to dress involves enormous boots like a Keystone Kop from the silent movie days.

But even when characters aren't dressed for laughs, they're old-fashioned in their fashions. Apart from the cigar that never leaves the corner of his mouth (even when he's in bed, or locked in a trunk, or blown up by a bomb), Rocky's buttoned-up double-breasted blue suit, his bow tie, and especially his spats make him look like an old movie's idea of a gangster, a figure from the Prohibition era. The spats were such a gangster cliché that the chief villain of the movie *Some Like It Hot* is actually nicknamed "Spats," so there seems to be a link in the public mind between what a man wears on his feet and how he makes his living.

One general difference between the pre-1948 TV package, which this cartoon belonged to, and the post-1948 package, is that the pre-1948s were heavier on topical references, especially to celebrities and show business. Bugs's first line in the picture is a joke about a popular radio show, and his last line is an Edward G. Robinson impression. Robinson was a frequent choice of directors looking for a celebrity to parody, since he was a Warner Bros. contract star, and his appearance and voice were instantly recognizable. Chuck Jones's unit also released a cartoon in 1946 where the antagonist was Edward G. Robinson, although in the form of a cat (rather unimaginatively named "Edward G. Robincat"). But the celebrity cameo was a go-to gag everywhere, and most years there would be at least one cartoon that had a bunch of them: 1946 gave us Bob Clampett's "Book

Revue," written by Warren Foster, with Benny Goodman, Frank Sinatra, Danny Kaye, and anyone else Foster could think of to connect with the title of a book, and Bob McKimson's "Hollywood Canine Canteen," also written by Foster, a series of gags about dogs who resemble famous movie stars, where the first dog we see is a parody of, yes, Edward G. Robinson.

Toward the end of the 1940s, this kind of thing became rarer, and in the early 1950s, it was all but extinct. The next time Freleng did a cartoon with a major part for gangsters (1950's "Golden Yeggs"), he kept the name Rocky but abandoned the Edward G. Robinson caricature: the new Rocky, who Freleng would use many times, is a tiny guy with a huge hat that covers his eyes. Later on there would be a few references to popular TV shows, especially *The Honeymooners*, but on the whole there were fewer recognizable people in the post-1948s.

It's hard to say why the celebrity parody passed out of fashion. It may be that Warner Bros. had a large backlog of cartoons and worried that celebrity caricatures or topical references might lose their currency by the time they made it to theaters. Warner Bros. also had a reissue program that increased the possibility that cartoons would be playing for an audience that hadn't heard of what was being referenced. The second Rocky's design is supposed to be inherently funny, rather than getting laughs through his resemblance to an actor. Theoretically, this gives the film more of a shelf life.

I say "theoretically" because one of the odd things about dated references in *Looney Tunes* is that they never seemed to top the cartoons' popularity or longevity. From many people who grew up with the cartoons on TV, you'll hear a variation of this: "When I was a kid, I didn't know who Edward G. Robinson or Humphrey Bogart were, I only knew them as the tough guys from Bugs Bunny cartoons, but I laughed anyway." If the adults who made and programmed the cartoons dropped the references out of concern that they would become dated and spoil the experience for kids, they forgot that children are used to not understanding everything they see and hear; almost anything kids watch is going to contain something incomprehensible to them. They roll with it.

* * *

Basic storytelling demands that the hero must confront the villain directly, but not in "Racketeer Rabbit." The final scene of "Racketeer Rabbit" is Rocky hiding in a trunk listening to a confrontation between Bugs and Bugs's imaginary cop. Bugs uses the confrontation as an excuse to torture Rocky, but Rocky's defeat has nothing to do with any of that: before his final fight (with his cop self) Bugs quickly opens the trunk and hands Rocky a big cartoony bomb, which explodes just after Bugs is done beating himself up. What does that have to do with the premise of the scene? Nothing, it's just a bomb.

All this shows how useless conventional storytelling theory is when confronted with the inexplicable logic of a great *Looney Tunes* cartoon. The scene works. It works on the level of music, not words. Bugs's cop act, with the completely pointless costume changes, is the biggest, most ridiculous con he's pulled on Rocky. In musical terms, it's the grand climax. Nothing can follow it, and the bomb is an acknowledgment of this, a way of wrapping things up as fast as possible and making Rocky run away to turn himself over to the cops. It's the quick coda that follows the grand climax. We don't need to see a grand confrontation between Bugs and Rocky because that's not what the story is about, it's about seeing how many gags the creators can spin out of the theme of crime and gangsters. Almost nothing else needs to be done after the magnificent trunk scene. Just move on to the final shot and iris out.

The final shot of a cartoon usually has the star of the cartoon, or one of the stars, if there are two, alone in the frame. It's often a place where the star can talk directly to us, looking slightly down (remember, the director expects the audience to be in a theater looking up) and delivering a quick one-liner. The writers rarely wasted their best one-liners on these moments, since the point is not to get the biggest laugh—we're already laughed out, if the cartoon was any good—but to put a button on it. So Bugs looks at us and imitates Edward G. Robinson's vocal tics ("Some guys just can't take it, see? Nyeah!") and twists his face into a Robinson caricature, with the prominent lips and the exaggerated squint.

That's the cue for the two things that usually end a *Looney Tunes* cartoon: the iris out, and Carl Stalling's musical sting. Even though most live-action movies ended in a fade-out, the standard ending for most short cartoons was an iris out, where the screen blacks out at the edges and moves toward the center, closing in on the main character's face. Whether intentionally or not, it suggests the kinship of animated comedy with the silent era, when this device was common in live-action film.

Stalling also liked to end a cartoon score by playing a cadence to signal that it was over. It's usually four loud notes in the same basic rhythm with a lot of orchestral volume. *Looney Tunes* viewers grow to recognize this particular cadence, so that even with our eyes closed we would know it's over.

But as I said at the start, it's not *completely* over.

"That's all Folks!" is written out on the screen.

"The Merry-Go-Round Broke Down" is played on the soundtrack. *Now* it's over.

Acknowledgments

"JUST WORK ON THE damn *Looney Tunes* book with me," Ken Whyte said. I had written a proposal for what eventually became this book, but I didn't have the confidence to try writing it. Ken, who first hired me at *Maclean's* magazine, had faith in my ability to deliver, and wouldn't let me get away with procrastinating. Those are the two things every writer needs from an editor.

Thad Komorowski, author of *Sick Little Monkeys: The Unauthorized Ren & Stimpy Story*, was the first person to read a draft of this book and offer notes on how to improve it. Greg Ford was generous with his time and in helping me to see what I needed to add or cut. Mark Mayerson, whose blog posts made it possible for me to write the "Timing" chapter, provided additional notes and comments on the entire manuscript.

Michael Barrier's interviews have helped preserve the stories of many Warner Bros. creators in their own words, and his books have made the classic era of Hollywood animation come alive for me and many others; he was also generously willing to answer some questions from me. Christopher P. Lehman's book *The Colored Cartoon: Black Representation in American Animated Short Films, 1907–1954*, was an essential resource, particularly for chapter 11, and he was kind enough to suggest additional reading, including Donald Crofton's *Before Mickey: The Animated Film 1898–1928*, Henry T. Sampson's *That's Enough Folks: Black Images in Animated Cartoons, 1900–1960*, and Nicholas Sammond's *Birth of an Industry: Blackface Minstrelsy and the Rise of American Animation*.

Others whose research and writing inform this book include Devon Baxter, Jerry Beck and everyone at *Cartoon Research*, Amid Amidi and *Cartoon Brew*, Jenny Lerew of *The Blackwing Diaries*, Jon Cooke, Kevin McCorry, Don M. Yowp of *Tralfaz*, Mark Kausler, Jim Korkis, Keith Scott, Vincent Alexander, Bob Jaques, Terry Teachout, and in general, the online community of classic animation experts. Dwight Macdonald once said that the "amateur scholar—'just a hobby, really'—is a species little known over here," but this book could not have been written without the people who made *Looney Tunes* scholarship available to anyone who cared to click on a link.

Unlike Huckleberry Finn, I knew in advance how hard it was to make a book, because I'd watched my brilliant sister, Sarah Weinman, go through the experience of publishing her first book and working on her second. Her faith in my work, along with her own superb writing and research, gives me something to live up to.

Finally, I could not have gotten to this point without the faith and good humor of my mother, Judith Weinman, to whom this book is dedicated, and my late father, Jack Weinman.

Notes

CHAPTER 1

1 Rob Long: Conversations with My Agent (London: Faber and Faber, 1996), 31.
2 "Warner's To Lease 110 Films," The Atlanta Constitution, July 13, 1960, https://www.newspapers.com/image/397770597/.
3 Chuck Jones, Chuck Amuck: The Life and Times of an Animated Cartoonist (New York: Avon, 1989), 88.
4 Kathryn Harris, "Warner's Million-Dollar Rabbit : TV's Classic Cartoons Earn Top Ratings, Huge Profits for 32 Years," Los Angeles Times, September 25, 1992, https://www.latimes.com/archives/la-xpm-1992-09-25-fi-942-story.html
5 Manny Farber, "Short and Happy," New Republic, September 20, 1943, p. 394.
6 Jim Korkis, "In His Own Words: Bill Scott at UPA," Cartoon Research, December 9, 2013, https://cartoonresearch.com/index.php/in-his-own-words-bill-scott-at-upa/.
7 Wade Sampson, "Chuck Jones: Four Months at Disney," Mouse Planet, September 2, 2009, https://www.mouseplanet.com/8944/Chuck_Jones__Four_Months_At_Disney.
8 Albert Burneko, "Of Course Osama Bin Laden Loved 'Tom and Jerry.' Of Course," Huffington Post, November 2, 2017, https://www.huffpost.com/entry/bin-laden-tom-jerry_n_59fb56b2e4b01b474048fef9.

CHAPTER 2

1 "Pacific Title and Art Studio," Art of the Title, https://www.artofthetitle.com/studio/pacific-title-and-art-studio/.
2 "Lloyd Turner: An Interview by Michael Barrier," last modified February 6, 2008, www.michaelbarrier.com/Interviews/Turner/interview_lloyd_turner.htm.
3 Scott Eyman, John Wayne - The Life and Legend (New York: Simon & Schuster, 2014), 61.

4 "Frank Tashlin: An Interview by Michael Barrier," last updated December 16, 2004, http://www.michaelbarrier.com/Interviews/Tashlin/tashlin_interview.htm.

5 Jeff Lenburg, "Who's Who in Animated Cartoons: An International Guide to Film and Television's Award-Winning and Legendary Animators (New York: Applause Theatre & Cinema Books), 153-155.

6 Michael Barrier, The Animated Man: A Life of Walt Disney (Berkeley: University of California Press, 2007), 54.

7 Later on, Merrie Melodies began producing cartoons in Technicolor, and that became the only difference with Looney Tunes. When the latter switched to color, there was no difference between the two. Still, Warner Bros. continued releasing cartoons under both banners, even though directors didn't know, or care, which label a short would receive. It was only later that Looney Tunes became the generic name for all the films, partly because it came first, but mostly because it's a better name. You can't really trust a cartoon series that can't spell "Merry."

8 Mark Langer, "The Disney-Fleischer Dilemma: Product Differentiation and Technical Innovation," in The Classical Hollywood Reader, ed. Steve Neale (New York: Routledge, 2012), 313.

9 Thad Komorowski, email message to author, November 30, 2020.

10 Tom Klein, "Tex Avery Loses an Eye, 1933," Cartoon Research, June 27, 2015, https://cartoonresearch.com/index.php/tex-avery-loses-an-eye-1933/.

11 Komorowski, email message to author.

12 Michael Barrier, Hollywood Cartoons: American Animation in Its Golden Age (New York: Oxford University Press, 1999), 329.

13 Keith Scott, "Mel Blanc: From Anonymity to Offscreen Superstar (The advent of on-screen voice credits)," Cartoon Research, September 12, 2016, https://cartoonresearch.com/index.php/mel-blanc-from-anonymity-to-offscreen-superstar-the-advent-of-on-screen-voice-credits/.

CHAPTER 3

1 One of the big problems for a Looney Tunes fan is trying to identify a cartoon by its title, because most of the titles are puns, alliterations, or rhymes that have nothing to do with the actual story of the cartoon. Why would a cartoon where Daffy Duck is tormented by an offscreen animator be called "Duck Amuck?" Does "Kitty Kornered" sound like it's about Porky trying to put cats out and getting thrown out by them instead? Say what you will about "Sinkin' in the Bathtub," but at least you know someone will probably be taking a bath.

2 Ibid.

3 Jerry Beck and Will Friedwald, Looney Tunes and Merrie Melodies: A Complete Illustrated Guide to the Warner Bros. Cartoons (New York: Henry Holt & Co., 1989), tk.

4 "Dogs urinate on trees" is a very common subject for punch lines in Warner cartoons. A later cartoon, Friz Freleng's "A Hare Grows in Manhattan," ends when a gang of dogs see the title of the book A Tree Grows in Brooklyn, stop menacing Bugs, and run across the bridge to Brooklyn. These gags are usually not that funny, but it seems like the directors couldn't resist a bodily function joke that the censors were willing to allow on a regular basis.

5 Later we see that the doctor's "patient" is a football that he was stitching back together, and while the gag is amusingly corny, it keeps Daffy from screwing up on a sick patient.

CHAPTER 4

1 Sometimes Stalling's musical in-jokes were so complicated they seemed to be for his amusement alone. Given a cartoon with the title "I Got Plenty of Mutton," he chose a patriotic song called "This Is Worth Fighting For," pointing out, in a deadpan way, that this tune, owned by his employers, sounded like it was borrowed from Gershwin's "I Got Plenty of Nuttin'."

2 Mark Mayerson, email message to author, January 17, 2021.

3 Ibid.

4 "Carl Stalling: An Interview by Michael Barrier, Milton Gray, and Bill Spicer," last updated October 29, 2007, www.michaelbarrier.com/Funnyworld/Stalling/Stalling.htm.

5 Donald Crafton, "The View From Termite Terrace: Caricature and Parody in Warner Bros. Animation," in Reading the Rabbit: Explorations in Warner Bros. Animation, ed. Kevin S. Sandler (New Brunswick, NJ: Rutgers University Press, 1998), 110.

6 Mark Mayerson, "Six Authors In Search of a Character: Part 7, Directing," Mayerson On Animation, June 4, 2007, mayersononanimation.blogspot.com/2007/06/six-authors-in-search-of-character-part.html.

7 Mark Mayerson, "Six Authors In Search of a Character: Part 6, Sound, Bar Sheets and Timing," Mayerson On Animation, May 31, 2007, mayersononanimation.blogspot.com/2007/05/six-authors-in-search-of-character-part_31.html.

8 Avery parodied this in some parts of "Porky's Preview," a collection of crudely drawn animated shorts supposedly created by Porky. One of the segments has Porky trying to animate a dancer, but constantly getting the rhythm wrong and crossing out his drawings when he does. Eventually he gives up and simply moves the dancer's whole body from side to side in some vague semblance of a rhythm.

9 Mayerson, "Six Authors in Search of a Character: Part 7, Directing."

10 Barry Putterman, "A Short Critical History of Warner Bros. Cartoons," in Reading the Rabbit: Explorations in Warner Bros. Animation, ed. Kevin S. Sandler (New Brunswick, NJ: Rutgers University Press, 1998), 29.

11 Joe Adamson, Tex Avery: King of Cartoons (New York: Film Fan Monthly, 1975), 162.

12 John Province, "Termite Terrace Tenancy: Virgil Ross Remembers," Animato! no. 19 (1989), 17.

CHAPTER 5

1 David Bossert, "Rediscovering Oswald," Animation Magazine, September 26, 2017, https://www.animationmagazine.net/features/rediscovering-oswald/.

2 Joe Adamson, Bugs Bunny: Fifty Years and Only One Gray Hare. New York: Henry Holt , 1990, 54.

3 Christopher P. Lehman, The Colored Cartoon (Amherst: University of Massachusetts Press, 2007), 64.

4 "Frank Tashlin: An Interview by Michael Barrier."

5 Adamson, Tex Avery: King of Cartoons, 162-4.

6 Tom Shales, "Chuck Jones and the Daffy World of Cartoons," Washington Post, November 26, 1989, https://www.washingtonpost.com/archive/lifestyle/style/1989/11/26/chuck-jones-and-the-daffy-world-of-cartoons/6615424f-79a3-4f1b-94c4-d5bfe1e84e8e/.

7 Province, "Termite Terrace Tenancy: Virgil Ross Remembers," 17.

8 Adamson, Tex Avery: King of Cartoons, 162.

9 Hogan was a story man who, at this time, was writing stories for both Avery and Jones, and he also wrote "Prest-o Change-o," "Elmer's Candid Camera," and "Elmer's Pet Rabbit" for Jones. He would soon follow Avery to MGM and write many cartoons for him in the 1940s and '50s.

10 Michael Barrier, "Remodeling the Rabbit," last updated February 16, 2011, www.michaelbarrier.com/Interviews/McKimson/RemodelingRabbit.html

11 "Cartoon Man Walks Out On Leon Schlesinger," Hollywood Reporter, July 2, 1941, http://texaveryatwb.blogspot.com/2019/10/the-heckling-hare-cartoon-man-walks-out.html

12 Barrier, Hollywood Cartoons, 609.

13 Adamson, Tex Avery: King of Cartoons, 126.

CHAPTER 6

1 Erskine Johnson, "Movie Items: Cooper to Star In Bathtub Scene!," The Pittsburgh Press, Monday, February 1, 1943, 14.

2 "Frank Tashin: An Interview by Michael Barrier."

3 Erskine Johnson, "In Hollywood," The Burlington (N.C.) Daily Times-News, April 17, 1943, 7.

4 Clampett directed the first color cartoon in the Looney Tunes series, "The Hep Cat" (though, for reasons we'll get into a bit later, you will never see it released in the Looney Tunes series).

5 Mark Nardone, "Robert McKimson Interviewed," in Gerald Peary and Danny Peary, eds., The American Animated Cartoon (New York, 1980), 148

6 Komorowski, email message to author.

7 The famous difference between this version of Pepe and the one who would get his own series a few years later is that this one isn't actually French: his pursuit ends when his wife shows up, and he sheepishly abandons his fake French accent and tries to make excuses: "Just . . . removing a cinder from this lady's eye, dear."

8 Barrier, Hollywood Cartoons, 474-77.

9 "Lloyd Turner: An Interview By Michael Barrier."

10 The best gag in the cartoon, though, is a nonviolent one: Instead of trying to think of a new plan, Sylvester simply walks on air up to the tree branch, holding up a sign that informs us, "Anything is possible in a cartoon!" Maltese loved sign gags. He wrote most of the Road Runner and Wile E. Coyote cartoons, and was constantly having them pull out signs to communicate.

CHAPTER 7

1 Modern Screen, vol. 26, no. 1, December 1942, 83.

2 "Schlesinger Sells Out to Warners," The Lowell Sun, June 22, 1944, 9.

3 Linda Simensky, "Selling Bugs Bunny: Warner Bros. and Character Merchandising in the Nineties," in Reading the Rabbit: Explorations in Warner Bros. Animation, ed. Kevin S. Sandler (New Brunswick, NJ: Rutgers University Press, 1998), 175.

4 Showmen's Trade Review, July 6, 1940, 17.

5 Simensky, "Selling Bugs Bunny," 175-6.

6 Michael Barrier, Funnybooks: the Improbable Glories of the Best American Comic Books (Oakland: University of California Press, 2015).

7 Maggie Thompson, Comics Shop (Iola: Krause Publications, 2010), tk.

8 Donald D. Markstein, "Mary Jane and Sniffles," Don Markstein's Toonopedia, www.toonopedia.com/maryjane.htm.

9 Edward Summer, "Of Ducks and Men: Carl Barks Interviewed," in Carl Barks: Conversations, ed. Donald D. Ault (Jackson; University of Mississippi Press, 2003), 90.

10 Ibid.

11 It's sometimes said that Looney Tunes were mostly aimed at adults, which isn't exactly true. This statement is at best an overreaction to the years when they were primarily part of children's programming lineups. Adult jokes were made, but the subject matter was usually at a child's level of understanding: there's a reason the studio released cartoons every year that parodied classic fairy tales.

12 Farber, "Short and Happy."

13 Aline Mosby, "Bugs Bunny box office film champ," Columbus Daily Telegram, March 30, 1956, 5.

CHAPTER 8

1 Devon Baxter, "Bugs Bunny in 'A-Lad-In His Lamp (1948)," Cartoon Research, August 15, 2018, https://cartoonresearch.com/index.php/bugs-bunny-in-a-lad-in-his-lamp-1948/.

2 "Disney Vs Warners," Tralfaz: Cartoons & Tralfazian Stuff, May 23, 2020, https://tralfaz.blogspot.com/2020/05/disney-vs-warners.html.

3 Barrier, Hollywood Cartoons, 477.

4 "Phil Monroe (1976): An Interview by Michael Barrier and Milton Gray," last updated June 22, 2015, http://www.michaelbarrier.com/Interviews/Monroe/Monroe1976.html.

5 "Lloyd Turner: An Interview by Michael Barrier."

6 "Disney Vs Warners."

7 Keith Scott, "The Origin of Foghorn Leghorn," Cartoon Research, February 22, 2013, https://cartoonresearch.com/index.php/the-origin-of-foghorn-leghorn-2/.

8 "Robert McKimson: An Interview by Michael Barrier," last updated February 24, 2011, www.michaelbarrier.com/Interviews/McKimson/McKimson.html.

9 Billboard, September 29, 1951, 95.

10 "Robert McKimson: An Interview by Michael Barrier."

11 "Lloyd Turner: An Interview by Michael Barrier."

CHAPTER 9

1 When Warner Bros. had to redesign the Looney Tunes opening in the early 1950s due to changes in movie screen formats, Daffy's special intro was quietly dropped.

2 Michael Barrier, email message to author, March 9, 2021.

3 Letter, Chuck Jones to Linda Jones, February 16, 1953, quoted in Chuck Jones Blog, Post # 37, https://webcache.googleusercontent.com/search?q=cache:crvxagqpWNEJ:https://blog.chuckjones.com/chuck_redux/2009/09/chuck-jones-letters-to-his-daughter-linda-14.html+&cd=5&hl=en&ct=clnk&gl=ca

4 Here's how much difference a few seconds of screen time makes. In 1954's "Captain Hareblower," Freleng repeats a gag he used in one of his best, 1948's "Buccaneer Bunny." In that cartoon, Bugs twice throws a match into a ship's gunpowder room, and Yosemite Sam twice rushes to put out the match before it can blow up the whole boat. He then tells Bugs: "If you does that once more, I ain't a-goin' after it!" Bugs calls his bluff, throws a third match, and Sam actually tries to make good on his words, playing jacks and humming nervously while he waits for Bugs to crack first. In "Captain Hareblower," a cartoon that's about forty seconds shorter, the gag is the same except that Sam says his "If you does that once more . . ." line after Bugs has thrown only one match. Well, there's a reason why comedy always comes in threes: without that second match, no pattern is established, and the whole gag falls flat.

5 Komorowski, email message to author.

6 "Wile E. Coyote and the Road Runner," First Versions, https://www.firstversions.com/2015/11/wile-e-coyote-and-road-runner.html.

7 Letter, Chuck Jones to Linda Jones, October 1, 1952, quoted in Chuck Jones Blog, Post # 10, https://chuckjones.com/blog/chuck-jones-letters-to-his-daughter-linda-4-9/

8 Freleng had already paired them in a "cheater" cartoon, a parody of television's "This Is Your Life," where new Bugs/Daffy material surrounded a collection of old clips . . . a format that would soon become very, very familiar to Looney Tunes fans once the characters went into actual television.

CHAPTER 10

1 "Movies From A.A.P.: Programs of Quality From Quality Studios, Warner Bros. features and cartoons, Popeye cartoons" (Associated Artists Productions Corp. 1957), https://archive.org/stream/moviesfromaappro1957asso/moviesfromaappro1957asso_djvu.txt

2 UA Signals Aggressive TV Drive". Broadcasting Telecasting, October 27, 1958, https://archive.org/details/broadcastingtele55unse_0/page/n429/mode/2up.

3 Jon Cooke, "Misce-Looney-Ous: That Wasn't All, Folks!: Warner Bros. Cartoons 1964-1969," https://www.intanibase.com/gac/looneytunes/1960sarticle.aspx

4 Barrier, Hollywood Cartoons, 562-3.

5 'Sandy Speaks! a candid conversation with Don Sandburg," Chicago Television Alumni Club, www.chicagotelevision.com/Sandy2001REV03F.htm.

6 Kevin McCorry, "The Other Television Shows Starring the Warner Brothers Cartoon Characters," www.kevinmccorrytv.ca/others.html.

7 Bernard F. Dick, Engulfed: The Death of Paramount Pictures and the Birth of Corporate Hollywood (Lexington: University Press of Kentucky, 2001), 168.

8 Larry Jackson, Audio Commentary, Bugs Bunny Superstar, Warner Home Video.

9 Lenita Drew, "The Guy Who Ruffled Donald Duck's Feathers: 'What's up Doc?'," Reno Gazette-Journal, December 10, 1974, 15.

10 "Unadulterated Hogwash," Letters of Note, October 21, 2009, https://web.archive.org/web/20190808075659/www.lettersofnote.com/2009/10/unadulterated-hogwash.html.

11 Mike Mulvey, "Freleng Still a Leader in Cartoon Field," Lincoln Journal Star, April 16, 1984, 12.

12 Lafayette–West Lafayette Journal and Courier, Tuesday, September 10, 1985, p. C3.

13 Thad Komorowski, "Bob Clampett Superstar," What About Thad, November 28, 2012, https://www.whataboutthad.com/2012/11/28/bob-clampett-superstar/.

14 One seemingly minor but actually quite significant difference: the contract for the AAP cartoons stipulated that broadcasters were not allowed to alter the cartoons in any way, and they couldn't even cut out the opening and closing titles. Warner Bros. was allowed to edit its own material, so The Bugs Bunny Show and its successors would usually start

"cold" with the beginning of the cartoon proper, even when this meant cutting out gags that happened under the opening credits. The classic "That's all, folks!" [please check that phrase for consistency] tagline was common in local TV but much rarer in the upscale packages.

CHAPTER 11

1 Herman Hill, "Film City Cartoonists Act To Correct Race Caricatures," Pittsburgh Courier, October 7, 1944, 13.

2 Greg Ford, personal communication, March 1, 2021.

3 Jim Korkis, "Animation Anecdotes #131," Cartoon Research, October 11, 2013, https://cartoonresearch.com/index.php/animation-anecdotes-131-2/.

4 Keith L. Thomas, "Old Cartoons, New Outrage," Atlanta Journal-Constitution, November 12, 1990, D1-4.

5 Christopher P. Lehman, "The Censored 11: 'Coal Black and The Sebben Dwarfs" (1943), Cartoon Research, June 2, 2018, https://cartoonresearch.com/index.php/the-censored-11-coal-black-and-the-sebben-dwarfs-1943/

6 "Protest Movie Poking Fun At Negro Soldiers," The New York Age, May 8, 1943, 10.

7 Lehman, The Colored Cartoon, 79.

8 Province, "Termite Terrace Tenancy: Virgil Ross Remembers," 17.

9 "Coal Black and De Sebben Dwarfs," The Big Cartoon Database, https://www.bcdb.com/cartoon-info/7484-Coal-Black-And-De-Sebben-Dwarfs.

10 David Johnson, "Jump For Joy: Duke Ellington's Celebratory Musical," Indiana Public Media, February 5, 2008, https://indianapublicmedia.org/nightlights/jump-for-joy-duke-ellingtons-celebratory-musical.php.

11 Jim Korkis, "Jim Korkis on Bob Clampett's 'Coal Black and de Sebben Dwarfs' (1943)," Cartoon Research, May 20, 2017, https://cartoonresearch.com/index.php/jim-korkis-on-bob-clampetts-coal-black-and-de-sebben-dwarfs-1943/

12 The character is never actually referred to as "Coal Black," but the original title, "So White and de Sebben Dwarfs," was vetoed for fear of retaliation from Disney.

13 "Coal Black and De Sebben Dwarfs," The Big Cartoon Database.

14 The Way We Were, In Cartoons," Boston Globe, September 4, 1982, 7.

15 This also applies to the fact that all the jobs were held by men except for a few tasks, like cel washing, usually reserved for women. Back when there was only one woman animator at a major studio, Walter Lantz's employee La Verne Harding (who later did some Warner Bros. work through Friz Freleng's company), this was just considered standard; that doesn't make it right, but it does mean that most of us, thrown back into the past, would have accepted it; people who want to change the status quo are always outliers to start with.

16 Amid Amidi, "The Remarkable Life of Frank Braxton, Hollywood's First Black Animator," Cartoon Brew, February 27, 2016, https://www.cartoonbrew.com/

animators/remarkable-life-frank-braxton-hollywoods-first-black-animator-137356.
html.

17 Thomas, "Old Cartoons, New Outrage," D4.

18 Carolina Moreno, "Is Speedy Gonzales A Mexican Hero Or a Stereotype In Cartoon
Form?" Huffington Post, April 7, 2016, https://www.huffingtonpost.ca/entry/
is-speedy-gonzales-a-mexican-hero-or-a-stereotype-in-cartoon-form_n_5706a852e4
b0537661890eaa.

CHAPTER 12

1 Dana White, George Lucas (Minneapolis: Lerner Publications Company, 2000), 35.

2 Michael Mallory, "They dare to 'Duck'," Los Angeles Times, August 22, 2003,
https://www.latimes.com/archives/la-xpm-2003-aug-22-et-mallory22-story.html.

3 Leonard Maltin, Of Mice and Magic: A History of American Animated Cartoons
(New York: New American Library, 1987), 287.

4 Jerry Beck, "The Return of Duck Dodgers Storyboard by Michael Maltese," Cartoon
Research, December 25, 2017 and January 1, 2018, https://cartoonresearch.com/index.
php/the-return-of-duck-dodgers-storyboard-by-michael-maltese-part-1/ and https://
cartoonresearch.com/index.php/the-return-of-duck-dodgers-storyboard-by-michael-
maltese-part-2/.

5 Greg Ford, personal communication.

6 Ibid.

7 Bob Miller, "The New Looney Tunes," Comics Scene Yearbook #1 (New York:
Starlog Communications International, Inc., 1992), 23-29, 72.

8 Ben Ohmart, Mel Blanc: The Man of a Thousand Voices (Duncan: BearManor
Media, 2012).

CHAPTER 13

1 Ian Failes, "The Oral History of 'Space Jam': Part 1 - Launching the Movie," Cartoon
Brew, November 15, 2016, https://www.cartoonbrew.com/feature-film/oral-history-
space-jam-part-1-launching-movie-144935.html.

2 Tom Weaver, "Merrie Monstrosities & Looney Toons," Starlog Magazine 317
(December 2003), 32.

3 "The Year In Quotes: Two Michaels and Only One Mickey," Los Angeles Times,
December 29, 1996, https://www.latimes.com/archives/la-xpm-1996-12-29-ca-
13350-story.html.

4 "Interview: Ivan Reitman Reflects on Space Jam, 20 Years Later," Mr. Wavvy,
November 22, 2016, https://mrwavvy.com/blog/interview-ivan-reitman.

5 Erik Malinowski, "'Space Jam' Forever: The Website That Wouldn't Die," Rolling Stone, August 19, 2015, https://www.rollingstone.com/movies/movie-news/space-jam-forever-the-website-that-wouldnt-die-70507/

6 Imagine - From Pencils To Pixels, YouTube video, https://www.youtube.com/watch?v=lnsBLF5cYpg.

7 "Joe Dante," Suicide Girls, June 4, 2007, https://www.suicidegirls.com/girls/anderswolleck/blog/2679865/joe-dante/..

8 G. Michael Dobbs, Escape! How Animation Broke into the Mainstream in the 1990s (Albany, GA: BearManor Media, 2015), tk.

9 Honey Bunny: A Very Unofficial Website, 2012-2015, https://www.honeybunnyworld.com/honeybunny,en,home.html.

10 Brian Boone, "The Untold Truth of Space Jam," Looper, May 20, 2020, https://www.looper.com/211131/the-untold-truth-of-space-jam/.

11 Derek Lawrence, "New Legacy, New Lola: Why Space Jam wanted to do better by one Tune," Entertainment Weekly, March 5, 2021, https://ew.com/movies/space-jam-new-legacy-lola-bunny/

12 David Edelstein, "Holiday Movies; That's Not All, Folks!" New York Times, November 2, 2003, https://www.nytimes.com/2003/11/02/movies/holiday-movies-that-s-not-all-folks.html.

13 Scott Eyman, "Wascally wabbit still making twacks," Southern Illinoisian, May 1, 1990, 6.

CHAPTER 14

1 Kevin McCorry and Jon Cooke, "Looney Tunes on Television," The Internet Animation Database, https://www.intanibase.com/gac/looneytunes/looneytunestv.aspx.

2 "Wideo Wabbit: The Complete, Illustrated History of the Warner Bros. Cartoons . . . on Home Video," www.dohtem.com/bugs/history/history3.htm

3 Greg Ford, personal communication.

4 "Bugs Bunny gets an extreme makeover," Today, February 17, 2005, https://www.today.com/popculture/bugs-bunny-gets-extreme-makeover-wbna6989380

5 Adam Buckman, "Looney Tune-Ups," New York Post, February 17, 2005.

6 "Eleven-Year-Old Fuels Animated Debate," Washington Post, April 28, 2005, https://www.washingtonpost.com/archive/lifestyle/2005/04/28/todays-news/07eaa1ec-a12e-4be5-bda1-a8a0c2aa2c0a/.

7 Ryan Ball, "Legal Buzz Kill for Warner's Loonatics?" Animation Magazine, March 1, 2005, https://www.animationmagazine.net/tv/legal-buzz-kill-for-warners-loonatics/.

8 "Ottawa animator bashed for Looney Tunes changes," CBC News, May 26, 2010, https://www.cbc.ca/news/canada/ottawa/ottawa-animator-bashed-for-looney-tunes-changes-1.916930.

9 Jerry Beck, "'Wabbit - A Looney Tunes Production' Toplines Cartoon Network Upfront Presentation," IndieWire, March 10, 2014, https://www.indiewire.com/2014/03/wabbit-a-looney-tunes-production-toplines-cartoon-network-upfront-presentation-124337/

10 Bugs had already done his own version of "Duck Amuck" in 1955's "Rabbit Rampage," where the animator turned out to be Elmer Fudd. That was one of the weakest classic Bugs Bunny cartoons, a lesson in why a story that works for Daffy Duck might not work for Bugs Bunny, and vice versa.

EPILOGUE

1 Komorowski, personal communication.
2 Komorowski, personal communication.